W9-ATE-304

A History of Medieval Christianity

PETER LANG
New York • Washington, D.C./Baltimore • Boston • Bern
Frankfurt am Main • Berlin • Brussels • Vienna • Oxford

Jeffrey Burton Russell
and Douglas W. Lumsden

A History of Medieval Christianity

Prophecy and Order

PETER LANG
New York • Washington, D.C./Baltimore • Boston • Bern
Frankfurt am Main • Berlin • Brussels • Vienna • Oxford

Library of Congress Cataloging-in-Publication Data

Russell, Jeffrey Burton.
A history of medieval Christianity: prophecy and order /
Jeffrey Burton Russell and Douglas W. Lumsden.
p. cm.
Includes bibliographical references and index.
1. Church history—Middle Ages, 600–1500. 2. Europe—Church history—
600–1500. I. Lumsden, Douglas W. II. Title.
BR252.R8 270.3—dc21 99-29432
ISBN 0-8204-4511-8

Die Deutsche Bibliothek-CIP-Einheitsaufnahme

Russell, Jeffrey Burton:
A history of medieval Christianity: prophecy and order /
Jeffrey Burton Russell and Douglas W. Lumsden.
–New York; Washington, D.C./Baltimore; Boston; Bern;
Frankfurt am Main; Berlin; Brussels; Vienna; Oxford: Lang.
ISBN 0-8204-4511-8

Cover design by Nona Reuter

The paper in this book meets the guidelines for permanence and durability
of the Committee on Production Guidelines for Book Longevity
of the Council of Library Resources.

275 Seventh Avenue, 28th Floor, New York, NY 10001
www.peterlangusa.com

Printed in the United States of America

Table of Contents

Preface

Thirty years ago, most people (including far too many historians) perceived the medieval Church as an impersonal corporation whose primary purpose was the acquisition of power and the furthering of its own existence. Wielding such formidable and fearsome weapons as excommunication, interdict, and inquisition, the Church (always displayed in print with an oppressive capital "C") crushed medieval society beneath the weight of its rigidly dogmatic doctrine. In this popular vision of medieval Christianity, new ideas were extinguished before they could undermine the unified and monolithic structure of the Church. Knowledge was suppressed; ignorance was sown and harvested under the vigilant eye of the tyrannical overseer. It was the Church that prevented the light from illuminating these Dark Ages.

In 1968, Jeffrey Burton Russell challenged this powerful image of the immobile medieval Church, declaring that the history of medieval Christianity could be better understood by investigating the tension within the Christian community between two opposing "spirits": the spirit of order and the spirit of prophecy. These spirits were equally necessary for the survival of Christianity; both were ultimately spirits of light. As Dr. Russell put it, "both of these spirits were opposed to the self-satisfied defense of the status quo that has often characterized Christianity since the end of the great persecutions. But the spirit of order has attempted to reform men and their institutions to correspond with the will of God, while the spirit of prophecy has sought to *transform* them, to lift them out of this world into the world and life of God." Rejecting traditional approaches, Dr. Russell offered a more meaningful perception of the medieval Church as a dynamic community comprised of people with a wide variety of ideas, motivations, and perspectives.

Dr. Russell's synthesis has held up remarkably well over the subsequent three decades. His approach freed historians to examine the medieval Church, not as an obstacle that needed to be pushed aside in order to clear the way for "renaissance" and "enlightenment," but as a process that underwent significant change and development through time. Or to put it another way, rather than regarding the medieval Church as a thousand-year incident in the history of Christianity, Dr. Russell allowed medieval Christianity to have a history of its own.

When Dr. Russell asked me to "update" his work, my initial concern was to make sure that his synthesis remained intact. Popular portrayals of the medieval Church still tend to promote old images of deliberately ignorant and power-crazed bullies zealously striving to resist progress and maintain a stagnant and subservient society. But most serious scholars, at least, now recognize the history of medieval Christianity as the history of a variety of ideas, sometimes harmonizing, often clashing, always working within the context of a vibrant community, weaving a bright tapestry of many colors and shapes. My goal was not to revise Dr. Russell's work, but to tend it, to remove a few items that have not withstood the test of time, to enhance some areas that have received recent attention, to convert some of the language to newly established standards. But above all, my goal was to maintain Dr. Russell's excellent vision of medieval Christianity: not the function of a stationary Church after all, then, but the product of an ever-moving church comprising the widest possible variety of souls, representatives of the spirits of order and prophecy.

I owe Dr. Russell a great debt of gratitude for his confidence in my abilities to do justice to his efforts. I wish to express my appreciation to my parents, Bill and Carolyn, and my sisters, Teri and Karen, who have offered tremendous enthusiasm and support for my career decisions. I also owe many thanks to my wife, Karolyn, for her encouragement, patience, and love, and for reminding me whenever I'm ready to quit that the goal is just another step away.

D.W.L.

Chapter One

Prophecy and Order

The Christian spirit has always been ambivalent toward this world. On the one hand, the spirit of prophecy, rooted in the tradition of Isaiah and Jeremiah, has insisted that this world, its men and its institutions, are under judgment. Our duty, it says, is to strive for a radical transformation of the world in order to destroy the obstacles erected by society between ourselves and the transcendent God. On the other hand, the spirit of order has called for a progressive, creative, and often very moderate program of reshaping this world and its institutions on the model of God's world. Both prophecy and order seek the Kingdom of God; but prophecy seeks the end of the world and uncompromisingly hopes for an immediate meeting with God, while order works more patiently within the world and with the imperfect materials at hand.

In medieval Christianity, as in Christianity as a whole, both the prophetic spirit and the spirit of order were at work, sometimes in cooperation and sometimes in conflict. There are other ways of viewing the medieval church; but as history is not a bare account of "what happened," but an investigation of what happened with the intent of discerning significant patterns, the study of the church in terms of the complementary forces of prophecy and order adds to our understanding of its development.

Medieval Christianity was an integral part of medieval society, affecting as well as affected by the other human institutions and ideas surrounding it. The study of medieval Christianity both illuminates and is illuminated by medieval history as a whole. Therefore, the study of medieval Christianity is also one phase of the study of medieval Europe, and vice versa.

But equally important, the medieval period is one phase, and chronologically the longest phase, of the history of Christianity itself. For at least a century now, all reputable scholars have accepted the notion of development in the history of the Christian church. Old-fashioned Catholics liked to believe that the Catholic Church of the nineteenth century was in essentials identical with the church of the first century; old-fashioned Protestants insisted that only what was explicitly biblical was true Christianity. All now recognize that in the beginning the apostles had only a very disorganized and inchoate set of ideas about Christ and that all the elaboration of Christian theology, ethics, anthropology, and sociology had gradually and painstakingly to be worked out in the course of centuries. The historian, whose raison d'être is to study change in society, is primarily concerned with the study of the development of the church.

The history of Christianity is far more than the history of the church as an institution. It is the study of the life of the Christian people (the *ecclesia*—the church in its broadest sense as the entire Christian community, clergy and laity alike), their ideas, their ways, their feelings, without undue scrupulosity or concern for formal institutional definitions. When seen in this proper historical perspective, the church is not a well-designed architectural construction—let alone the monolith that the ill-informed suppose it to be—but a diverse structure housing artifacts of varying designs, some large, some small, some beautiful, some ugly. Historians recognize that to describe the development of such complex patterns is inevitably to do them violence, and if they do not therefore shirk the task, it is only with the wholesome understanding that no problem is ever really done justice by the human mind.

Being human, and studying humans, historians are not content simply to describe the mechanics of the development of medieval Christianity. It is true that they are not concerned with "the descent of the Dove" as the English novelist and historian Charles Williams put it: the action of the Holy Spirit within the church. Whether or not they are believers, historians have no access, at least as historians, to the mind of God, and they do not presume to interpret that mind to their audience. They are obliged by the limitations of their knowledge and of their method to examine religions and religious institutions as the products of human enterprise, reserving their judgment of the metaphysical implications for such times as they act, not as historians, but as speculative philosophers. The tools used by historians are not suited to determine the truth about religious doctrine—or anything else, for that matter. The most that the historian can hope to accomplish is to gain an understanding of what people in historical communities *believed* to be true about religious doctrine. But historians do judge (without denominational prejudice) whether or not the development of the medieval church was a true expression of religion, a true expression of the pristine Christian spirit.

There were many varieties of religious expression in the Middle Ages. But was medieval Christianity as a whole conducive to a valid expression of the religious experience? It would be uncommonly presumptuous to claim to know for certain what constitutes true religious experience, and historians shun judgments based upon orthodoxies established by any denomination or upon the whims of personal conscience. But philosophers of religion (to name only a few from different generations, William James, Rudolf Otto, and Mircea Eliade) have given us something to work with. These philosophers would at the very least offer a measure of support to the statement that the religious experience is the immediate and personal sense of the holy: the always inexplicable, incomprehensible, and often terrifying majesty and mystery of the "Wholly Other" who is nevertheless here, now, and always everywhere. The attitudes that proceed from a generalization of this experience constitute a *sacred view of the world.* In the sacred view of the world, nothing is profane but all things are sacred; in the profane view, presently far more common, nothing is sacred but all things are profane. Wordsworth, oppressed by the rise of the profane view of the universe, complained:

> The world is too much with us; late and soon,
> Getting and spending, we lay waste our powers;
> Little we see in nature that is ours;
> We have given our hearts away, a sordid boon!
> This Sea that bares her bosom to the moon,
> The winds that will be howling at all hours,
> And are up-gathered now like sleeping flowers,
> For this, for everything, we are out of tune;
> It moves us not.—Great God! I'd rather be
> A Pagan suckled in a creed outworn;
> So might I, standing on this pleasant lea,
> Have glimpses that would make me less forlorn;
> Have sight of Proteus rising from the sea;
> Or hear old Triton blow his wreathèd horn.

The sense of the sacred is that everything in the universe is either God (pantheism or emanationism) or filled with God like a sponge immersed in the sea (panentheism or immanentism). This sense is at the base of all religions; but it tends to fade somewhat as they become institutionalized. The ecstasies of the early Orphic religion in Greece, for example, contrast with the publicly ordained and publicly performed worship of the not wholly compelling Olympic pantheon of classical times. In the search for order, the prophetic spirit is often denied. The tradition of the Christian church has been to straddle the sacred and the profane and persistently to maintain that some things are holy, like churches, and others profane, like marketplaces. It is against this dichotomy that many current theologians are striving, either to restore to the churches the immediate sense of the otherness of God or else to convince them of the infinite worth of the "secular city" they had scorned as profane.

Did the medieval church, then, encourage a true religious sense? A German Protestant historian, Rudolf Sohm, once accused the church of transforming itself from a sacrament to a corporation. The medieval church did become involved in the pursuit of wealth, status, and political power. It did invest much time and energy in the construction and the maintenance of its own hierarchical structure. St. Bernard once observed with prophetic dismay that the pope spent not every day, but every hour of the day in administrative matters. St. Peter has always been the type of the church: cowardly, stupid, and indecisive; yet in the end Peter proved faithful and brave. The church was necessarily a failure in that its organizational structure muffled the immediacy of the religious experience. Its search for *order* frustrated *prophecy.* Yet this search was also completely necessary. Christianity can get along neither within the church nor without it. The demise of Gnosticism, which had no lasting ecclesiastical organization, is evidence that without a structure and a system of authority, no body of doctrines can long endure: either it will undergo such strange metamorphoses as to make it unrecognizably different from its origins, or else it will simply perish. It was the necessary work of the church, and a work in which it was quite successful, both to keep the doctrines of Christ alive and to keep its development of his teachings within the boundaries of a recognizable tradition.

Like Peter, the church is necessarily a failure, yet absolutely necessary. The search for order and the urge to prophecy, the progressives who make necessary adjustments and the conservatives who check the tendency to proceed too far or too fast, the constitutional structure of the church and the mystics and ascetics who decried or ignored the structure, the orthodox and the heretics: all these opposites are necessary. Christianity was able to preserve its doctrinal and institutional identity while at the same time producing (or at least permitting) a wealth and variety of religious experience unparalleled in the history of other religions. It was able to do this through the salutary and never-resolved tension between prophecy and order.

It is indisputable that, regardless of the need for order in the development of society and institutions, the founder of Christianity was a prophet. Christ taught the uprooting and reversal of most of the values that characterized society in his day. He did not, as some of his more extreme followers maintained, teach that the world was unreal or that it was evil, but neither did he come, as many supposed, to build a kingdom of this world. Christ vehemently rejected the status quo. He insisted that his mission was a complete transformation of the world as we know it in preparation for a world to come.

To go much beyond this in describing the career of Jesus in a book of this kind would be unfair to a subject that perplexes scholars and believers alike and has produced a literature that exceeds both in volume and in complexity that on any other problem. Yet since it is impossible to understand medieval Christianity without some reference to its backgrounds, it is necessary to raise, while not presuming to answer, some of the outstanding questions.

The problem of the historical Jesus is enormously complex. In his own time, the Romans thought him a fanatic, many of the Jews despised him as a charlatan or hated him as a blasphemer, and even his friends at times wondered whether he was not mad (Mark 3:21). But shortly after his death and resurrection, a community called Christians existed who accepted none of these explanations but rather that of Peter. "Who do you say that I am?" Peter was asked, and he replied, "You are the Christ, the Son of the living God." And Jesus said, "Flesh and blood have not revealed this to you, Simon son of Jonah, but my Father who is in heaven" (Matthew 16:16–17). This was accepted absolutely uncritically by Christians until well into the eighteenth century and rejected by non-Christians equally uncritically. Before the eighteenth century, the techniques and philosophy of historical investigation and textual criticism had not yet been developed to a level permitting a critical, analytical historical approach to the personality of Jesus. From the eighteenth century, through Albert Schweitzer in 1906, to the present, historians of all varieties tried to answer the question, What really *was* the personality of Jesus? The quest led them into areas shunned by previous Christians as untouchable. Catholics had argued that their church was essentially the same as that of the apostles; Protestants had argued that it was necessary to return to the pristine religion of the Bible.

But modern historians and critics questioned the reliability of both the apostles and the Bible.

The attempt to approach the Bible and the personality of Jesus historically in much the same way as one approaches the *Commentaries on the Gallic Wars* and the personality of Caesar makes sense from a scholarly standpoint. There is no area of either natural or human history that human reason should not freely investigate to the limits of its ability. But the historians underestimated the difficulty of their material. Problems of biblical criticism have grown more and more complex, and new questions have been raised more frequently than old ones answered. Furthermore, the personality of Jesus, unlike that of Caesar, is one that has had a deep meaning for people in every generation, so that each generation tends to interpret him to fit its needs. The historians of the Enlightenment tried to rationalize away the miracles; some late-nineteenth-century historians, carried away by the emerging science of anthropology and mythology, declared that Jesus was only a myth; progressive liberals made him a social worker and teacher; a businessman of the 1920s painted him as the most successful salesman of all time. In the twentieth century one of the strongest schools, championed originally by Rudolf Bultmann (who, like all good scholars, modified his views with time), declared Jesus to be an eschatological prophet: one who predicted the imminent end of the world and its transformation into the Kingdom of God. The duty of the individual Christian is, then, to face the ultimate reality he or she is about to encounter. This eschatological interpretation has many merits, and its defenders, particularly Bultmann, have bolstered it by a rigorous textual analysis of the Scriptures known as "form criticism." Yet the present popularity of the interpretation seems due at least partly to the readiness with which it can be incorporated into existentialist philosophies urging the necessity of the individual's facing reality in each present moment.

Schweitzer and many other twentieth-century theologians have argued from these changes in fashion that the historical search for the personality of Jesus is futile and that therefore each individual in every generation must in fact interpret him for him or herself. Bultmann said, for example, that though the Resurrection could not be accepted as an historical fact, it rightly remained the center of the individual's experience of Christianity. Lately such views, which were on their way to becoming standard, have been cogently questioned. The earlier historians had asked too much. They had assumed, as good nineteenth-century positivists, that history could tell them "how it really happened," and when they found that it could not, they either gave up or retreated into solipsism. But historians today do not believe that history can say fully how any event "really happened," because they know that the matter of history is far too complex, and that the human mind is far too limited, ever to construct a truly objective history. What historians do today is use the evidence they have to create a coherent, consistent picture of how individuals *appeared* to themselves and to others—whether the individual under study is Jesus of Nazareth, Julius Caesar, or Franklin D. Roosevelt.

Though we shall never know *exactly* what Jesus—or Caesar, or Roosevelt—was or thought, each new investigation and interpretation brings us a bit closer, so that at least we can say what he was not. Jesus was much more a prophet than a reformer, and he was no defender of any political order.

Chapter Two

Primitive Christianity

Christianity was established by Christ, but it was established in a particular social and intellectual context. The teachings of Christ did not seem alien to his listeners, but were instead the words of a fellow member of the community. The origins of Christianity are to be sought not only in the personality of Jesus, but also in the first-century milieu of the Hellenized Roman province of Judea.

Jesus and his immediate followers were all Jews, and the strongest influences upon Christianity derive from Hebrew religion. Many of the teachings of Jesus are rooted in orthodox Jewish tradition: his strict monotheism, for example; his reverence for the Scriptures; and his attention to Jewish festivals and the Jewish law. Many of the ethical teachings of Christ resemble very closely those of the noted rabbis of his time and of the preceding century. For example, his insistence that the law is made for humanity and not the other way round, and that it therefore must be modified when mercy and justice demand, closely parallels the thought of the great Rabbi Hillel. It is clear that the writers of the Gospels, particularly Matthew, took care to show how the events of Christ's life and death fulfilled the traditional prophecies. Many of the Jews supposed that Jesus had come as the Messiah: a leader who would deliver his people out from the grasp of foreign rulers and into God's promised kingdom. These people received Jesus into Jerusalem with joy on Palm Sunday, only to be disappointed when he refused to lead them in an uprising against the Romans. But there was another messianic tradition that Jesus' followers claimed he did fulfill: that of the "suffering servant" (Isaiah 53) who lays down his life for the people. Behind this tradition were two ancient Jewish customs, that of the scapegoat, an animal upon whom all the sins of the community were ceremonially placed and who then was driven out and killed, and that of the *go'el*, a relative responsible for the actions and the welfare of each family.

When Jesus began teaching, it was to a Jewish community heavily influenced from within by four religious groups—two in the social mainstream, and two on the fringes of society. The first mainstream group consisted of the Sadducees, an organization of priests that held a monopoly over the ritual and sacrifices in the Temple. The Sadducees awaited a spiritual messiah who would lead the Jews out of a world of care and into a blessed Kingdom of God. They believed that this world was transitory, and that cooperation with the foreign rulers of Palestine in the time remaining was preferable to resistance. The other mainstream group was the Pharisees, consisting primarily of pious laymen. The Pharisees called for a life of morality, by which they meant a strict adherence to the letter of the Law (or Torah) as they interpreted it. Like the Sadducees, the Pharisees believed that a spiritual messiah would one day deliver the Jews from the dominance of foreigners. In the meantime, their policy toward foreign leaders was to ignore them and wait for deliverance. Between them, the Sadducees and the Pharisees provided the most representative expressions of religious tradition in the Jewish community of the early first century.

Not all members of the community were drawn to the mainstream, however. First-century Jerusalem was a hotbed of religious thought, expressed alike by Talmudic scholars, street-corner preachers, and organized religious societies. The most notable fringe groups were the militaristic Zealots and the monastic Essenes. The Zealots awaited a messiah who would drive the Romans out of Palestine by force. By publicly advocating the violent overthrow of the Roman provincial government, the Zealots gained special attention from the local Roman leaders. The other fringe group, the Essenes, was considered less troublesome. These were ascetics who had withdrawn from the city and settled as small communities in the wilderness near the Dead Sea. The Essenes awaited the imminent arrival of a messiah who would oversee the end of the world and lead worthy Jews into a kingdom of the spirit. The Zealots and Essenes had relatively few members, but attracted a good deal of attention during their own period because of their extreme views and practices.

Into this community came Jesus of Nazareth. After a ritual baptism by John the Baptist, who was probably a member of an Essenic community, Jesus withdrew into the wilderness. But after a short time, he returned to preach in the cities. Jesus refused the life of withdrawal practiced by the Essenes. Traveling from city to city, Jesus preached a morality based on the spirit of the Law, a message that alienated the Pharisees. He taught that ritual was not as important as humble faith and ethical behavior, and thereby earned the hostility of the Sadducees. Jesus summed up the Law as follows: "Hear O Israel, you shall love the Lord your God with all your heart, with all your strength, and with all your soul. And you shall love your neighbor as yourself." This message, often called the Great Commandment, was later identified in Latin as the principle of *caritas*, the love of God and neighbor. In accordance with this teaching, Jesus refused the leadership of the Zealots; the message of the Christian church remained one of love and peace for the first 300 years of its existence. In short, although Jesus preached a Jewish message in a Jewish community, he led his church in a unique direction, charting a path through mainstream and fringe groups alike.

Judaism at the time of Jesus was influenced not only by internal debate, but by cultural forces from outside. The Jewish settlements in Palestine had interacted with other Palestinian communities, such as the Canaanites and Phoenicians, both peacefully and otherwise for centuries. The ancient Hebrew people had not always worshipped their own God at the exclusion of all others; the Book of Judges, for example, notes that the early Israelites lived among the other tribes of Palestine and worshipped foreign gods. Later, after the establishment of the Kingdom of Israel, its capital city of Jerusalem developed into a noted cosmopolitan center where people from many cultures and civilizations rubbed shoulders and exchanged ideas. The fifty-year Babylonian Captivity in the sixth century B.C. immersed a large and important segment of the Jewish community in yet another foreign climate. Afterwards, the Jews maintained a mostly peaceful contact with the Persians, who had delivered them from Babylonian dominance. Finally, in the late fourth century B.C., Greek culture came to Palestine in the wake of the conquests of Alexander the Great. The Jewish culture of Jesus and his followers featured historical and theological interpretations that had been greatly affected by these foreign contacts. Influences from these contacts, then, helped shape early Christianity.

Christianity was strongly colored by a dualism rooted partly in the ancient Canaanite religion and partly in Persian Zoroastrianism. The latter was a dualist religion postulating a God of Light (Ahura Mazda) and a God of Darkness (Ahriman). These two spirits were independent and fought a constant cosmic struggle that would continue for ages, though Light would eventually triumph over Darkness. It was humanity's duty to align itself with the forces of Light. This notion seems to have influenced the teaching of Jesus and Paul about the struggle between God and the "Prince of this World," the ruler of an evil eon that would pass in a cataclysm, after which the world would be replaced by the Kingdom of God.

Jesus was ambivalent in his attitude toward the world, sometimes appearing to accept it with the hope of reforming it, in the tradition of orthodox Judaism, and sometimes appearing to reject it utterly, in the tradition of dualism. From the former attitude derives the spirit of order and the notion that Christ came to found a church that would bring about Christian order in the world; from the latter comes the spirit of prophecy and the determination to cast down and shatter the illusions of this world in order to penetrate immediately to the Kingdom of God. It is precisely this ambivalence that has been the enduring strength of Christianity: it has wholly capitulated neither to the demands of society nor to the cries of fanatics for the overthrow of society.

To this basic balance of forces in Christianity the Greek tradition made its contributions. Judea was at the time of Jesus a minor province of the Roman Empire, and it was located in the part of the empire that had been heavily Hellenized for three hundred years. Since the time of Alexander the Great, the eastern Mediterranean had been bound by the informal but very real ties of Greek civilization. The *koine,* or common Greek tongue, was the language of commerce, literature, and philosophy throughout Asia Minor, Syria, Egypt, and Palestine, as well as Greece. Alexandria, in the Nile Delta, was the greatest center of Greek learning at that time; there, at the end of the third century B.C., the Old Testament was translated into *koine* Greek. It was in Alexandria in the first century A.D. that Philo, one of the greatest Jewish philosophers, read the Torah in Greek and wrote Greek commentaries on the sacred text. The Gospels and the Epistles were written not in traditional Hebrew or in the Aramaic commonly spoken in the Palestine of apostolic times, but in *koine* Greek.

Jesus himself does not seem to have been directly influenced by Greek thought, but it is clear that at least some of his followers were. These followers imbibed both the content and the method of Greek philosophy. When St. John wrote, "In the beginning was the Word," he was thinking not only of the Israelite tradition of Wisdom, but of the Platonic traditions in which the world is created by a Demiurge or an emanation from the primal God. The *Word (Logos* in Greek) is the *Thought* of God by which he creates the universe. The concept of the *Logos* is at least as old as the sixth-century B.C. pre-Socratic philosopher Heraclitus, who proposed that the *Logos* was the means by which the created universe was linked to an eternal, unchanging God. The Stoics believed that the *Logos* kept the world in harmony, and not only linked humanity to the rest of the cosmos, and ultimately, to God, but provided humans with the ability to think, speak, and plan. Through the Apostle John, the Greek concept of the *Logos* found its way into Christian theology.

After the death of Jesus, his followers scattered. Soon, however, they reunited and began telling a strange story. Jesus had risen from the dead, they declared, and after spending a short time among his followers, he had departed and been carried away to heaven. His resurrection was the first of what would be a general resurrection of the dead. Many of the Greek and Egyptian mystery religions featured the concept of a resurrected god. The resurrected Dionysus was a prominent deity in several Greek cults. The resurrected Osiris was the featured deity in Egyptian traditions. But Dionysus and Osiris were remote beings, whose deaths and resurrections occurred in long ago times of legend. Jesus had been a contemporary man, only recently executed. The idea of such a resurrection was as strange in the first century A.D. as it is today; a substantial part of Paul's first letter to the Corinthians, probably the oldest document in the New Testament, attempts to convince the members of the church in Corinth that the resurrection of Jesus did indeed occur (I Cor 15:12–58). Even more difficult to explain was the subsequent relationship between the resurrected Jesus and the God of Jewish tradition. In the Gospels, Jesus always referred to God as his Father in Heaven. Throughout the New Testament, Jesus is referred to as the Son of God. After the Resurrection and Ascension, Jesus himself was described as divine. Some said that Jesus now sat at the right hand of God (Eph 1:20). He was called the image of the invisible God, the firstborn of all creation (Col 1:15). Jewish monotheistic tradition would not allow a second God, yet Jesus was apparently more than human. How could God the Father and the resurrected Son of God be reconciled to a monotheistic belief? And where did the mysterious Holy Spirit fit into this relationship? How could Christianity allow three apparently divine beings and yet remain true to its monotheistic foundation?

These questions did not trouble the people of the Hellenistic world as much as they might trouble people of the modern western world. During the Hellenistic period, it became common for educated Greeks to think of deities as abstract concepts, perhaps best represented by Plato's eternally unchanging forms. In the fourth century B.C., Plato had suggested that true reality is eternal and unchanging. The world of phenomena that we perceive with our senses changes constantly; thus, sensory things cannot be as real as the absolute principles we perceive with our minds. These unchanging ideas, which Plato called "forms," constitute one absolute Truth. Being real, forms exist in a real realm of forms somewhere beyond the reach of our senses. Moreover, these forms exist within an all-encompassing hierarchy. The highest of all forms not only caps the hierarchy, but embodies it wholly, so that all forms are permeated by and participate in the highest form. Plato referred to this ultimate form as the One, the Good, or simply, God.

In the years following Plato's death, his followers considered the nature of the One, the highest of all Truths. They concluded that the One was perfect in every way. It existed as a sphere, the most perfect of all shapes, and it was by nature eternal and unchanging, since any change would imply imperfection. As the most perfect of all entities, its only conceivable activity was the contemplation of perfection, that is to say, itself. But how does a perfectly self-contained form interact with the cosmos? Greek philosophers proposed that the One produced an emanation, as the sun produces light. This emanation, the *Logos*, created the cosmos and links the cosmos to the One. The *Logos*, in turn, produces an emanation, as light produces heat. This third emanation is the Soul of the cosmos, which causes living things to be filled with life. These emanations are in every way identical to that which produced them, except that they are the *begotten* of the original. To the Greeks, these three *hypostases* (individual beings that are nonetheless united as a whole) suggested a god with a trinity of aspects. God would not be God without these aspects, just as the sun would not be the sun without light and heat.

When Christianity spread to educated Greeks, they were already familiar with the trinitarian nature of God. The One, the *Logos*, and the Soul of the cosmos corresponded quite easily to the Father, Son, and Holy Spirit. When the Gospel of John added the concept of the incarnation of the *Logos* (John 1:14), Christians were able to adapt Platonic ideas to explain the existence of the Son as the *begotten* of the Father, the identical image of the Father in every respect. The explanation of the nature of the Trinity was further refined by later Christian theologians: the Son is the Father's Thought of himself; and the Holy Spirit is the Love that the Father and the Word have for each other. The idea of the Trinity conveys the eternal dynamism of a perfect, eternal, and unchanging God, a God that was acceptable in principle to both Platonists and Christians alike.

Christianity was compatible with Hellenistic philosophies in other ways, as well. Ethically, the humane but strict rabbinic morality of Jesus proved very congenial to Stoicism, the most rigorous ethical philosophy current in the Roman Empire. Christian thinkers readily assimilated the rational Stoic principles of moderation and right reason to the revealed principles of the Mosaic and rabbinic laws, Sometimes it became difficult to tell Christian saint from Stoic philosopher, as when St. Clement wrote: "Everything that is contrary to right reason is sin.... Virtue itself is a state of the soul rendered harmonious by reason in respect to the whole life.... And Christian conduct is the operation of the rational soul in accordance with a correct judgment and aspiration after the truth." Clement was not alone among the thinkers of Late Antiquity and medieval Europe when he expressed the belief that Plato must have studied under Jewish rabbis, since his philosophy came so close to the Truth revealed with the advent of Jesus.

Christianity assimilated the method of Greek philosophy even more readily than its content. Christ left his followers with the impact of his ministry, his death, and his resurrection, but he had not bequeathed any carefully worked-out system of theology. In another cultural context this would not have mattered. Other religions in other places—Confucianism or Buddhism, for example—have prospered without a theology, but with a fundamentally ethical emphasis. Some religions, such as the religions of Babylonia, or of early Greece and Rome, have flourished with a wholly mythological system. But Christianity, though it had mythological underpinnings and was the inheritor of the strong ethical tradition of Hebrew religion, was not content with these. The Hellenistic cultural context of Christianity demanded that the questions *why* and *how* be asked, and that an intellectual system of religion be created by means of rational reflection upon revelation. This rational reflection, this philosophical investigation of the nature of God and of God's relationship to man, is called theology. If doctrine contains the rules of a religion, theology attempts to discover how and why the rules work. St. Paul became the first Christian theologian when he began constructing a doctrine *about* Christ in addition to spreading the teachings *of* Christ, and this tradition was carried on and greatly reinforced by the fathers of the church, many of whom were more intellectual and more Greek in their way of thought than Paul. This intellectualizing process has sometimes been called "the Hellenization of Christianity." It has produced one of Christianity's most distinguishing characteristics: insistence upon intellectual truth as well as upon right action.

Another kind of Hellenistic influence upon Christianity was that of the mystery cults, which derived from ancient religions and were elaborated and syncretized in the Hellenistic civilization of the eastern Mediterranean. These were fertility cults, uniting the believer with the deity through certain ceremonial rites and emphasizing the personal salvation of the individual. At a time when the old public religion of Rome had ceased to command widespread belief or support, these religions were making great headway not only in the East but in Italy and Rome itself. Certain similarities between them and Christianity have long been observed. Most of the cults centered upon the ancient myth of the fertility god or goddess who died and rose again from the dead; most had a rite of sacrifice and of communion by eating the god's flesh in a symbolic manner; most taught personal salvation. Mith-raism, a religion derived from Zoroastrianism, declared that Mithra, the Son of the Sun, was born of a virgin at the winter solstice (December 25), and the Mithraists had a midnight service to commemorate this nativity—although this particular coincidence is easily explained by the fact that the church fathers deliberately chose the date of Christmas (no one knew at what time of year Christ was actually born) to discourage Christians from participating in Mithraic rites as well as their own.

Christian writers sometimes borrowed the language and expression of the mystery cults, but Christianity was not merely another of the mystery religions. Their nature was purely mythological and ceremonial; but Christianity had in addition a very advanced ethical and intellectual system. Further, the gods of the mystery religions were generated in some undefined mythical time, while the Christians always took care to press the historical existence of their own founder, who was born in the time of Augustus and who "suffered under Pontius Pilate" in the reign of Tiberius. Still, the similarity of Christianity to the mystery cults helped make Christianity acceptable to people who found Christian doctrine familiar and comfortable.

But there was one ancient cult which, though indirectly, had enormous influence upon Christianity, and that was Orphism. Orphism was a set of Greek religious ideas existing without formal organization from as early as the eighth century B.C. and named after its legendary founder, Orpheus. Its central myth was that of the god Dionysus. Born as Zagreus, the child of Zeus, the boy was seized by evil Titans and devoured; his father, however, was able to procure his heart and to consume this himself; thereafter Zagreus was reborn again from Zeus as the god Dionysus. Zeus killed the Titans with thunderbolts, and men arose from their ashes—hence men share in both the evil nature of the Titans and in the divine nature of the god whom they had devoured. This myth sets forth the central teaching of Orphism, that the body is the prison of the soul: Zagreus-Dionysus is life and spirit; the Titans are the forces of matter, which devour and entrap the spirit; and the resurrection of Dionysus is the salvation of the spirit. The point is that Orphism was a dualistic religion, postulating a conflict between spirit (Good) and matter (Evil). Orphic ideas colored much Greek thought, particularly that of Plato, whose philosophy postulates a dichotomy between a real world of ideas and a less real, illusory, world of matter.

In Christian thought as early as the first century, this Greek dualism was wedded to Persian dualism. The equations were early made in Christian thought that Good is light and spirit and that Evil is darkness, matter, and flesh. The world-rejecting aspects of Christianity were thus underscored at the expense of the moderate, world-accepting aspects, and the formation of a strong, sometimes fanatical, distrust of matter and of the body was encouraged. This tradition often burst the bounds of orthodoxy and was condemned as heretical; more often it stayed within the church, urging it to extremes. It appeared in ancient and medieval heresies, in the more extreme practices of monastic asceticism, and in seventeenth-century Jansenism; and it is still manifest in many segments of both Catholic and Protestant Christianity.

The ideals of Hellenistic kingship came to play a large part in Christian political thought. When Alexander the Great conquered the East and his successors divided it, they adopted the style and manner of the ancient rulers of the East. The Hellenistic ruler was not only an autocrat, as the Great King of Persia had been, but also divine, as Pharaoh had been supposed to be. The awesome qualities of the Hellenistic king were later ascribed, in a modified form, to the Roman emperor. This had two consequences. In the first place, the Christians respected the authority of the emperor, even when he was unjust or unfavorable to Christianity, some of the church fathers arguing that unjust authority had to be accepted as a punishment visited upon us by God for our sins. In the second place, the majesty of the imperial office persisted, even when the emperors became Christian; and the strong position occupied by the later Byzantine, and to some extent the Holy Roman, emperors in relation to the church was in this tradition. The idea that in some fashion the emperor had divine authority was a strong element in the medieval conception of order and of the organization of Christian society.

The most important problem of the church of the first three centuries, apart from its survival in a hostile pagan world, was the development of its doctrine in a way that encouraged discussion and resolution of important points and at the same time discouraged undisciplined speculation that led to heresies and schisms. Even during the lifetime of the apostles, the Christian community was divided between those who wished to hold to the strict dictates of the Mosaic law (including, among other things, circumcision for male converts) and those who wished to modify that law to make it easier for the Gentiles to embrace Christianity. By the time the apostles had died, the number of compelling questions and the variety of traditions in the eastern Mediterranean milieu were such that it was impossible to secure a universal consensus.

The greatest difficulty the Christians faced was with the Gnostics. Gnosticism is difficult to define, since it took a great variety of forms. It sprang out of late Hebrew religion at about the same time as Christianity; and like Christianity, it was strongly influenced by Canaanite, Persian, and Greek dualism and by Platonic philosophy. Some of the Gnostic sects were purely dualistic; others were closer to Christianity. The Gnostic approach to religion was mythopoeic: the warfare between Good and Evil was clothed in terms of an elaborate cosmogony and cosmology involving intricate generations of gods and demigods. According to Christian Gnostics, Jesus had imparted secret knowledge (*gnosis*) to his immediate followers, revelations that were never written down. These Gnostics claimed to be the inheritors of this secret knowledge, which represented the true path to salvation. It was difficult for Christianity both to overcome the competition of Gnosticism and to prevent Gnostic doctrines from exercising too great an influence upon Christian believers. In spite of all efforts of the church fathers to the contrary, some of the Gnostic spirit rubbed off on Christianity, strengthening the otherworldly aspects of the religion. Gnosticism itself remained an independent force in the Middle East, spreading to the Balkans and eventually to western Europe by the twelfth century in the form of Cathar heresy.

Gnosticism and other heresies were provoked by raising the basic issues inherent in the construction of a Christian theology: What is Christian morality and on what basis does it repose? What is the nature of the Trinity? What is the nature of Christ? How is Christian worship to be conducted? What are the sacraments? Is man saved by his own efforts or solely by the will of God? These questions were met with a variety of answers by people who believed that they were following the true message of Jesus. How could the average member of the Christian congregation know who was right and who was wrong?

With these kinds of questions multiplying, and with the growth of the Christian community in size and importance, it became clear that some kind of system of authority was needed in the church. The prophetic Spirit had created Christianity, but the spirit of order was needed to preserve it. By the end of the third century, in spite of sporadic persecutions, Christianity had spread throughout the Roman Empire and into Persia and India. By 300, perhaps a quarter of the population of the eastern half of the empire was Christian, and a tenth of that of the western half. The concentration of Christians in the cities was probably higher ("*pagan*," the word Christians commonly used to denote non-Christians, meant "country bumpkin," an indication that early Christians perceived the countryside to be less Christianized than the cities). From its beginnings, the Christian community included not only the poor and dispossessed but some of the nobility and many intellectuals. As time passed, more and more notable citizens were adhering to the new religion. A pattern of organization had become necessary.

The transformation of the Christian community into an organized church was the result both of metaphysical and of pragmatic considerations, and it happened very early. Historically, Christianity was always an "organized religion." At the Last Supper, Christ had already brought the apostles into personal union with him by giving them his body and blood; and St. Paul elaborated the idea that all Christians were one with Christ in a "Mystical Body." In the earliest years following the Passion of Christ, Christians assumed that the apostles were heirs to his authority, and as the apostles died one by one, their survivors elected new men to fill the empty places. Already in the Book of Acts, Matthias was chosen by the apostles to replace Judas Iscariot. Whoever the apostles consecrated as a successor by the laying on of hands was deemed to share equally in the responsibility and authority conferred upon the apostles by Christ. This transmission of authority is called apostolic succession, and Orthodox, Catholic, and Anglican bishops today believe that their authority stretches back unbroken through the laying on of hands to the time of Christ. These direct successors to the apostles were the bishops. Within 75 years of the Crucifixion, Ignatius of Antioch (c. A.D. 30–107), one of the greatest church fathers, had already argued that "we should look upon the bishop even as we would look upon the Lord himself."

More than anything, the doctrine of apostolic succession provided the answer to the "secret knowledge" of the Gnostics. Many Christian leaders reasoned that if Jesus left hidden revelations to anyone, he must have left them to his closest disciples. And these disciples surely would have passed any secret knowledge to their successors, and so on and on through the generations. Through the practice of apostolic succession, each new bishop received the gifts of his office from a predecessor, who through an unbroken line had received his gifts from an original apostle, and ultimately from Jesus himself. If a direct successor to an apostle had not received any secret revelations, then, the leaders of the church reasoned, these secret revelations must not really exist.

The practical need for organization continually increased, and it became necessary to establish rules for the election of the successors of the apostles and to create definitions of the scope and nature of the church. In the pristine Christian community, there was no distinction between clergy and laity: all were simple followers of the Lord. But almost immediately the Mass, or Lord's Supper, became the center of Christian worship, and some of the community were given the authority to break the bread and offer the cup as Christ had done at the Last Supper. Those who had the power of distributing the sacrament were called priests (Greek *presbyteroi,* "elders") or bishops (Greek *episkopoi,* "overseers"). Soon it was found useful to have one man in each community with authority to resolve disputes on matters of practice or doctrine, and a distinction was then made between the priests and the bishop. Within the first 200 years of the spread of the church, every important town or city with a Christian community came to have its bishop. Since the largest Christian communities naturally existed in the largest and most important towns of the Roman Empire, it was natural that ecclesiastical organization came to parallel Roman civil administration: the civil administrators and the bishops dwelt in the same towns; and the most important bishops, like the most important administrators, were those who occupied the major cities like Alexandria, Rome, Antioch, or Milan. It was the bishops who generally received consecration from the apostles, and so it was upon the bishops that the powers of the apostolic succession devolved.

At the same time, a definition of the Christian community was necessary. The community was defined as the church (Greek *ekklesia,* "community," "assembly," or "congregation" was translated as *ecclesia* in Latin and *church* in English), and the church was identified with St. Paul's Mystical Body of Christ. All who were joined to Christ in the Mystical Body were saved. But how was membership in the Mystical Body, or indeed in the church, to be defined? Were all good people members of the church? But then professed pagans would have to be considered Christians. Were all those who professed belief in Christ members? But there were many, among the Gnostics for example, who claimed to be Christians while teaching eccentric doctrines and even, like Simon Magus, practicing magic. Were only those professed Christians who were pure of heart really members of the church? This is the idea of the "invisible church" professed much later by some Protestants, but the difficulty lay in building an effective organization out of something invisible.

It therefore became common, though by no means universal, to assume that membership in the church was limited to those who were in communion with the bishops, the successors of the apostles. St. Ignatius wrote, "Apart from [bishops, priests, and deacons] there is no elect church, no congregation of holy ones." Through apostolic succession, the bishops had the right to grant Holy Communion to those whom they deemed pure in conduct and correct in doctrine, and otherwise to refuse it. "Let that be deemed a proper Eucharist which is administered by the bishop or by a person whom he has delegated," said Ignatius. This was an enormous step toward a principle of order in the church, and it had an immediate effect upon prophecy. In the earliest years of the church there were men who imitated Paul and Barnabas by wandering around preaching Christ to all people. But they were under the authority of no bishop, and some naturally came to teach in an eccentric manner uncongenial to the nascent ecclesiastical authority. Such prophecy was therefore discouraged, and it ceased to exist much beyond the end of the first century.

All the organizational developments mentioned above had been effected by the early years of the second century. But several enormous questions remained to be resolved. As the priests and laity in each community had disputed among themselves, so the bishops of the whole church began to disagree on matters of jurisdiction, of discipline, and of doctrine. Who would be the shepherd of the shepherds and resolve these disputes? Who, in short, constituted the ultimate authority in the church?

The Bible could be no such authority, for it was centuries before a general agreement was reached as to which books it should include, the official canon being set only in 369 by St. Athanasius. There were several possible answers. In the first few centuries, the teachings of the fathers of the church were given great weight, though of course they frequently disagreed with one another. Public meetings of bishops called synods or councils also had enormous prestige, but there could still be disagreement within the councils; moreover there was the question of who had the authority to call the councils and to select their membership. Then, particular authority came to devolve upon the bishops of those cities most important for their size or for their place in Christian tradition: Jerusalem, Antioch; Alexandria, Rome, and, later, Constantinople. In the Latin West, the bishop of Rome gradually came to be the most important; later, in the Middle Ages, the bishops of Rome would extend the identification of the Mystical Body with the church to the church of Rome, and indeed to the church of Rome with its governing body, the pope and his cardinals. This was to be the ultimate statement of the principle of order within the church in western Europe.

Against growing order, the spirit of prophecy protested. In the first three centuries, when the Christians were often persecuted, the witness of the martyrs was itself an expression of the individual, prophetic spirit. Moreover, many refused to bow to the authority of the bishops in matters of discipline or doctrine and were therefore expelled from the church as heretics. Of these, a number were unworthy by virtue of their cowardice in the face of persecution, laxity in morals, or absurdity in doctrine; but there were also many in whom dwelt a righteous prophetic spirit, repulsed by an often narrow and unsympathetic ecclesiastical authority.

Monasticism was the most important of the prophetic movements in the early church. From the second century it was not uncommon for men, often of wealth and prestige, to withdraw into a desert place to live a life of utter poverty and renunciation. Dressed in rough skins, eating only what they could glean from the nearly barren land, shunning human comfort and company, they followed the ascetic spirit of John the Baptist or imitated Christ in his own withdrawal for forty days into the desert. Only by renouncing this world completely, these hermits argued, could they wholly fulfill St. Paul's injunction to empty out the self and to install Christ in its place. At first the monks (Greek *monachos,* "one who dwells alone") dwelt each in his complete solitude; but soon the numbers seeking retreat were so many that communities sprang up in the desert; and in order to avoid confusion and anarchy, some sort of rule or order had to be placed even upon the prophets.

The first monastic community was founded in the Egyptian desert by Pachomius in 323. His sister, Mary, formed a monastic community for women in 330. Pachomius modified the solitary monastic life by bringing the monks together on a regular basis for communal meals to celebrate the love between God and humanity. When the monks came together, they prefigured the eschatological community that would join Christ at the end of time. By awaiting the second advent of Christ outside the institutional church, the monastic community represented the prophetic spirit. At the same time, however, by coming together in communion, the monks imposed order upon their community. Moreover, the monastic community did not cut itself off completely from the world: the prayers of the monks were for the benefit of the world in its entirety.

Prayer was the principal duty of the monk and the real function of monasticism. The prayers of the monk were active and constructive, rather than self-centered. These prayers were a real weapon against the powers of evil, calling down the blessings of God upon the entire Christian community. There was nothing merely symbolic or simply metaphorical about the war that the monks were waging. Monks regarded themselves as warriors on a spiritual battleground, struggling against an enemy whose presence was as literal as a host of earthly soldiers.

Monasticism spread rapidly in the East, especially in Syria and Egypt, during the third and fourth centuries. In 410, eastern style communal monasticism passed into the West, when the Syrian monk, Cassian, established a monastery in Massilia (modern-day Marseilles). Subsequently, monasticism became one of the most visible examples of the prophetic spirit of Christianity in the western world.

Monasticism has its roots deep in the tradition of Christ. But it is necessary to explain the enormous numbers of people, young and old, who poured into the desert during the third and fourth centuries. It used to be argued that they were fleeing hard times: persecution, economic depression, the general malaise of the later Roman Empire. But depression or malaise was not keenly felt in the population as a whole. Moreover, an extraordinary proportion of the monks were people who had wealth and influence in their communities and were the least prone to the effects of moral or economic depression. Finally, the only other period of enormous monastic expansion, in the eleventh and twelfth centuries, is one of great moral and economic advance and optimism. What the two periods, the second and third and the eleventh and twelfth centuries, have in common is that each was a period of rapid growth of organization within the church. In each era, the advance of the spirit of order called forth a corresponding thrust from the spirit of prophecy. The call of Christ seemed to the monks to demand sacrifice and wholehearted devotion greater even than that preached by the organized church.

The most spectacular advance of the spirit of order was soon to come. Soon the Roman state, which since the Crucifixion had sporadically prosecuted and persecuted Christianity, would adopt a new policy of tolerance. Soon the divine emperor himself would lay claim to being the supreme authority over the Christian church. Soon, through the Christianization of the empire, the spirit of order would be able to equate the church with society as a whole and to strive to build a Christian society on earth.

Chapter Three

The Peace of the Church

The "Peace of the Church"—the end of persecution by the Roman state and people—transformed the problems and even the nature of Christianity. Though the persecutions had been sporadic, and though their ferocity has sometimes been exaggerated (Nero probably did not, for example, use Christians as human torches to illuminate his nocturnal revels), they were harsh enough and deeply rooted in popular support. They were usually launched, not by official decree, but by the fanaticism and prejudice of the common people. Eusebius of Caesarea's graphic and detailed account of the persecution of the Christians of Lyon in the early third century is typical: first the people of Lyon rose up and heaped abuses upon the Christians, and *then* they dragged the Christians before the authorities, who responded to the public pressure. Christianity was despised by the intellectual and cultured as an absurd doctrine suitable only to the vulgar, and it was loathed by the vulgar as something strange and, therefore, obscene. In a dark psychological process, people have always accused little-known religions of the most heinous crimes imaginable, particularly sexual orgies and child-murder or cannibalism. Some Protestants still charge Catholics with such crimes; Christians have so accused Jews; medieval Catholics the heretics; and the Roman people the Christians. Christianity seemed wicked or detestable. One of the earliest known depictions of the Crucifixion is a graffito of a crucified donkey with the mocking inscription "Alexamenos [evidently a local Christian] adores his god." But the most serious charge leveled against the Christians, one which enlisted state support for the persecutions, was that of atheism.

The charge of atheism was made in deadly earnest. The religion of ancient Rome, as indeed the religion of most societies, was public and official in nature. The Romans and the Greeks knew no distinction between religion and the state, between devotion to the public cult and patriotism. Every Roman was required to perform certain public acts of devotion to the gods who maintained Rome's strength and property; what private citizens believed in their own homes was up to them. The

Roman state objected to religious cults characterized by human sacrifice or ritual mutilation, but otherwise accepted a wide variety of private religious practices as long as the public manifestations of patriotism were retained. Most religions found no objections to this point of view, which had been normal for millennia. Only a few refused to participate in public rituals; of these the Jews and Christians were the most numerous. Unlike the Jews, the Christians proselytized vigorously, and were therefore highly visible. Christians reasoned that there was but one God, and he had commanded them to have no other gods but him. But to the Roman state and people, disloyalty to the gods of Rome bespoke disloyalty to the Roman state. In vain did the Christians fulfill all the other duties of citizenship, including military service; in vain did they plead that their high morality made them even better citizens than the ordinary. They would not fulfill their duties to the state gods, and so they were not only atheists, but traitors.

Persecutions flared up here and there throughout the empire, but in the third century they expanded in scope and thoroughness. After the Christians spurned the generous offer of the Emperor Aurelian (270–275) to include Christ in a pantheon along with Mithra as a manifestation of the Unconquered Sun, the state determined to root out these subversives. It was the best emperors, those who were most energetic in trying to pull together the weakening bonds of Roman society, who could least tolerate the Christians' refusal to submit totally to the imperial will. So the great Diocletian, whose persecution began in 303, and his successors Maxentius (d. 312) and Galerius (d. 311) launched the most merciless pogroms of all. Even this "Great Persecution" was limited, however; by the fourth century, Christianity was too widespread and too well organized to destroy. Moreover, the persecutions no longer enjoyed much public support. The majority of the Roman population had grown accustomed to Christians in their midst and no longer regarded them as threatening.

Still, imperial policy resulted in a substantial number of organized persecutions, especially in the eastern Empire near the centers of imperial authority. Though many Christians lapsed, many suffered bravely under persecution; often, groups of Christians went cheerfully to their deaths, holding hands, smiling through their pains, and singing hymns. Christians who died in persecutions were known as martyrs, from the Greek word for "witness." By going willingly to their deaths, these martyrs were testifying to the presence of a better life to come. More than a few of the Romans observing these Christians found themselves quite impressed by this testimony, and conversions after persecutions more than replenished the ranks of the Christian community. As the moralist Tertullian (fl. 190–210) remarked, "the blood of the martyrs was the seed of the church." Most of the church fathers taught that the proper attitude toward persecution was passive obedience, in recognition that it came from God as the just punishment of sin, and in anticipation of the advent of the Kingdom of God.

This passive acceptance of what Christians considered a bad order of society became an active acceptance of a good order of society when the persecutions stopped and a new era of tolerance and support was ushered in by Constantine the Great.

Constantine was born in Britain of a soldier father, Constantius Chlorus, one of the four ruling tetrarchs in the Roman Empire. Constantine's mother was a Christian, later known as St. Helena. Late in her life, Helena claimed to have been successful in discovering in Palestine the remnants of the True Cross upon which Jesus had died. Her success in making her son a Christian was less marked, however. During the political and military upheavals following the retirement of Diocletian as emperor in 305, the empire was divided, and Constantine's father laid claim to the imperial title in the West. He died before he could recognize his ambitions, but he bequeathed them to his son. The legions stationed in Britain proclaimed Constantine emperor, and he proceeded to engage his rivals in a series of battles from which, with the help of his ally Licinius, he emerged victorious. Eventually he also deposed Licinius and assumed the rule of the entire empire in 324.

It has long been debated whether Constantine was a Christian. The church father Lactantius tells a story that was adapted by Constantine's biographer, Eusebius, and entered into popular belief: before the battle of the Milvian Bridge, in which Constantine defeated one of his rivals and thus was able to occupy the city of Rome, he is supposed to have seen the symbol ☧ in the sky (χρ, the first letters of the name Christ in Greek) with a legend in Greek meaning, "by this sign you shall conquer." Not only is it doubtful whether Constantine saw the vision, but many people doubt whether he was ever really a Christian at all. As emperor he continued the public religion of Rome, with special attention to Sol Invictus, the Unconquered Sun; he struck coins and medals in honor of the Sun and other deities, including himself as divine emperor. If he ever formally professed Christianity, it was probably not until he was on his deathbed.

Nonetheless the reign of Constantine marked a great advance in Christian fortunes. In the decade 310–320, Constantine, Licinius, and even the dying and repentant Galerius issued a number of edicts in which persecutions of the Christians were halted, tolerance of all religious beliefs and practices was proclaimed, and the obligation of public sacrifice was lifted. Then, in 324, when Constantine had completed his reunification of the Roman Empire, he publicly declared his support for Christianity even while maintaining traditional religious institutions and practices. In a letter to one of his government officials, he wrote, "Favor the Christian clergy, since their conduct of worship towards the divinity will in my opinion bring immeasurable benefit to the commonwealth." Though Constantine stopped short of establishing Christianity as a state religion, he showed his favor by putting Christian bishops in charge of religious disputes, Christian and non-Christian alike. Perhaps Constantine perceived that the Christian church was becoming the most numerous and influential cult in the empire. Perhaps he felt the genuine stirrings of Christian faith. More likely, Constantine simply believed that Rome was big enough to accept Christianity alongside more traditional religions. In any event, the age of persecution was over, and the age of Constantine began: the age of alliance of church with state that has endured in at least some countries into the twentieth century.

In later years—up to the present day—people in the western world looked back to the time of Constantine as a period in which the Christian community overthrew the pagan world in a bitter life-or-death struggle. Since Christianity is an exclusive religion, one that does not perceive other religious faiths as legitimate, it has been hard to accept the idea that pagans and Christians could live together side-by-side without conflict. But Constantine was a Roman emperor first and a Christian second (if at all). By the time he became emperor, the state religion of Rome had undergone significant changes. Old notions of a polytheistic pantheon composed of anthropomorphic, childishly emotional gods had long been dismissed by philosophers and intellectuals. By the beginning of the fourth century, most thoughtful expressions of religious belief tended to support an essentially monotheistic system, in which a central deity intervened in nature through emanations or divine aspects. Constantine, not noted for his acumen as a theologian, seems to have considered one monotheism as beneficial as another. He did not perceive a great deal of difference between Sol Invictus, the Unconquered Sun, and Jesus Christ, the Light of the World. He proposed that if Christians and non-Christians could each agree upon the principles of one God in Heaven and the divinely appointed authority of the emperor, then everyone should get along happily. His goal was internal peace and harmony within the Empire, rather than dogmatic theological consistency.

Constantine asked the Christian leadership for one important concession: acknowledgment that the emperor was the natural head of the church. The bishops agreed to this concession with unanimity. There was no Christian precedent for such an acknowledgment, but there was plenty of Roman precedent. Since Caesar Augustus, the Roman emperors had each carried the title *pontifex maximus*, highest priest in the state religion of Rome. In assuming the leadership of the Christian church, Constantine was demonstrating its legitimacy as a publicly authorized cult in the Roman state. The bishops, themselves Roman citizens, were understandably happy to receive such recognition—it meant an end to the church's status as an outlawed and persecuted cult. Christians could now practice their faith without compromising their Roman citizenship.

To some Christians, notably Eusebius of Caesarea, the admiring chronicler of the deeds of Constantine, the alliance of Christianity with the empire was natural. There was a theory of history derived from the Hellenistic period in which four or five universal monarchies succeeded one another in progression. Some of the Christian fathers, such as Irenaeus and Tertullian, affirmed that the Roman Empire was the last and greatest of the universal monarchies and that its fall would bring about the appearance of the Antichrist, dreadful war and ruin, and the end of the world. Because of this theory, as well as because many Christians assumed implicitly, along with their pagan fellow-Romans, that Rome was eternal, there was universal consternation and horror when the city of Rome was sacked by barbarians in 410. A hundred years earlier, at the time of Constantine, Eusebius and other Christians believed that the preservation of the Roman state was necessary for the preservation of the world and that the union of Christianity and the empire under Constantine and his successors was wholly desirable.

The effects of this union—the Peace of the Church—were several. In the first place the Christian community was relieved of a great dread and fear. It was now possible to practice Christianity without danger to life or limb. Yet even this was a mixed blessing. Heretofore only those with strong convictions had entered the church, which had been a community of martyrs and heroes. Even some pagan writers observed that Christians stood out from the population by virtue of their morality and their acts of love and mercy. Now the lukewarm diluted the fervor of the Christian community even while swelling its numbers.

Further, after Constantine made it legal to bequeath property to the church, and as the emperor gradually came to prefer Christians over pagans for promotions in the army and the civil service, the church grew rich and powerful. During the first 300 years of the Christian church, its leaders were motivated by religious conviction. Bishops did not occupy positions of power; indeed, they daily faced the very real prospect of arrest, torture, and execution. Under Constantine, however, bishops found themselves in positions of high authority. No longer the leaders of an outlaw community, bishops now helped govern the Roman state. The new status of the Christian community could not help but change it. Not only the lukewarm but also the timeservers now entered the church, which became a road to advancement within society more than a tribunal of judgment upon society. As the church grew wealthier, corrupt practices such as simony (the sale or purchase of the sacraments or of ecclesiastical offices) became more common. The history of medieval Christianity really begins with the Age of Constantine, for it was then that the intricate involvement of the church with the state began, with all of its dilemmas. Few people in the church resisted this new dispensation, in which the order of society was identified with the order of the church. They were too relieved to escape persecution; they were too eager to Christianize society by the use of political influence; and they were too accustomed to the formal attachment of religion to the state. The idea of real religious pluralism was almost inconceivable to a religion that was convinced that it possessed the only ethical and metaphysical truth.

The effects, both good and dubious, of the alliance of Christianity with the state appeared immediately. On the one hand, the involvement of the church in politics significantly modified the laws and customs of society. For example, Christians put an end to the hideous spectacles in which men and animals tortured one another to death in the coliseums to the screaming delight of a brutal mob. Yet, on a deeper level, some accommodation of the church to society was necessary. A religion that through exaggerated conservatism ceases to express the true life of the community or ceases to speak in a language which the community can understand condemns itself to isolation and eventual impotence or even extinction. The ability of Christianity to adapt to society at the same time as it adapted society to itself is one of the secrets of its long endurance.

But for these advantages medieval Christianity paid a price. The acquisition of political power and influence invited, indeed almost demanded, interference on the part of any energetic ruler determined to secure order by the use of every tool at his disposal. For Constantine and his successors, the church became such a tool.

Perceiving that the balance of wealth, population, and power had shifted to the East, Constantine determined to build a new capital at Byzantium, a second Rome that he adorned with all the splendors of the first. He renamed the city Constantinople, took up his residence there, and caused its bishop to be elevated to the level of the four other patriarchs, Rome, Alexandria, Jerusalem, and Antioch. He prepared a shrine for the twelve apostles in which he caused to be erected a thirteenth tomb reserved for himself; and his biographer Eusebius bestowed upon him the title of "Equal of the Apostles." In order to integrate the Christian church into the overall harmony of the empire, Constantine not only patronized it but undertook to direct it. When Constantine arrived in the East, he did not find the smoothly unified Christian community that he expected. Instead, he found the Christian leadership at odds over theological issues that were beyond his comprehension. Constantine determined that if the Christian church was going to function as a focus for religious stability, then its leaders were going to have to solve the issues dividing them. Constantine took direct action. The first great ecumenical council, that of Nicaea in 325, was summoned and presided over not by a patriarch, but by the emperor, who even intervened in the theological discussions and used the authority of the state to compel assent to doctrinal decisions. It was at this council that the Arians, followers of the Alexandrian priest Arius who argued that the Father was superior to the Son and Holy Spirit, were condemned. Constantine first supported the Arians, but perceiving that the majority of bishops in attendance opposed the doctrine, he shifted his support to the majority view. Clearly, Constantine was more interested in consensus than doctrinal truth. Under his influence, the bishops left the council with an agreement that all parties could accept. By the time Constantine died in 337, he had established the tradition of "caesaropapism," in which the chief authority over the church is supposed to be delegated by God directly to the emperor. Although there was no Christian precedent for imperial rule over the church, Roman tradition held that the emperor was the highest priest (*pontifex maximus*) of Roman religion in all of its forms. Constantine did not need to personally declare himself to be a Christian in order to assume the highest position of authority in the Christian church.

Constantine's successors were even less reticent. Now openly Christians, they argued imperial authority in the church with all the conviction that material force and influence could lend. Though some supported one side of the great doctrinal controversies of the time and some the other, they all argued that it was the emperor who was entitled to determine what was Orthodox; and the Emperor Constantius went so far as to declare that "whatever I will must have the force of ecclesiastical law." The alliance between church and state was finally sealed in 391 under the Emperor Theodosius the Great, who formally established Christianity as the official religion of the empire and outlawed paganism. The tables were turned, and the religion that had suffered persecution with patient dignity now eagerly encouraged stiff civil penalties for paganism and for heresy. In such a church the prophetic spirit found expression increasingly difficult.

Prophetic resistance to these trends sometimes took extreme forms. The first conflict between extreme purists and moderates took place even before the reign of Constantine. During the great persecutions at the end of the third century and the beginning of the fourth, many Christians had nominally abjured Christianity in order to save their lives. When the persecutions were over, they sought to return to the church. The majority of the faithful were willing to accept them, but a minority refused, condemning the cowards as apostates. The extremists' greatest strength was in the province of Africa and in neighboring Numidia, where they were called Donatists after their bishop, Donatus. The Donatists refused to recognize any bishop or priest who had apostasized, however temporarily, and they even condemned anyone who was willing to be in communion with such alleged cowards. Donatism spread widely and persisted until the Vandal conquest of Roman Africa in 429, a conquest hastened by the bitter feuds between Catholics and Donatists. Perhaps the most important significance of Donatism is that it represented a reaction of purists against worldly compromise that became typical of many protest movements within the church down to the present. Many medieval heretics, though unconnected with historical Donatism, held identical beliefs, refusing to accept the validity of sacraments administered by an immoral priest, as against the teaching of the church that sacerdotal powers were independent of the worthiness of the priest.

In the meantime, the establishment of order within the church was growing. By the end of the fourth century, when Christianity was established as the official religion of the empire, the majority of the Roman population were nominally Christian. The new religion had first spread to the Jewish communities of the commercial cities of the Mediterranean, and subsequently to the non-Jewish peoples of those cities. The peasants in the hinterland ("pagans" in the original sense), always conservative, clung longer to the old ways. (Later, "pagan" was translated by the English as "heathen": "inhabitant of the heath," or English countryside.) By 400, when even the country people had been converted, there was need to expand and modify the organization of the church. In the beginning, there had been no organization of the dioceses into parishes, the priests living instead at large in the city or with the bishop. By the fourth century, the growing numbers of Christian people and the growing stability and wealth of the church made it possible to build several churches in every major town. The chief of these churches was called the cathedral (Latin *cathedra,* "chair," i.e., the chair where the bishop sat) and was designated the bishop's residence. The other churches were usually designated parish churches, and a priest was in charge of each. Large and important churches would be staffed by several priests, the leader of whom was called the rector or pastor. The older system, in which the priests of the diocese all lived together with their bishop, continued to be used in wild and newly converted areas. During the conversion of the English, for example, the priests of a diocese lived with the bishop in his "minster." The English countryside, as yet devoid of parish churches, was studded with rude stone crosses, to which the priests of the minster would journey as often as circumstances permitted in order to say Mass for the faithful. In the East, and sometimes in the West, bishops chose *chorepiscopi,* "country-bishops," as auxiliaries in rural areas, but this custom slowly disappeared.

As more territory was Christianized, the number of dioceses grew. In the East, it was common for even smaller towns to have their bishops; in the West, only major cities were generally made into episcopal sees. The official recognition of Christianity made it natural to draw the boundary lines of the dioceses to correspond roughly with Roman administrative boundaries. As smaller Roman administrative units were grouped into larger, so it also became the custom in the church to group dioceses into larger units called provinces. The Council of Nicaea of 325 urged bishops to gather periodically in provincial councils in order to discuss common problems and to coordinate policies. The bishop of the most important metropolis in the province (such as Rome, Milan, Alexandria, or Lyon) was called the metropolitan bishop, and it was his authority to call the provincial synods and to preside over them. Thus the beginnings of a hierarchy were established: the priest of the parish was responsible to the bishop of the diocese, and the bishop of the diocese to the metropolitan of the province.

There were in the fourth and fifth centuries two obstacles to further elaboration of the hierarchy. First, the bishops were the successors of the apostles. As no authority higher than apostolic authority was conceivable, there was consecration to no higher office than that of bishop. The metropolitans remained bishops, and as a result their authority over other bishops was always tenuous and disputed. By the seventh century the institution of metropolitans gradually faded away. Second, the authority of the civil power, particularly that of the emperor, made itself so strongly felt as to inhibit the growth of any other authority over the entire church. In the fourth and fifth centuries there were two major possibilities for such authority: the bishops of the great patriarchal sees and the ecumenical councils.

After the establishment of Constantinople, there were five patriarchal sees. From the end of the first century at least, these sees were accustomed to receive requests from lesser communities for advice and arbitration. In about A.D. 95, for example, the church of Corinth asked the church of Rome to help resolve a local dispute. Of the five patriarchs, those of Rome and Constantinople emerged preeminent by the fourth century because of their location in the seats of empire. Even their power was inhibited both by the influence of the emperors and also by an ancient rule against the transfer of bishops from one diocese to another. This meant that the ablest bishops of minor sees had no chance of being elevated to the patriarchate, and that upon entering into their office the patriarchs had no episcopal experience. Nevertheless the growth of the power of the patriarchs of Rome and Constantinople was impressive.

That of Constantinople was the more striking in that the city was of little importance until Constantine made it his capital, yet in 381 the First

Council of Constantinople conferred upon the patriarch a primacy in honor second only to that of Rome. Though Alexandria was the most venerable see of the East, it found its power gradually slipping to that of Constantinople, which enjoyed special imperial patronage, the prestige of the capital, and the advantage of being near when dignitaries and bishops from all over the empire came to call upon their ruler. Yet the very presence of the emperor proved in the long run disadvantageous. Constantinople enjoyed immense ecclesiastical power; but that power was more often imperial than patriarchal, and the bishop of the Second Rome, patronized and often appointed by the emperor, was obliged to be obedient to his master. It was not the patriarch but the Emperor Constantine who called the First Nicene Council, the Emperor Theodosius who issued edicts against pagans and heretics, and the Emperor Justinian who erected the great cathedral of Hagia Sophia.

The rise of the bishops of Rome was less spectacular but more enduring. In the first place, they had the advantage of certain theoretical claims to primacy. When Christ bestowed authority upon the apostles, he appears to have given Peter preeminence (see, for example, Matthew 16:17–19). Since Peter journeyed to Rome, probably led the Christian community there, and was finally crucified there, the bishops of Rome could claim that they were his successors. They argued that they had inherited not only the general authority of the apostles but the special authority of Peter.

It is now no longer necessary to dispute at length over the pristine powers of the bishop of Rome. Old-fashioned Catholics used to imagine that they were obliged to argue that the popes of the second century exercised, at least implicitly, the same plenitude of power accorded Pius IX in 1870; old-fashioned Protestants supposed that they had only to disprove this in order to demonstrate that the institution of the papacy was fraudulent. Neither argument is particularly cogent. The early papacy certainly did not possess anything remotely resembling its later powers; but these powers were gradually acquired through a process of development typical of many historical institutions. Whether or not this development was metaphysically legitimate is a question for the theologian, not the historian.

In the development of papal powers there were several conceptual as well as chronological stages. Conceptually, the papacy first obtained recognition of its primacy in honor throughout the church. Second, it obtained the right to judge disputes submitted to it by other dioceses. Third, it gradually obtained the right to administer the church as a whole in matters of jurisdiction and discipline. Fourth, it gradually secured the right to define doctrine. Fifth, for a while it even claimed the right to rule all of Christian society not only in spiritual but even in temporal matters. None of these claims were uncontested; the supporters of papal authority were faced continually with the task of persuading the church as a whole to accept the spiritual (and at times, temporal) leadership of the pope.

Chronologically, the acquisition of these powers is difficult to define, for it was full of false starts and retreats as well as gradual progress. To begin with, the bishop of Rome had several advantages in addition to his theoretical primacy. First, he occupied the ancient capital of the empire and so even here had the upper hand over his brother at Constantinople. Second, the imperial power in Rome declined markedly over the centuries. For most of the fourth century there was no emperor in Rome at all, and Constantinople was responsible for the entire empire. In the fifth century there were emperors at Rome until 476, but their powers were greatly reduced by the effects of internal dissension and the barbarian invasions. After 476, Constantinople resumed the sole rule of the empire, but, except for the time of Justinian (527–565) and his immediate successors, it was unable to control much of Italy. There were certain handicaps to being away from the center of civil power, but on the positive side the opportunities for independent action were greater. The imperial presence did not overshadow the bishop of Rome as it did the bishop of Constantinople. The popes pursued a policy independent of, and sometimes antagonistic to, that of the emperor; and if Rome remained the Eternal City, it did so because of the prestige of the papacy, not that of the empire. Finally, while the East had three patriarchates (including the powerful Alexandria) that rivaled Constantinople, Rome was the only patriarchate in the West. Aside from the bishop of Carthage, who enjoyed great prestige throughout Africa, Rome was without a rival in fully half of the empire, and the fall of Carthage in 439 to the heretical Vandals enhanced the position of Rome even more. In the second century, St. Irenaeus (120–202) said, “It is a matter of necessity that every church should agree with this church [of Rome], on account of its preeminent authority.” Pope Victor (189–198) intervened in Asia to order the churches there to conform to the Roman date of Easter. Pope Siricius (385–399) established a papal vicariate in Thessalonica.

Yet as late as 400, papal powers were very ill-defined. In the first ecumenical council the papacy and the West as a whole were scarcely represented. More common than theories of papal primacy were those of episcopal collegiality: St. Cyprian (200–258) argued that it was upon the episcopate *as a whole* that the church was founded and that the bishops *as a whole* were the supreme authority in the church. This argument found many supporters until the triumph of papal monarchy in the eleventh century. It has always been held by the Eastern Orthodox church, and it has been revived since, by the conciliar movement of the fifteenth century, by Anglican and Lutheran Protestants, and, to a limited extent, even by the Roman Catholic church at the time of the Second Vatican Council of 1962–1965.

It was really owing to the labors of a few great popes of the fifth and sixth centuries that the power of the papacy in the West was firmly established. The first of these was Pope Leo the Great (440–461), who ruled Rome while the western empire was coming rapidly to an end. The Visigoths had already taken the Eternal City (410) and passed on to southern Gaul and Spain. The Franks occupied northern Gaul; the Vandals had conquered Africa and the Anglo-Saxons much of Britain. Only Italy remained to the empire, and there the imperial military forces, from the lowest infantryman to the commander-in-chief, consisted almost entirely of barbarian mercenaries. The moral authority of the emperor was even more tenuous. Into this situation burst the Huns, a pagan, savage group of conquerors from the plains of central Asia, their powers recently united under the bloodthirsty Attila. After ravaging the Balkans and central Europe, Attila invaded Gaul, where he was defeated by an alliance of Romans, Burgundians, Franks, and Visigoths at the decisive battle of Châlons in 451. Repulsed from Gaul, Attila invaded Italy and from Milan announced his intention of conquering Rome itself. Helpless to prevent the conquest by military force, the emperor abdicated his responsibility to the pope. As the Huns advanced toward the city of Rome, it was Leo, rather than the emperor, who led a delegation to meet with Attila. Leo somehow managed to turn the Huns aside, perhaps by convincing Attila, whose warband was ravaged by disease and exhaustion, to accept a small portion of Rome's wealth in peace rather than fighting for it all. Later accounts say that Leo was accompanied by an angelic host. In any case, Leo was credited with saving Rome, and the reputation of the papacy received an enormous boost.

As the power of the emperor and the Roman civil administration decayed in the West, it had in part passed to the bishops, who were the only other authorities of note in the cities. In many localities the bishop had been entrusted with the civil, financial, and even military administration of the town. In Rome similar powers passed to Leo from the hands of an impotent emperor. It was Leo who led the embassy to meet the tired and aging Attila in Milan and there persuaded him by means of a sizable tribute to refrain from his projected conquest. It was Leo who took charge of the repair of the fortifications of Rome and the repair of the public buildings. In all this, Leo was appropriating to the papacy a certain temporal authority.

Leo's prestige was not limited to administrative affairs or to the West alone. When he intervened in the doctrinal dispute between the Nestorians and the Monophysites and persuaded the Council of Chalcedon (451) to accept as orthodox his definition of the nature of Christ, it was the first time that a pope had exercised such influence at a general council. When his letter was read to the assembled bishops, they agreed that "this is the faith of the Fathers; this is the faith of the Apostles. This is the faith of us all. Peter has spoken through Leo."

It is his insistence upon the pope's role as the successor of Peter that makes Leo one of the earliest proponents of a Christian order dominated by the papacy. Leo was the first pope to argue that the pope was the vicar of Peter: that he had the right to rule the church as the Fisherman's successor. It was he who for the first time emphasized that Christ had given the keys and the power to bind and loose to Peter alone. Just as Peter in turn had delegated these powers to the other apostles, so the pope delegated power to the other bishops. The next step, which would not be taken until the papacy had reached its zenith, would be to state that Peter and his successors functioned as vicars of Christ. The superiority in honor over other bishops of Peter's successors was accepted by the Council of Chalcedon, but that body also promoted an idea of order somewhat different from Leo's. It declared that the see of Constantinople, though second to Rome in honor, was equal in rank and power, and it affirmed that even as Rome had authority over the West, so Constantinople had authority over Pontus, Thrace, and the province of Asia. This idea would have great consequence, eventually dividing Christendom into two orders and two societies: Roman Catholicism and Eastern Orthodoxy.

Gelasius I (492–496) pressed the claims of the papacy further. The Emperor Zeno attempted to impose upon the church his own doctrine of Christ's nature, but Gelasius responded to this effort and to that of Zeno's successor, the Emperor Anastasius I, by asserting the independence and indeed the supremacy of the priestly authority. It was the pope's function to teach, and the emperor's to learn, what was the good in society. As successor of Peter, the pope had authority over all of Christian society, and the emperor was only his most important helper.

This Gelasian doctrine was often cited and much developed by the papalists in the long struggle between papacy and empire in the later Middle Ages.

The most important pope of the early Middle Ages was Gregory I the Great (590–604). Born into a noble Roman family, Gregory first pursued a career in civil administration, but as a young man he perceived the contradiction between the teachings of Christ and the pursuit of wealth and prestige. He withdrew from the world and established a monastic community on his family property. But he could not remain long in isolation. His reputation as an administrator of rectitude and skill was too great, and he was persuaded to return to public life in the ecclesiastical administration of the city. Elected pope in 590, he continued the policies of Leo the Great, acting as the emperor's representative in the city of Rome, collecting taxes, providing for welfare, arming and training soldiers, repairing public buildings and fortifications, and taking chief responsibility for the defense of Roman interests against the invading Lombards, who were both barbarians and Arian heretics. By exercising these powers and by adding to the papal patrimony (land owned directly by "St. Peter" —i.e., the papacy), he increased the temporal power of the papacy.

A clear and cogent theologian and political theorist, Gregory did not confine his talents merely to administration and to Italy. He was one of the greatest architects of medieval order. The foundation of his theory of Christian society was that it must imitate or reflect heavenly society. As heaven was organized hierarchically, each spirit in its proper place and rank, so Christendom must be. St. Augustine had already written, "Order is an arrangement assigning their proper places to equal and unequal things"; and Gregory added, "Universal society could subsist by no other principle than that of a great system of order preserving its diversity of operations." Order establishes tranquillity and unity, and it preserves and protects the right of each creature to occupy its proper place and to fulfill the functions assigned to it by God. Gregory argued that, in practice, order was to be achieved by the construction of a chain of command linking priest to bishop to pope. Such notions of hierarchical order became the basis of the unified and structured organization of the church that progressed from the eighth century and culminated in the political theories of Gregory VII in the eleventh.

With such a view, Gregory I could not but contest the dispensation of Chalcedon, which divided Rome's authority with Constantinople. The pope made a practice of hearing appeals against the patriarch on the part of eastern clergy; in theory he objected openly to the patriarch's use of the term "universal bishop." This term implied a universal authority on the part of Constantinople that properly, Gregory argued, pertained only to the Roman see, which has *principatus—prime authority—over* the whole church.

It was the desire to establish order, with the *principatus* and the hierarchical organization it entailed, that led Gregory to initiate what was perhaps his most significant policy: the extension of papal influence and prestige north of the Alps. Until that time northern Europe had formally recognized the primacy of Rome while paying little attention to papal decrees. With extraordinary vigor, witnessed by his voluminous correspondence, Gregory now intervened in the affairs of local churches everywhere. In 595–597 he launched the conversion of the English to Roman Catholicism by sending St. Augustine of Canterbury to convert Kent and to establish the see of Canterbury. The English eventually became the strongest supporters of the papacy in the north, and in the eighth century their missionaries to the Continent would do much to establish papal authority in both Gaul and Germany.

At Gregory's death in 604, conditions both in the church and in society as a whole were still unsettled, but the papacy had become a leading force for order. It had developed the potential for becoming the center and focus of an orderly Christian Society, a potential that would be further actualized by a succession of very effective popes in the eighth century.

Another great force for order in the church was the ecumenical council. Yet the ecumenical council has always had the weakness of depending for its direction upon whatever authority summoned it. The early councils were all called by emperors and were closely bound to imperial policy. Constantine and his successors called general councils to remove dissension and to promote unity; this they did for the welfare of the state as well as the church. Accordingly, the councils addressed themselves primarily to healing doctrinal and jurisdictional disputes.

The first major doctrinal dispute in the church concerned the nature of the Trinity. Christ had spoken both of his Father and of the Holy Spirit but had not defined their functions. The Christian community from its inception believed in a divine Trinity—Father, Son, and Holy Spirit—but there was no general agreement as to the function of the Three Persons. Most of the early fathers of the church were subordinationists, believing that the Son and the Holy Spirit were subordinate in time and in power to the Father. The consensus, however, moved in the direction of considering the Three Persons equal in every respect, so that by 300 the subordinationist position had become old-fashioned. When, therefore, a priest and theologian of Alexandria, Arius, openly defended a variety of subordinationism, he was roundly attacked and eventually excommunicated by his bishop. Arius' chief opponent was a deacon of Alexandria named Athanasius, and soon Christians, particularly in the East, were divided into an Arian and an Athanasian party. Constantine summoned the First Council of Nicaea in 325 to deal with the question, and the assembled church fathers, after lengthy debate, approved the Athanasian position.

Arianism did not perish with the Nicene Council, however. Some of the successors of Constantine were themselves Arian and not only supported Arianism at home but encouraged Arian missionaries. These missionaries were successful in converting many of the barbarian tribes, notably the Ostrogoths, Visigoths, Vandals, Burgundians, and Lombards, so that all of these people were Arians at the time of their irruption into the empire. A second ecumenical council (I Constantinople 381) confirmed the decisions of Nicaea and approved the Nicene Creed in the form still recited in churches. The emperor Theodosius embraced the Catholic (Athanasian) position and proscribed the Arians as heretics. But Arianism remained a potent force in the barbarian kingdoms of the West into the seventh century.

The second great doctrinal dispute concerned the nature of Christ. Everyone agreed that Christ was the Son of God, but what did this mean? The school of Antioch and its followers, notably Nestorius, patriarch of Constantinople from 428, argued that Jesus had both two natures and two separate persons: one person was wholly human and the other person wholly divine. Mary, in consequence, was not the "Mother of God," of the divine Christ, but only the mother of the human Jesus. The Nestorians were condemned at the third ecumenical council (Ephesus, 431); but some of their opponents, particularly the school of Alexandria, went to extremes and argued that Christ had but one person and one nature, the divine. This was known as the *monophysite* ("one nature") position and was condemned at the fourth ecumenical council (Chalcedon, 451) on the grounds that it ignored the humanity of Christ. At Chalcedon the teaching of Pope Leo the Great was accepted as orthodox: Christ is but one person, but that person has two natures, the human and the divine. This doctrine was confirmed at the fifth ecumenical council (II Constantinople, 553), though both the Nestorians and the Monophysites remained strong, particularly in Syria and Egypt. The present Coptic church of Egypt is Monophysite, and the Nestorians were such effective missionaries in Persia and central Asia during the Middle Ages that they converted many tribes and established churches as far east as Mongolia and China.

The most significant aspect of the conflict between the Nestorians and the Monophysites is the way in which it illustrates the development of doctrine. At first there had been an open question: the exact nature of Christ. On this question there had been for centuries a variety of opinions. After much consideration, by the fifth century two of these opinions emerged as cogent and popular. The question was publicly raised and debated; a council made a decision and defined a doctrine. In the Arian dispute, the church affirmed one side of the question; in the argument between Nestorians and Monophysites it took a compromise position. In both cases, once the question was resolved and an official doctrine proclaimed publicly, only those who affirmed that doctrine were considered orthodox; others were condemned as heretics. In this way Christian doctrine grew; in this way too the intellectual emphasis of Christianity—the search for metaphyscal truth—was confirmed.

The exercise of imperial power, the growth of the papacy and of diocesan organization, the definition of doctrine, the acquisition by the church of political influence in society as a whole, all these were signs of a growing Christian order that was soon wholly to supplant the order of classical Rome.

Chapter Four

The Mind of the Church, 300–700

Order and prophecy both found a place in the intellectual and cultural expression of the early medieval church, but it was the spirit of order under the influence of Greek philosophy that generally prevailed in the formation of Christian theology. Doctrine was confirmed not only by the decisions of bishops and councils but, more basically, through reflection upon the ethical and metaphysical implications of the Christian message on the part of theologians. To put it simply, the fundamental beliefs of Christianity are the products of revelation, and therefore fall into the realm of prophecy. But attempts to understand and explain these beliefs required the use of an orderly system of rational thought.

The first four centuries of the church constitute, in terms of Christian intellectual formation, the age of the church fathers, teachers who first systematically elaborated these implications. The higher schools of the Roman Empire, like the Academy in Athens, were long dominated by pagans, and the Christian intellect had to find expression outside the classical system of education. Till the middle of the second century, the so-called "Apostolic Fathers" usually taught in the Jewish manner. Beginning with Justin Martyr, who was converted about 130, the "Apologist Fathers," in defense against the philosophical assaults of their pagan antagonists, adopted both the method and the matter of classical civilization. The adoption of philosophy by the Christians was hastened by the conversion of pagan philosophers like Justin, and by the demand for an antidote against the intellectual heresy of Gnosticism. The resulting wedding of reason and revelation was fruitful for the development of Christianity as a vehicle of thought and culture.

Justin was born to a pagan Greek family in Samaria about 110; he received a classical education and determined, in the classical manner, to seek out truth. He became in turn a Stoic, a Peripatetic, and a Pythagorean, but no system seemed to him adequately sophisticated. He was surprised to find that sophistication in Christianity, which all intellectuals were supposed to disdain. Justin's significance is that, unlike most earlier converts from Greek paganism, he did not feel an obligation to reject his classical background altogether. Rather than sneering at the limitations of the ancient philosophers, Justin argued that their teachings were in many ways parallel to those of Jesus and that they therefore, like the writers of the Old Testament, must have received some seminal divine inspiration.

Many Christian writers, such as Tertullian (145–220), remained very suspicious of the classics. "What indeed has Athens to do with Jerusalem?" he asked. "What concord is there between [Plato's] Academy and the church?" Even Justin's pupil Tatian (110–172) held that the Greek philosophers were all vain boasters and the Greek gods all demons. But the attitude of Athenagoras (fl. 177–180), who searched not only the philosophers but the poets for presentiments of divine truth, was becoming more common. As more and more educated Greco-Romans converted to Christianity, Christian doctrine became increasingly a synthesis of Greek with Jewish thought. St. Irenaeus (120–202) may have been the first systematic theologian, combining Scripture with careful philosophical reasoning in order to refute the heretics of his day.

Typical of the efforts to reconcile Judeo-Christian revelation with Greek rationalism was the development by the school of Alexandria of the allegorical method of interpreting the Bible, an approach that was to have immeasurable influence on medieval literature as well as theology. It was at Alexandria in the first century A.D. that the Jewish philosopher Philo first applied an allegorical method to the understanding of the Old Testament. For Philo, the problem was this: the Scriptures are the revealed word of God; yet the revered patriarchs and kings of the Old Testament often behaved in a fashion difficult to reconcile with right reason. Jacob defrauded Esau, Lot slept with his daughters, and David seduced Bathsheba and sent her husband off to be killed. Even Yahweh seemed on occasion vengeful, cruel, or even whimsical. In order to preserve intact both revelation and reason, Philo concluded that the Scriptures must have a meaning other than that of the literal. For example, when Isaac was obliged to marry Leah in preparation for taking to wife his beloved Rachel, this is to be interpreted, said Philo, as the necessity for the student to undertake preliminary studies before devoting himself to understanding divine revelation.

Such ideas were embraced by the Christian teacher Clement of Alexandria (153–217) and the Alexandrian theologian Origen (185–254). Similar approaches have always been followed throughout the church, although within the last few centuries many Christian leaders have come to insist that the Bible is absolutely true in the literal sense. The more open approach to biblical interpretation remains the norm in most mainstream Christian communities.

Little is known of Clement apart from his writings. He settled in Alexandria after travelling extensively and studying under a number of Christian teachers. Alexandria was a noted seat of learning, and the Christians there often found themselves on the defensive not only against pagan masters of classical literature and philosophy, but also against Gnostics who found inspiration and support in those same classical works. Uneducated Alexandrian Christians distrusted these pagan works, which seemed to reinforce beliefs that they found repugnant. Educated Alexandrians were reluctant to join a religious sect that forced them to reject their educational heritage. But Clement believed that classical works could be reconciled with Christian faith without leading to heretical Gnostic beliefs. He argued that, far from supporting Gnosticism, the logical systems of Greek philosophy refuted its basic doctrines. He wrote that classical philosophy prepared educated Greeks for Truth, just as Hebrew Law had prepared the Jews for the revelation of Jesus. In fact, Clement believed that Plato had come so close to Truth, he must have been trained by Jewish rabbis! Moreover, Clement believed that many works of classical literature taught a natural morality that could be used to make better Christians. Clement helped make Christianity acceptable to the intellectuals of Alexandria, the leading educational center of its time. He opened a door that allowed the passage of some of the brightest minds in the history of the Christian church. One of the first to pass through this door was an arrogant genius named Origen.

Origen was born at Alexandria to devout Christian parents. As a young child he showed such interest in theology that his father, Leonides, became convinced that the child was the special dwelling place of the Holy Spirit. When the persecution launched during the reign of the Emperor Septimius Severus deprived Leonides of both his property and his life, Origen, the eldest of eleven children, undertook to support them by teaching grammar and literature. His devotion to theology matured with his talents, and he was ordained to the priesthood and appointed head of the cathedral school of Alexandria; but his brilliance was matched by a stubbornness that provoked the ecclesiastical leaders of the city. He was defrocked and spent the remainder of his life in exile in Caesarea. His writings are voluminous and original. His greatest contribution was the further elucidation of the allegorical method of interpreting the Scriptures.

Both Testaments of the Bible are the work of God and the Holy Spirit, Origen argued, but the real meaning of the Old Testament is less in its literal signification than in its hidden meaning, which becomes clear only after being illuminated by the new revelation of Jesus and by the principles of philosophy. The Old Testament is to be understood on several levels, of which Origen originally specified three. St. Augustine used four, which came in the Middle Ages to be accepted as standard: the historical, the tropological (moral), the analogical (the Old Testament seen as prefiguring the New), and the soteriological or eschatological (referring to the salvation of the Christian community at the end of history). For example, the story of Joshua at the battle of Jericho means (1) literally and historically, that Joshua took Jericho; (2) morally, that the walls of sin will crumble before the man of faith; (3) analogically, that Jesus entered Jerusalem in triumph; (4) eschatologically, that on the Last Day the old world will crumble to make way for the Kingdom of God when the trumpet of judgment sounds. Not only did medieval theologians search the Old Testament for such meanings, but they carefully composed their own works on several planes. The poets and historians took up the method; and in the *Divine Comedy,* Dante, as he explained to his friend Can Grande della Scala, carefully used the four levels of meaning. This complex pattern of thought and expression was woven into the fabric of medieval Christian culture.

After the Peace of the Church, the great schools of the empire were opened to the Christians, but the schools themselves had deteriorated considerably from the days of Plato and Aristotle. They had become dry, narrow, and unfit for the expression of the life of either the pagan or the Christian community. They gradually lost their importance, even the Academy of Plato closing its doors by order of the Emperor Justinian. Intellectual leadership now being in the hands of the Christians, it was up to them to evolve new educational institutions. The chief sources of Christian education were in the catechetical schools operated by the bishops; the writings and preachings of great teachers like Jerome, Augustine, and Gregory the Great; or, increasingly, the monasteries.

There have been in the West two very different educational traditions. One stresses the needs of order and society and insists that the young are to be taught both the conventional values and morals and the skills useful in performing tasks deemed valuable by society. This was the tradition that dominated the Christian schools, both episcopal and monastic. Conventional Christian values and doctrines were taught unquestionably; and the poets and philosophers were used not for their own sakes, but as treasure-houses from which one extracted passages and sentiments congenial to Christianity and edifying to the spirit. Students were given the skills necessary to train them to fill the needs of society as lawyers, educators, priests, and monks. The other tradition is that which encourages independent thought and original ideas. It concentrates on teaching the young not only the content of a specific subject but also how to think. It is a tradition much more congenial to the prophetic spirit, and like prophecy itself, it has never been popular; for the independent thinker, like the prophet, is often obliged to stand in opposition to the accepted values of society. Socrates was obliged to drink hemlock, and Jesus to carry his cross to Golgotha.

In medieval Christianity, great thinkers like Augustine, Abelard, Bernard, and Aquinas were able to create and develop their own ideas; but on the whole, independence was discouraged. Education conducive to order and social tranquillity prevailed in the medieval, as it had in the ancient world. But the idea of a liberal education, involving both breadth and independence of thought, is a product of the medieval university, and has enjoyed at least a tenuous existence ever since.

Toward the end of the fourth century two great fathers of the church appeared: St. Jerome (c. 347–419) and St. Augustine of Hippo (354–430). Jerome, the son of a well-to-do Dalmatian family, received an education in the classics at Rome and then in the schools of Trier. Although he enjoyed the best prospects for success in the world, he became convinced that the best way to follow Christ was to renounce the world; thus, he withdrew to the Syrian desert as a hermit from about 374 to 376. He returned to civilization to finish his education in the great centers of Christian intellectual life at Antioch, Alexandria, and Constantinople. Eventually he went to Rome, where he acquired great influence at the court of Pope Damasus (366–384). Even at Rome, however, Jerome spurned the exercise of worldly power and devoted himself to preaching the virtues of the ascetic and monastic life. This devotion to asceticism, which appears in all his works and letters, was

Jerome's chief contribution to developing Christianity: he was probably its strictest moralist since Tertullian. Jerome was also the translator into Latin of the Hebrew Old Testament and the Greek New Testament. This translation became known as the Vulgate *(vulgus,* "the crowd"), from its wide use as the standard Bible of the Middle Ages. Jerome spent the last three decades of his life in withdrawal from the world at a monastery in Bethlehem.

St. Augustine was, after Jesus himself and Paul, the most formative figure in the history of Christian thought and, with Plato and Aristotle, one of the fundamental influences in western culture as a whole. Philosophy and theology were for six hundred years after Augustine's death largely devoted to the elaboration of his thought.

Augustine was born in 354 in Numidia to a pagan father of the class of *curiales—citizens* with influence and responsibility, whose wealth, however, had been eroded by the oppressive tax policies of the later Roman Empire. His mother, Monica, was a Christian and was later canonized. Like Origen, Augustine early gave evidence of a questing mind, but unlike the Alexandrian, he was not as a youth committed to Christianity. He lived a boy's and young man's life that he later repudiated as sinful. At the age of seventeen he went off to study in the schools of Carthage, where "there sang all around me in my ears a cauldron of unholy loves." There he lived "seduced and seducing, deceived and deceiving, subject to a variety of lusts." He acquired a mistress, and the following year she bore him a son, whom he named with sincere devotion Adeodatus, "Gift of God." His restless mind led him not only to taverns: He felt that he had a shattered and bleeding soul, but no place to rest it. "Not in calm groves, not in games and music, not in fragrant spots, not in exotic parties, not in the pleasures of the bedroom and dining room; not [finally] in books and poetry." He sought all the philosophers and teachers of Carthage—like Justin Martyr before him—trying, and being disappointed by, one philosophy and religion after another.

Augustine's eventual conversion to Christianity was a product as much of his sense of sin and of the influence of his mother as of purely intellectual considerations. For some years Augustine was an adherent of Manichaeism, a religion with a morbid disgust for the flesh. Founded in the third century by a Mesopotamian named Mani, it was based upon Zoroastrianism with an admixture of Buddhism, Judaism, Christianity, and Gnosticism. Its morality was exceedingly dualistic and strict. Even while embracing this religion, Augustine had many questions and doubts that he could not answer, and he eagerly awaited the arrival in Carthage of Faustus, the most renowned of the Manichaean teachers. When Faustus proved unable to resolve his perplexities, Augustine removed to Italy with his mother, his mistress, and his son, in order there to seek other teachers and other doctrines. For a while he was a Neoplatonist, but in the meantime he had come under the influence of St. Ambrose, who himself had a good knowledge of Greek and a thorough understanding of Neoplatonic doctrines.

Ambrose (339–397), like most of the leaders of the early and medieval church, came from a wealthy and influential background. The son of a powerful praetorian prefect, Ambrose himself rose quickly in the civil administration. At the time that the bishopric of Milan fell vacant in 374, Ambrose was the civil governor of the province, and his experience, skill, and popularity won him election to the vacant see by acclamation. As bishop, the confidence that sprang of family background and administrative experience permitted Ambrose to exercise considerable influence, not only in the church but in the state. When the powerful Emperor Theodosius, for example, permitted the massacre of a rebel mob in Thessalonica by his troops, Ambrose excommunicated him and compelled him to do penance and to amend his life.

Under the influence of Ambrose, whose intellectual strengths were as great as his administrative virtues, Augustine began to study seriously the religion his mother had tried to teach him as a child. One day, while sitting in the garden meditating, Augustine heard the voice of a child at play calling out what sounded to him like "Take up and read!" Receiving this as an omen, he rushed into the house and opened the Bible at random to the passage: "'Not in rioting and drunkenness, not in sexual profligacy, not in strife and envying; but put on the Lord Jesus Christ.'... Instantly at the end of this sentence, by a light of serenity infused into my heart, all the darkness of doubt vanished away." No more terse description of the experience of conversion is possible. He was shortly baptized. Subsequently he returned to Africa. At Carthage he went into semimonastic retirement with a group of intellectual friends; he took Holy Orders; and he eventually was elected bishop of Hippo, in which post he remained until his death in 430.

The works of Augustine include quantities of sermons, letters, and treatises, like *On Christian Doctrine* and *On the Free Choice of the Will;* but his most justly famous monuments are his *Confessions, a* spiritual autobiography "confessing," or "witnessing to," divine mercy, and his *City of God.* This last was written following the sacking of Rome by the

Visigoths in 410, in defense against pagan polemicists who argued that Christianity had weakened the empire and prepared the way for disaster.

It is possible only to sketch some of the most important arguments of this great thinker, who developed and elaborated the thought of St. Paul on such important points as the nature of God, the nature of the world, and the relationship between God and humanity. For Augustine the existence of God is unquestionable, not only by virtue of revelation but by the dictates of philosophy. Indeed, to ask whether there is a God is a meaningless question, for God is Being itself. If anything is, God is. Because God is pure Being, he is the "isness" of anything that is: he is perfect Truth, perfect Goodness, and perfect Beauty. All things that are derive their being from God: insofar as they exist at all, they exist with the being of God. Insofar, therefore, as they are good, they are good with God's goodness; insofar as they are beautiful, they are beautiful with God's beauty; insofar as they are true, they are true with God's truth.

Experience informs us that there are defects in things, and these defects proceed from a lack of Being. Ugliness and evil are not qualities in themselves, but merely the lack of Beauty and Good. Insofar as a tree is ugly, it derives its ugliness not from any positive source, but from the fact that its share of Beauty is deficient. Augustine was thus able to postulate a chain of being, an organization of the universe that was further developed by later theologians, particularly Aquinas, and that became one of the commonest and most deeply rooted assumptions of western civilization. It lent an order to nature similar to the order that was so fervently sought in Christian society.

In the chain of being, at the top stands God, perfect Being, Goodness, Beauty, and Truth. Since matter is subject to change and decay, while spirit is simple and unchanging, God is pure Spirit. Below God in descending order are ranked things according to the degree in which they participate in God's being: according to the degree in which they too are good, beautiful, and spiritual. Of created beings, angels, who are pure spirits, are the highest. Below angels are humans (Augustine would have included sentient beings of other planets had he conceived of any). Humans are partly matter, but of all material creatures they are the most spiritual. Because they alone of earthly creatures have self-knowledge and a comprehension of good and evil, they have an immortal soul. Below humans are the animals in order of their intelligence (for intelligence is equated with spirituality); below animals, vegetables; and below vegetables, inanimate objects. Close to the very bottom of the scale is something that we have never seen and can only conceive of:

pure matter, the *hylē* of Aristotle, matter upon which no forms have been impressed. Matter is, as the French philosopher Etienne Gilson put it, tottering on the verge of unreality. The polar opposite of God is total nonbeing, utter nothingness, complete deprivation and lack of everything, nonexistence. On this scale, things are more good and more real the more spiritual they are; less good and less real the more material they are. This is rooted philosophically in Platonic idealism and is almost the opposite of modern materialism. Augustine would not have been impressed by Doctor Johnson's reply to Bishop Berkeley that if he kicked a stone and it hurt, he knew it was there. Knowledge did not come primarily from sense observation, but, as in the thought of both Socrates and St. Paul, from internal illumination.

In his expression of the chain of being, Augustine created one difficulty that plagued Aquinas later. The chain of being we have just described is purely ontological: it has to do with being. In the ontological sense it is proper to speak of things being "good" to the degree that they partake of Spirit and "evil" insofar as they are deprived of Spirit. Both Augustine and Aquinas, however, confused morality with ontology and tried to interpolate the moral with the ontological scale, claiming that moral evil was also deprivation, lack of Good. But the two scales are not easily conjoined. Ontologically, a human is always "better" than a cow because a human is more real, that is, more spiritual. But we speak of good cows and bad people; further, when we do so, we are usually using "good" and "bad" in different senses. A human is capable of moral evil, and a cow is not. To take another example, an angel is always ontologically better, because more real, than a human. But morally, Satan, a fallen angel, is clearly less good than, say, St. Paul. In the moral scale, in fact, Satan would occupy the lowest rank, for Satan is the most morally evil creature in the universe; yet ontologically he is as close as any angel to pure spirituality. This confusion of the moral and the ontological was to haunt moral theology throughout the history of the medieval church.

To return to Augustine's view of the world: in opposition to the Manichaeism that he had once professed, Augustine denied that the material world was illusory or evil. He agreed with Plato that the world around us was less real than the world of ideas or the world of God, but that it was by no means devoid of reality. Further, since it was created by the good God, it must itself be good. It is impossible to overstate the importance of this attitude of Augustine's. His acceptance of the intrinsic value of the world, and therefore of the value of observing it, prevented

Christianity from adopting a wholly otherworldly attitude that would have made it impossible for western science to develop. At the same time, Augustine was extremely important for the development of historical thought. Where most of the Greeks had dismissed time as cyclical and of no inherent importance, Augustine argued that since God had created time, it must have meaning. If God allowed time to elapse between the Creation and the Redemption, he had some purpose in doing so; God must have been gradually preparing the Jews for the Incarnation. Events in time are therefore real, they move in one direction, they change through a process of development, and they proceed toward a predetermined goal. This teleological premise established a new foundation for historical study that lasted into the twentieth century, and has only recently been challenged.

For Augustine, then, the study of the world is important. But its importance derives not from itself, but from the fact that it points the way to God who, as absolute Truth and Being, is the natural aim of all our investigations. But how can humans, who are limited, comprehend the eternal God? Augustine's answer is that we cannot. The theology of Augustine is essentially analogical. Humanity calls God "good," but God's goodness is utterly beyond humanity's comprehension, as are his beauty, his eternity, and all his other qualities. Augustine never lost sight of the sense of the Wholly Other and therefore wholly unknowable.

Humans cannot comprehend God, according to Augustine. Yet Augustine reasoned that God would not create understanding creatures and then deny them all access to truth. We see, therefore, as if through a glass darkly. We examine the things of this world and find in them analogies of God's world. In the beauty of a tree we find the analogy of God's incomprehensibly greater beauty. In the order of the planets we find the analogy of the infinitely greater order of God; from the endurance of the hills we draw the analogy of God's eternity; in the grandeur of mountains we see his tremendous majesty.

Thus the senses have their utility. But there is something other than the external world that we can examine, something that is a better analogy of God than anything we can see: our own minds. In our intellectual ascent to God, we mount one step higher and meditate upon our consciousness, which of all things on earth is the thing most directly formed in the image of God. Like Socrates and Plato, Augustine affirmed that the truest knowledge comes from internal illumination, for it is within us that the Holy Spirit dwells. As Augustine's acceptance of the world encouraged science, so his emphasis upon the light within greatly encouraged the development of Christian contemplative spirituality; the final step in self-understanding is the complete opening up of the soul, so that, as Paul had said, I live no longer, but Christ within me. At the apex of Augustine's intellectual order was, again, the spirit of prophecy.

Augustine's view of humanity's relationship to God was based upon the Pauline notion of sin and grace. God in his goodness had created humans with the potentiality for moral goodness. But moral goodness requires free choice, and so God gave humans absolute freedom to choose to obey God or to follow their own selfish wills. Adam and Eve, who represented all humanity, made the choice: they disobeyed God. The picking of the forbidden fruit is a symbol of this disobedience. In his *Confessions,* Augustine used a similar incident in his own life to illustrate the nature of sin. While playing as a boy with some friends, he helped them steal pears from an orchard. The stealing of pears is to the secular mind not such a great crime, but for Augustine the important thing is the disposition of the conscience. He knew that God wished him not to pick the pears. He had no reason to desire those particular pears: they were not special in any way, and he was not especially hungry at the time. He picked the pears simply because he wished to do something wrong. The essence of sin is comprehended in this act: to say to God, "Not your will, O Lord, but mine, be done."

The original sin of Adam and Eve had enormous consequences. Not only was humanity expelled from Paradise, but it bore in its very nature the mark of its sin. Adam and Eve were wholly free to choose good or evil, but having made their choice, the nature of humanity was then inclined to sin. Adam ("the Man") and Eve (the mother of the human race) represent humanity, so that every baby is born with this inclination. All humankind is afflicted, therefore, not only with the punishment but also with the guilt accruing to sin.

Augustine went further, and argued that since the Fall we have been not only inclined but actually bound to sin. Humanity made its choice in Adam, and we, as components of humanity, are therefore inherently corrupt. Augustine shared a Platonic view of reality: the abstract whole is more real than the sensory manifestation. There is nothing whatever that we as individuals can do to save ourselves from sin or to storm the gates of Paradise. In strict justice, God is obliged to do nothing for us. He made a contract with Adam that Adam should be happy as long as he obeyed God. The contract was with humanity, rather than with an individual man. Since Adam did not fulfill his obligations, the contract with humanity is consequently void. Hell is separation from God, and it is not God who has condemned humanity but humanity that has damned itself. Yet God is not only just, but merciful, and he wills to redeem us. He gives us a second chance. Since humanity cannot save itself, it is incumbent upon God to save us. This is the meaning of the Incarnation: God becomes human and dies for humanity in order to redeem the human race from its guilt. The Passion of Christ opens again the road to Paradise that humanity has blocked. As the Old Adam ("the Man") represented all humans in their guilt, so Christ, who was also called "the Man" or "the New Adam," represents all humans in their redemption. We are part of the mystical body of Adam, and we are part of the Mystical Body of Christ.

If Christ's redemptive act was cosmic in significance, what can the individual do to participate in his own salvation? Through our own most grievous fault in Adam and Eve, individuals are born damned and incapable of saving themselves. There is literally absolutely nothing a person can do to free himself or herself from sin, for there is nothing good in a human save that which comes from God. All we can do is open our hearts and await the gift of grace, of God's life. Grace generates faith, and a person heretofore spiritually dead becomes alive with God's life. The simplest modern analogy is to a radio set, which, silent until plugged into the circuit, comes to life when filled with electrical energy.

In the course of his meditations on grace and salvation, Augustine touched upon two of the most perennially difficult questions of Christian theology. The first is the problem of evil: if God is both good and omnipotent, how can there be evil in the world? The partial answer, Augustine suggests, is that the moral evil in the world comes from sinful humans (or angels), not from God. God tolerates this evil because it is the necessary consequence of a truly free will: if God had *obliged* Adam not to sin, Adam would have had no free choice, and without free choice there can be no virtue. God tolerates vice because its existence is necessary to that of virtue.

A second partial answer is that the ontological evil in the world, that is, the lack of perfect Goodness, is the necessary consequence of a created universe. God creates the universe from nothing; the universe is consequently other than God and lacking in perfection. The variety in the world means that, of necessity, some things lack perfection more than others. Again, the existence of imperfection is the logical consequence of the existence of anything at all. To blame God for putting imperfections in the universe is precisely like blaming the cheesemaker for putting holes in a Swiss cheese. The holes are necessary for the existence of a cheese that is Swiss; and in an ontological sense the holes do not exist at all: they are merely cheeselessness. So the imperfections of the universe are necessary. Ontologically, they do not really exist: they are simple deprivation and lack.

The other perennial problem is that of predestination. It has always been difficult to reconcile the freedom of humans with the omnipotence of God, though philosophically it can and has been done. Augustine left them unreconciled. He accepted the Christian doctrine of free will, but his theology leaves it little room; and he strongly condemned the theologian Pelagius for teaching that individuals might without grace form their own will to goodness and by means of a good life save themselves. At most, Augustine argued, free will is brought into play in an individual's response to grace: "We conclude that a person is not justified by the precepts of a holy life but by faith in Jesus Christ. That is to say, not by the law of works, but by that of faith; not by the letter, but by the spirit; not by the merits of deeds, but by gratuitous grace."

Augustine was in fact inclined to the even stricter position that the power of God's grace was such that no one could refuse it. Yet are we then all saved? Is God's life given to us all? No, Augustine answered, reluctantly but firmly. Remember that in strict justice God is obliged to save no one. It would be a great mercy if he saved only one among millions. Remember too that God damns no one; we have in Adam condemned ourselves. In his great mercy, God chooses those whom he wishes to save; he simply leaves others to their own just damnation. Many have found this doctrine of predestination and grace faulty in its apparent limitation of God's mercy as well as of individual freedom, and through the centuries there have been both dissent and modifications. Yet predestination remained, in one form or another, a common teaching of the Catholic Church as well as of those churches influenced by Luther and Calvin, who chose Augustine as their chief inspiration after the Bible. Bishop, monk, philosopher, and moralist, source of both Catholic and Protestant theology, Augustine died in 430 with his eyes fixed upon the penitential psalms while the Vandals were at the gates of his episcopal city of Hippo.

The monasteries were the main source of Christian education in the early Middle Ages. Monasticism was founded in the spirit of prophecy, and the monasteries came to be the most common homes for ascetics and contemplatives wishing to pursue an individual and prophetic road to God. But like the church as a whole, the monasteries came gradually to be both more ordered internally and more of a force for order in society.

In the beginning, the rules and regulations of monasticism varied greatly from community to community, but by the end of the sixth century a few were becoming general and common. Of these the most important were the Rule of St. Columba, followed by the numerous and influential monasteries founded by Irish missionaries, and the Rule of St. Benedict. The Rule of St. Benedict gradually prevailed in the West, and in the eighth and ninth centuries it was adopted by the Frankish kings as the official rule for all monasteries in their domains. By establishing one monastic order, the Benedictine, the rulers of church and state checked dissension and disparities within monasticism and turned it into an organized force for social order.

St. Benedict was born about 480 in the small town of Nursia in the Sabine hills near Rome. Like most monastic leaders, he sprang from a noble and wealthy family. He studied for a short while at Rome and then, renouncing the world, became a monk, eventually founding the abbey of Monte Cassino in the highlands of central Italy. There about 540 he established his "Rule"—his book of monastic regulations. For St. Benedict, the purpose of the monastery was to provide an environment where men might meditate away from the cares and distractions of this world. Some of the monks were priests; others were lay brothers. Monasticism was a fulfillment of the teachings of Christ and Paul to put away the world and to fill oneself wholly with Christ. Each monk had to vow poverty, chastity, and obedience to his ecclesiastical superiors, thereby suppressing the three greatest temptations: money, sex, and ambition. The chief duty of the monk was prayer. Benedict ordered that eight times in the twenty-four-hour day the monks would meet in the chapel to recite the community prayers called the Office. Throughout the rest of the day, they were to offer up privately not only their words and thoughts but also their other duties and labors as prayers to God. The monks were to live very simply and to do all their own work: carpentry, gardening, cooking, weaving, and the rest. A small portion of the day was set aside for sacred study, but the monasteries were not at first centers of intellectual endeavor. Classical learning was still feared as being pagan and corrupt: both monasticism and Christianity itself needed to be more firmly established before they could approach the classics with tolerance, much less with enthusiasm.

The central purpose of monasticism was prayer, which was considered a public duty. The monks prayed for the welfare of the entire world and believed that in so doing they were performing a social function more important than any other. The monastic life was not an escape from responsibility to one's neighbors.

Indeed, the monasteries came to fulfill social needs in other ways as well. From the fifth to the tenth century, when Europe was beset by internal dissension and decay and by frequent barbarian assaults from without, the civil and ecclesiastical structure of authority was badly weakened. In this situation the monasteries (though they, too, were subject to barbarian attack) stood as islands of relative tranquillity and order. In the midst of economic decline and the reduction of cultivated land, the monks cleared and tilled and rendered fields productive. In time of famine they fed the poor. They provided the only care for the sick available in most areas. They cared for penniless widows and orphans and provided shelter for those who traveled on the unsafe highways. And in the seventh and eighth centuries they became centers of education and learning.

Though Benedict himself had allowed little time for study, other monastic leaders encouraged it more. Cassiodorus, a scholar of sixth-century Italy, founded a monastery in which the chief duty of the monks, after prayer, was to study, to copy manuscripts, to write, and to teach. Cassiodorus and his contemporary Boethius, who was not himself a monk, evolved a curriculum based upon that of the classical schools, which became the basis of education throughout the Middle Ages. This consisted of the "seven liberal arts": grammar, rhetoric, dialectic, arithmetic, astronomy, geometry, and music. The Benedictines themselves gradually devoted a larger proportion of their day to teaching. This was not only owing to the inclination of the monks but also to the needs of society, for after the classical schools were closed, the monasteries became the chief centers of learning.

There were usually two schools in each monastery, the "inner school," which trained the boys who were destined to be monks, and the "outer school," where the others were taught. Though the laity was never wholly illiterate, most of the boys even in the outer school were planning to be priests, and it was this trained clergy to which the administration of both the church and the state was usually consigned.

The monks also labored in the *scriptoria,* where they copied manuscripts, the only way of reproducing books before the invention of printing. They copied not only Christian books but also the pagan classics, and we would possess nothing but a few fragments of the classical writers were it not for their labors. In the scriptoria those monks who were so inclined could also exercise their creative urge. Many of their manuscripts are beautifully illuminated, and these illustrations constitute the largest artistic genre of the early Middle Ages. The monasteries also produced original works of theology, saints' lives, chronicles, and even drama.

The monasteries were the most important cultural force of the early Middle Ages, not only in the formation of Christian order and culture within the boundaries of the old Roman Empire, but in the extension of the benefits of Christianity to previously pagan countries. The monks, particularly from Ireland and England, were the most vigorous and effective missionaries since apostolic times.

Thus in the period from the fourth to the seventh century the peace of the church, the growth of Christian institutions, and the spread of the Christian religion prepared the way for the establishment of a western Christian order in the eighth century.

Chapter Five

The Formation of Medieval Order, 700–900

In the eighth century the lines of the western civilization that was emerging out of the classical world were beginning to be discernible. The Mediterranean area, which had been the center of the commercial, administrative, and intellectual life of the Roman Empire, was now split into three distinct parts: the West, Byzantium, and Islam. Out of Arabia in the seventh century had come the warriors of Islam, a new religion based in part upon Judaism and Christianity, but transformed by the teachings of the Prophet Muhammad, who claimed to be the successor of Moses and Jesus and to offer a fuller revelation than theirs. Islam advanced with phenomenal rapidity, conquering Persia and thrusting eastward into India and central Asia. Westward, the Muslims seized Syria and Palestine from the Roman Empire and then moved rapidly to conquer all of North Africa as far as the Atlantic and the Straits of Gibraltar. From there, the Muslims advanced into Spain, and penetrated into the heart of Gaul before establishing borders along the Pyrenees. By 700, Islam had deprived Christianity of its wealthiest regions, its most intellectually prominent cities, and its most venerable shrines. Jerusalem, Syria, Egypt, Alexandria, Carthage, all fell into the hands of the Prophet's followers, who in 673–678 and again in 717–718 laid siege to Constantinople itself. Pressured by the forces of Islam, Byzantium could spare little attention to the fate of the western half of Christendom.

The Christian East and the Christian West had long been drawing apart. Since the death of Theodosius in 395, the political authority of Constantinople in the West had slowly declined. Owing to the general decline in population and commerce in the Mediterranean world since the third century, the economic contacts between the two regions also grew more tenuous. Intellectually, the gap was especially wide. Greek had always remained the cultural and commercial language of the East, but Latin had been widely used for centuries in administration and law. It had even made some progress as a language of culture, and in the sixth century, for example, there were more chairs of Latin than of Greek literature at the higher school of Constantinople. Gradually in the course of the seventh and eighth centuries, as the unity of the empire faded, the use of Latin also declined, and Greek reasserted itself in the East in every area of life.

The policies of the Emperor Leo the Isaurian (717–741) widened the gap between East and West. Leo reinstalled Greek as the sole language of law and administration; he reorganized his army and administration in an efficient and autocratic fashion; and he adopted and tried to enforce a religious doctrine, Iconoclasm, which was repugnant to the popes and to the people of the West as a whole. The papal resistance to the emperor's Iconoclastic edicts ordering the destruction of all statues and pictures in churches was very popular in the West and was a major step in the ecclesiastical separation of East and West, a separation that was already visible in the liturgy and practices of the two churches. Greek was the language of the eastern Mass, Latin that of the western; and while worship throughout most of the West was according to the rite practiced at Rome, the East used wholly different forms. The date of Easter came to differ. Married men might be priests in the East; but the western church took increasing pains to enforce the celibacy of the clergy. By the eighth century the West had adopted the doctrine of the double procession: the notion that the Holy Spirit proceeds from both the Father and the Son. The Greeks usually preferred the single procession from the Father and objected to the western insertion of the *Filioque* ("and from the Son") clause into the Nicene Creed. Of most practical importance, the patriarchs of Rome and Constantinople continued to argue over precedence and to dispute the jurisdiction of territories. By the eighth century, the divisions had become so great that from then on it is more proper to speak of a Byzantine rather than an eastern Roman Empire.

While the East grew more Greek, the West was moving toward a new cultural synthesis. To Christian culture, already a synthesis of Jewish, Greek, and Roman elements, were now added Celtic and Teutonic influences derived from the Germanic invaders and Celtic missionaries. By the eighth century, western Europe had a cultural identity that set it clearly apart from both Islam and Byzantium.

It was gaining a political identity as well. The unity of the empire had technically never been breached, and the barbarian kings often took Roman titles like that of consul and professed themselves subject to the emperor at Constantinople. In practice, however, the new kingdoms were quite independent. In 700, there were four major political entities in the West: the Visigothic kingdom in Spain, the Anglo-Saxon kingdoms in Britain, the Frankish kingdom in Gaul and Germany, and the Lombard kingdom in Italy. In addition, the Byzantine Empire retained footholds in Italy in the regions of Rome and Ravenna.

In the course of the eighth century, two of these four entities were removed by conquest: in 711–713 Spain fell to Islam, and by 774 the Franks had annexed Lombard Italy. Scandinavia, the Slavic countries, and vast tracts of Germany were yet to be convened and civilized, and the Anglo-Saxon kingdoms were small, divided, and isolated. This left the Frankish kingdom as the logical center for the formation of a Christian order in the West. The Franks had been pagans at the time of their irruption into the empire at the beginning of the fifth century, but by the end of that century they had been converted to Roman Catholicism. This made them naturally more favorable to the papacy than had been the Ostrogoths, Visigoths, or Vandals, who were all Arian heretics. An alliance of the political power of the Franks with the religious power of the papacy came in the course of the eighth century to provide the focus of unity for western civilization and the basis for the construction of a Christian society.

Franks and papacy were alike incalculably aided in this endeavor by the activity of Irish and Anglo-Saxon missionaries. The eighth-century synthesis was, curiously, less the result of a reaching out for power from the center than a centripetal movement by the people on the peripheries of western culture. Of the popes, for example, only Gregory the Great had taken the initiative in launching a great missionary effort: the sending of St. Augustine of Canterbury to England in 595–597. The Gauls also did missionary work, but the greatest numbers with the greatest enthusiasm came from Ireland and England.

Ireland, which had never been part of the Roman Empire, was pagan until the mid-fifth century. An ancient legend holds that St. Patrick came to convert the island in 432. Neither the date nor the personality of Patrick are at all well established, but it is clear that Christianity had taken root among the Irish by the beginning of the sixth century. Patrick probably came to Ireland from Lérins, a strict monastery in southern

Gaul, and the Christianity he imported was very ascetic and monastic in spirit. Particularly after the conquest of Christian Britain by the pagan Anglo-Saxons, Ireland was to some extent isolated from the continental church, and Irish Catholicism adopted certain distinctive characteristics. Some of these differences were minor, though they exercised theologians at the time considerably: the Irish celebrated Easter on a different date than the Romans, and Irish monks wore a different kind of tonsure. More significant was the role of monasticism in Ireland. The Irish church was the only one in Christendom to be dominated completely by monasticism, not only morally but even administratively. In Ireland the dioceses were centered not in towns (of which there were few), but in monasteries, and the abbot of the chief monastery of the diocese filled the function of bishop. Thus from the beginning Irish Catholicism had the ascetic coloration that has continued to distinguish it down to the present.

Most important for the development of the church as a whole was the Irish emphasis upon the Christian concept of life as a *peregrinatio,* literally, "pilgrimage." One of the basic assumptions of medieval Christianity was that human life in this world was a *peregrinatio,* a wandering through a valley of sorrows on the way to a person's true native land in God. The Irish monks took this idea literally and determined to imitate the apostles by going forth and preaching the Gospel to all nations. Before Gregory sent Augustine to carry Roman Christianity to the English, Irish missionaries like the sixth-century St. Colum Cille (Columba) and the seventh-century Sts. Chad and Aidan had converted what is now southern Scotland and northern England to Celtic Christianity. The English kingdom of Northumbria went on to become one of the great centers of Celtic culture, which from the sixth to the eighth centuries was one of the most brilliant in Europe for the originality of its poetry and painting, for the quantity and quality of its manuscripts, and for the erudition of its theologians. Nor did the Irish stop at Britain. St. Columbanus (fl. 600) and his followers founded monasteries in Gaul and in Italy, preaching the Gospel, establishing schools, and elevating moral .and intellectual standards.

By 650, in a process well described by the great English historian St. Bede, the Roman and Irish Catholics in Britain were at loggerheads owing to the divergence of their practices. With the intolerance of an age in which nice points of theology appeared very important, neither side wished to compromise. Accordingly, in 663 or 664 King Oswy of Northumbria called a great synod at the monastery of Whitby. There the

Irish monk St. Colman debated the virtues of Celtic Christianity against the English abbot Wilfred of Ripon, later bishop of York. After the arguments were concluded, the king decided in favor of Rome, declaring that he could find in Scripture arguments for the primacy of Peter but none for that of Ireland. Colman and the Irish packed up and returned sadly home, and by the end of the century most of Ireland had itself accepted the Roman customs. But Celtic Christianity had not been wholly defeated, for it made lasting contributions to the synthesis of the European church. It was the Irish, for example, who introduced private penance and secret confession, as against the old custom of public confession and penance. Meticulously, the Irish invented "penitentials," books describing in detail all sins with the appropriate penance attached to each. Nor did they slacken their missionary efforts after their absorption by Rome; throughout the Middle Ages they were found as far east as Warsaw and Kiev; there were Irish bishops in Austria and southern Italy, Irish monasteries all over Europe, and Irish scholars at the great schools and courts.

Meanwhile, the English combined a close devotion to the Roman church with a missionary fervor derived from the Irish; and throughout most of the Middle Ages the papacy had no more loyal supporters than the English kings and people, who paid the popes a yearly voluntary tribute called "Peter's pence." The English, Teutonic in blood, Roman in religion, and strongly influenced by the Celts, were the perfect vehicle for European synthesis; and English missionaries helped to cement Christian society by bringing the papacy and the Franks together.

The first of the English missionaries to the Continent was the victor at Whitby: St. Wilfred of York. Wilfred's mission began rather by accident: he was a politically inclined prelate with many enemies, and it was in the course of a mission to Rome in order to plead his case against his opponents that in 678 he found himself in Frisia (the present Netherlands). Learning that the Frisians were pagans, he preached to them awhile during the winter of that year. Returning home, he spread the word that there was need for missionary work just across the North Sea. St. Willibrord, St. Boniface (Winfrith), and many others answered his call, and for a century there was as great an outpouring of English missionaries as there had been of Irish. In Charlemagne's time, a

Frankish monk complained that the English swarmed through Gaul as thick as bees.

The most important, and certainly the most energetic, English missionary was St. Boniface (c. 680–755). Trained in a monastery from the age of five, Boniface absorbed both learning and zeal. He had built a reputation both as a scholar and an administrator when, nearly forty years old, he determined to follow the example of Willibrord and undertake a mission to the Frisians, whose paganism had proved violent and resistant to conversion. In 716 he arrived on the Continent and spent much of the spring and summer in Frisia. After initial difficulties, he realized that his work would have much greater chance of success if he could enlist the assistance of the two most prestigious men in western Europe: the chief minister of the Franks and the pope.

The Merovingian kings of the Franks had gradually lost their power by delegating it to the "mayor of the palace" or chief minister. At the time, the chief minister was Charles Martel (714–741), the future victor of Tours and grandfather of Charlemagne. Boniface applied to Charles for help, and both Charles and later his son Pepin the Short (741–768) supported the mission of Boniface, from political need as well as Christian duty. It was to their advantage to convert the neighboring savage pagans and so secure their borders, to improve the organization of the church and so enhance public order, and to raise the intellectual level of the clergy so as to obtain more qualified administrators. If English missionaries were willing and able to help achieve these ends, the Frankish leaders could only assent with Christian will. Continuing his journey to Rome in 718, Boniface also enlisted the support of Pope Gregory II and his successors, who welcomed the work of the English in converting the pagans and building a well-organized transalpine church with a strong sense of the prestige of the see of Peter. After preaching for three years in Thuringia and Hesse, he returned to Rome, where he was consecrated missionary bishop.

Boniface and his followers labored mightily throughout Gaul and Germany, founding monasteries and schools, preaching to the pagans, organizing ecclesiastical administration, and encouraging order and obedience to the pope and to the chief minister of the Franks. Boniface's mission was one of the most important episodes in European history, for it quickened a spirit of reform and renewal that would time and again reappear until it finally culminated in the papal revolution of the eleventh century. A tireless preacher, Boniface set in motion a spirit of moral reform that was implemented by episcopal synods and by the capitularies (ordinances or administrative edicts) of the Frankish rulers. The monasteries he founded became centers not only of moral but also of intellectual advance; and, with the encouragement of the Frankish rulers, this cultural progress was accelerated at the time of Charlemagne. Boniface and his fellow workers greatly advanced the conversion of Germany to Christianity, thus laying the foundations of medieval German culture. They founded and organized dioceses, Boniface himself being named archbishop of Mainz with a certain preeminence among the bishops of Germany.

The labors of Boniface worked in every way toward the formation of the new European synthesis. A somewhat intolerant as well as fervent man, he directed his saintly displeasure against illiterate priests who celebrated Mass badly, against ignorant peasants whose Christianity was still colored by pagan superstitions, and against heretics. He even combated the Irish monks and missionaries because their conformity to the practices of the Roman church was still imperfect, and he sought with much success to replace them in positions of influence by men more loyal to the pope. The transalpine hierarchy, heretofore virtually independent, was brought gradually into dependence upon Rome.

The hierarchy was beginning to take the general form that it would have until the papal revolution of the eleventh century. It was still usual for the priests of a diocese to live in the city with the bishop and to serve the countryside on circuit tours. Eventually, clergy came to live in the parishes, which were the smallest administrative units of the church. Each parish was headed by a priest who was responsible to the bishop of the diocese. Dioceses in turn were grouped into provinces, and though the old office of metropolitan had lapsed, its place was taken by that of archbishop. The archbishop's authority over the other bishops of his province was tenuous, but he at least had the right to call provincial synods. Sometimes the most important archbishop in a country would have the often merely honorary title of primate. In England, the archbishop of Canterbury was the primate; in Germany the primacy was disputed between Mainz and Cologne, and in France between Lyon, Sens, and Reims. In Italy, of course, there was no rival to Rome. All these were responsible to the pope to a degree that varied in proportion to their own strength compared with that of the papacy.

More than anyone between Gregory the Great and Charlemagne, Boniface advanced the cause of Christian unity and order. The energetic, indeed sometimes officious, saint was murdered in 755 by a band of robbers in Frisia, where he had returned at the advanced age of nearly eighty in a final effort to complete the conversion of that stubborn people.

The labors of the English missionaries were accomplished with only the moral support of the popes, who gave them honors and advice but very little practical aid. Yet in other respects the eighth-century popes were not only vigorous but almost revolutionary. To be one of the foundation stones of European order, the papacy needed three things: independence from interference by the imperial government in Constantinople, the establishment of an independent base of power in central Italy, and an alliance with an important western power. These aims were accomplished by a succession of four extremely able popes: Gregory II (715–731), Gregory III (731–741), Zachary (741–752), and Stephen III (752–757).

On the accession of Gregory II in 715, the position of the papacy was insecure in the extreme. Byzantine power was still considerable in Italy, and during the seventh century few popes had dared to resist the imperial will. One who did, Martin I (649–655), was summarily arrested and sent into exile. Early in the eighth century the Emperor Leo the Isaurian established a military officer at Ravenna with the title of exarch and the duty of imposing military and civil order in the peninsula. The pope himself was still considered an imperial administrator, responsible for the military as well as the civil affairs of Rome and its environs. The exarch, acting for the emperor, levied troops throughout Italy and imposed heavy taxes, which he sent to Constantinople. These impositions galled the Italian population, especially because the emperor seemed very little interested in using them to defend the West. Preoccupied with the massive Arab threat from the east, Leo the Isaurian and his successors used the money they collected in Italy for the defense of Constantinople and Asia Minor. Italy itself was left open to the inroads of the Lombards. By 715 these hostile and still largely savage people had conquered most of the interior of the Italian peninsula, and their announced aim was the occupation of both Ravenna and Rome.

The popes were in an untenable position. They were obliged to resist the Lombards, but they found themselves hindered, not helped, by their connections with the emperor. The issuing of the decree on Iconoclasm by Leo the Isaurian in 726 was the last straw. Gregory II not only refused to publish the decree, but also seized the opportunity to stop sending tax money or troops to the emperor or the exarch. The exarch threatened to march against him, and there was an unsuccessful plot against the pope's life, but Gregory had taken a long step toward independence.

At the same time, Gregory made other efforts to improve the position of the papacy. It was he who gave the initial encouragement to St. Boniface, a policy whose rewards, though somewhat delayed, were to be rich. The prestige of the see of Peter, already great, was enhanced, and many from northern Europe began to make pilgrimages to Rome.

Gregory made concerted efforts to build the temporal influence of the popes. This influence rested upon two bases, the first of which was the powers they exercised as Byzantine administrators, powers they appropriated as their own as the emperor grew weaker. Also, the pope was the possessor of the "patrimony of St. Peter," land bequeathed or given to the successors of the Prince of the Apostles by pious donors. This land, much of it rich and fertile and populated by serfs, yielded a steady source of income. Gregory II began to wed administrative to proprietary strength, a policy that helped eventually to establish the "Papal States" as a viable political entity.

Politically, however, the position of the papacy was still precarious. The popes played the Byzantines against the Lombards and the Lombards against the Byzantines, with the contradictory hopes that neither side would win and that peace and tranquility would be restored to Italy. It became clear that a third power must be invited to eliminate both sides. This could mean only one thing: the Franks. Spain was in the hands of the Muslims; the English kingdoms were distant and disunited. Only the Franks were nearby, Christian, and powerful. When the Lombard king, Liutprand, temporarily took Ravenna in 732, it looked as if the balance of power were finally going to be irremediably upset. Liutprand announced his intention of taking possession of Rome, and in 739 Gregory II's successor, Gregory III, accordingly appealed to Charles Martel. The Frankish minister, however, was indebted to the Lombard king, who had helped him clear southern Gaul of the Muslims, and he refused to help. Pope Zachary was able to establish an uneasy truce with the Lombards, but the final fall of Ravenna and the exarchate to the new Lombard king, Aistulf, in 751 set off a new crisis.

The popes continued to lay up Frankish support against their troubles. In 750, Charles Martel's son Pepin wanted to become king in name as he already was in power. He could not simply depose the weak Merovingian king; though the king was a ruler in name only, his person was sacrosanct. With no separation of church and state, the king held as much religious authority as he did secular. In order to overcome the holy aura surrounding the king, Pepin needed the approval of the highest possible religious authority. He asked the approval of Pope Zachary, who was delighted to concur and thereby to place the Franks in his debt. With the blessings of the pope, Pepin deposed the last Merovingian king and placed him in a monastery.

Zachary's successor, Stephen III, did not hesitate to submit the bill for services rendered. While Aistulf was threatening Rome, Stephen undertook the first recorded papal journey north of the Alps, meeting Pepin at Ponthion in southern Gaul in January, 754. He remained during the rest of the winter in Gaul, where he confirmed Pepin's royal dignity and consecration, granting him the further title of "Roman patrician." In return he secured Pepin's promise to invade Italy and to restore to the pope the lands overrun by the Lombards.

The events of 750–754 did much to enhance the alliance of the papacy and the Franks, but they also foreshadowed future conflict. For the time being, the interests of the two parties coincided: to defeat the Lombards and the Byzantines, to remove the influence of Constantinople from the West, and to create a viable Christian order in western society. But each party cherished its own particular view of the way in which that order was to be constructed. When Pepin was crowned by the Frankish bishops in 751, he was anointed with holy oil. The ceremony was deliberately and directly copied from the coronation of Solomon in the Book of Kings. The implication was that Pepin, like David and Solomon, ruled as the chosen one of the Lord and that, like the kings over Israel, he had a certain spiritual authority over the people of God, an authority that amounted to semi-priestly powers. In the actual conduct of ecclesiastical affairs, Pepin made it clear that, great though his respect for the pope and the authority of St. Peter might be, it was the king who had the duty to provide for the welfare of the church in his own domain, to call synods, to regulate the monasteries, and to issue administrative edicts concerning ecclesiastical order. The consecration of Pepin wrapped this practical power in a theoretical package. The precedents for royal control of the western church were established.

At the same time, the popes were busily enhancing their own power and prestige. Gregory II and his successors had taken care to build up the papal patrimony, but the weakness of their political situation never escaped their attention. It occurred to someone at the papal court, probably around 750 (although some historians place the date as much as sixty years later), that it was possible to exalt papal power immeasurably simply by producing a certain document. There was an old legend that Pope St. Sylvester had cured Constantine the Great of leprosy and that in return Constantine had granted him great dignities and wide lands. If only that document were now to be produced, the unknown papalists reflected, how much benefit might accrue! The only difficulty was that the document was missing from the papal archives. It was missing because it had never existed, the whole story being fictional; but the papal advisers supposed that it had merely been lost and undertook to supply the deficiency with their own pens. The result was the "Donation of Constantine," a forged document in which Constantine conferred upon Sylvester his crown, his insignia, and all his imperial dignities. These Sylvester modestly returned, but the impression was left that the emperor owed his powers to papal generosity. In addition, according to the document, Constantine gave the pope wide lands throughout the empire. It was possible to interpret part of the document as a grant of the entire western empire to the popes: "We give to…Sylvester, the Universal Pope...the city of Rome and all the provinces, districts, and cities of Italy and the western regions."

These papalist ideas seem to have had wide currency. When Pepin met Stephen III at Ponthion, the king's son, the future Charlemagne, saw his father dismount from his horse and perform ceremonially the function of a groom for the pope. And in 755, when Pepin fulfilled his promises and defeated the Lombards, wresting away many of the territories they had conquered from the Byzantines, the king received two embassies. One was from the emperor, thanking Pepin for his efforts and requesting the return of the conquered territories. The other was from the pope, adjuring him to "hasten to restore to St. Peter what, under your hand and seal, you promised for the good of your soul." It was to the pope rather than to the eastern emperor that the ruler of the Franks gave the disputed lands, in a "Donation of Pepin" that was confirmed by treaty in 756. The popes were now the temporal rulers of a strip stretching completely across the Italian peninsula from Rome to Ravenna.

These proceedings did much to widen the breach between the East and the West, a breach illustrated by documents and coins. Until the eighth century, Rome had used Byzantine coinage, but beginning with Gregory III the popes issued their own coins. Until 772, the popes dated their documents by the regnal year of the emperor at Constantinople; from 772 to 802, by their own regnal year; and after 802, by the regnal year of the king of the Franks as new emperor in the West. An enormous revolution had been effected: the papacy had extricated itself from dependence upon Constantinople and thereby made itself a focus for the emerging order of western Christianity. In the process the popes had greatly enhanced their theoretical position, their prestige north of the Alps, and their temporal power in Italy.

But for everything there is a price. The price was the growing dependence of the papacy upon the king of the Franks, who emerged as the other focus of western order. Relieved of the pressures of Byzantines and Lombards, the popes had now to struggle to retain their prestige and freedom of action within the powerful Frankish embrace. Though Pepin might have held the bridle of Stephen's horse at Ponthion, it was Pepin's armies upon whom the pope relied for protection; and from that moment on, the welfare of the papacy was firmly bound to the welfare of the Frankish state.

But this explicit dependence was only the most obvious, not the most serious, of the disadvantages of the new situation. The Constantinian Peace of the Church had been recreated in the West. The papacy became one of the two great pillars of society. The popes became temporal as well as spiritual rulers, with a material stake in the social order. The church increased its power in order that it might mold society according to the principles of Christian order. But society supported the church to the extent that it seemed socially useful. The goals of Christianity came to be confused with those of secular society. A Christian society was established in the West, and the church, forgetful of its prophetic duty of judging society, became its servant. Religiosity, the defense of the status quo, replaced religion. The new order was necessary, but it was also necessarily a failure.

The greatest and most successful proponent of the new Christian society was Charlemagne, Charles the Great, who restored the imperial title to the West. The *regnum Francorum* (kingdom of the Franks) was miraculously transformed into something called by Charlemagne's advisers the *imperium christianum* (Christian empire). Charlemagne completed the formation of the European synthesis that earlier in the century had been promoted by the labors of Boniface. His empire came to include almost the entire West, to unite the cultures of Latin, Teuton, and Celt, to enhance moral and intellectual order, and to knit the

Christian church and a Germanized Roman state together into one new order of society.

On the death of Pepin in 768, Charlemagne and his brother Carloman were both heirs to his powers; but in 771, when Carloman died, Charlemagne was left sole ruler. In 773, threatened by a revival of Lombard power, Pope Hadrian II issued an appeal to Charlemagne, who descended into Italy and captured the Lombard capital at Pavia. He thereupon assumed the Lombard crown and declared the Lombard kingdom annexed to that of the Franks. To the pope he confirmed a "Donation of Charlemagne" but he soon made it clear that the pope was supposed to rule in Italy as a representative of the Frankish crown. In the context of Charlemagne's whole policy, the conquest of Italy is one of a number of wars he fought to secure his borders. He completed the pacification and conversion of Germany, for example, by a series of bloody campaigns against the Saxons, whom he forcibly converted to Christianity. But the annexation of Italy had the further effect of consummating the alliance between the papacy and the Franks: the pope was no longer a Byzantine official; now he was part of the Frankish political structure.

Charlemagne made it abundantly clear that he believed that his anointing as king consecrated him to rule the church as well as the state. He could not have believed otherwise, since no one in the Middle Ages believed it was possible, let alone desirable, to separate the two. Religion and the state were together the public expression of the life of society. For Charlemagne, an orderly church was part of the general public order, and he was responsible for its direction, with the help of the pope and the other bishops.

Having embraced the idea of a Christian society, the church was obliged to serve the purposes of society. In practical terms, control of the church by the king was politically necessary. The church was one of the few institutions powerful enough to be an effective force for order, and its leaders had held secular responsibilities since the reign of Constantine. In many ways, the church represented the last vestige of Roman authority in the West. Accordingly, Charlemagne used clergymen in his administration. He employed bishops as his representatives in the provinces and invested them with military as well as civil authority. Bishops like those of Reims and Cologne came to have as much political power and influence as the greatest feudal lords had among the laity. Bishops and lay lords were sent out by the central government as *missi dominici* (envoys of the king) to see that local administrators were properly fulfilling their duties. The king, relying heavily as he did upon the support of the bishops, had to make sure that they were men he could trust, so he reserved the right to approve all episcopal elections and on occasion to depose refractory clerics. The Frankish assemblies issued capitularies dealing with ecclesiastical and civil problems alike.

Considering himself responsible for the intellectual and moral welfare of society, Charlemagne ordered the bishops to call reform synods and to enforce their decrees. He founded a system of education, with its center at his own palace school, to which he attracted great scholars from all over Europe, and he issued orders that each bishop should conduct a school in his diocese. Thus he took under the royal wing the reform movements begun by Boniface. This had the double effect of advancing moral and intellectual reform while bringing the church into greater dependence upon the state. So true was this that Charlemagne, like Constantine, did not hesitate in summoning councils to deal with matters of doctrine and in ordering his advisers to make theological pronouncements on his behalf. At the synod of Frankfurt in 794, for example, he condemned a Spanish heresy called Adoptionism (a doctrine related to Nestorianism; the argument was that the Virgin gave birth to a wholly human Jesus, who was later "adopted" by God as his Son). His chief adviser, Alcuin, and others wrote tracts modifying the decisions of the Second Nicene Council (787) in regard to Iconoclasm. This council outlawed Iconoclasm and thus brought the East back into closer conformity with the practices of the western church; but to Charlemagne's mind it went too far in encouraging the veneration of images, and he did not hesitate to say so.

Under Hadrian and Charlemagne the relationship of pope to king still resembled alliance as much as dependence. Conflicts between them were rare: Charlemagne wrote to Hadrian, "Your interests are ours, and ours are yours." And Hadrian preserved the church's moral independence by refusing to accept Charlemagne's criticisms of the Second Nicene Council. "We are more concerned," he wrote, "for the salvation of souls and the preservation of the true faith than for the possession of the world."

But Hadrian's successor, Leo III (795–816), was obliged to act otherwise. The papacy could raise its head morally only when the political situation in Italy was secure. But the security of Italy depended on the power of the Frankish king. Thus, the moral strength of the pope depended upon the king's being both strong and benevolent. This unhappy fact was demonstrated many times during the ninth century, but never more dramatically than in the events of 799–800. At this time the popes were often members of one or another of the great Roman noble families, who were frequently in deadly enmity. The enemies of Leo III's family ambushed the pope on April 25, 799, as he was riding through the city. They threw him off his horse, beat him savagely, and tried to blind him and cut off his tongue. Then, to justify their actions, they issued a public indictment accusing him of heresy and immorality. As his predecessors had called upon the Frankish king to help the Romans against the Lombards, so now Leo called upon Charlemagne for help against the Romans themselves.

The peace and tranquility of Italy were too important to Charlemagne for him to ignore the summons, and he came down to Rome in the following year, 800. There he heard the accusations, sifted the evidence, and finally declared that he was convinced of Leo's innocence and that a public trial was unnecessary. By strong implication a Frankish king had sat in judgment upon a pope in the same way that the Byzantine emperor used to do. On Christmas Day, 800, while Charlemagne was praying at Mass in the Cathedral of St. Peter, Leo rewarded him by placing upon the brow of the Teutonic ruler the imperial crown of Rome.

Historians have long debated the motives of the pope in granting, and of the king in accepting, the imperial honor. In point of fact, the significance of the coronation has varied according to the interpreter. For example, the pope's placing the crown upon the king's head might seem to imply that imperial powers were derived from the pope (at Christmas, 1804, Napoleon at his own imperial coronation seized the crown from the pope and placed it on his own head precisely in order to avoid this implication). Yet after Charlemagne was crowned, the pope fell down before him in the posture of submission with which his predecessors had signified their submission to the emperors of Rome. Theoretically the coronation could be interpreted as symbolizing either imperial or papal supremacy. In practice, it served primarily to enhance the prestige and power of the Frankish ruler.

So far had order prevailed over prophecy that the church was now an integral part of the *imperium christianum,* defending its values and dependent upon its welfare. Christianity was a part of the kingdom of this world. In the course of the ninth century, the limitations of this situation were already evident. Following the death of Charlemagne in 814, the Frankish Empire fell asunder under the internal pressures of civil war and of dynastic division and dissension, combined with the external pressures of a new wave of raids and invasions mounted by Vikings, Muslims, and Magyars. By 900 no farm or town in western Europe was safe from burning and ravaging by one or more of these peoples, and the stabilizing of European society that by 800 had seemed on the way was postponed for at least another century.

The natural consequence of dependence upon imperial power was that the church shared the decline of the empire. A kind of pattern was produced, recurring at several stages in medieval history, in which the papacy, reformed and strengthened by a powerful and benevolent monarch and subject to that monarch's will, would continue to be strong for a while after the succession of a weaker ruler. There would be a short period of papal domination of the empire. Then, unable to support its own political independence, the papacy would also collapse and be obliged to await revival at the hands of a revived empire.

Thus, during the decline of the Frankish Empire, there was a succession of three powerful popes: Nicholas I (858–867), Hadrian II (867–872), and John VIII (872–882). These popes were able to press the reform of the church, to force a bigamous emperor (Lothar II) to put away his second wife, and to issue statements of the theoretical supremacy of the spiritual over the temporal power. But the collapse of Carolingian power left the Roman nobles with a free hand, and in 882 the enemies of John VIII succeeded in bribing one of his servants to poison him. The poison proving not to be quick enough, the conspirators burst into the papal bedchamber and finished the job by beating out the pontiff's brains with a hammer. This outrage ushered in a long period of debasement. The papacy of the eighth century had been lifted up in the arms of the king of the Franks; the papacy of the tenth, still in the Frankish Empire's embrace, sank with it into the mire.

Chapter Six

Christianity in Society, 700–1050

The religious justification of the integration of Christianity with society is that it makes it possible for religion to influence society more strongly. Does this justification withstand the test of practice? To what extent did the Christian ideals taught by the church really affect the assumptions, attitudes, and actions of people in the medieval West? And, conversely, to what extent was Christianity transformed by the needs of society?

Most of the assumptions running through medieval literature and philosophy are Christian in origin. But writers in at least the early Middle Ages were almost all clergymen, and it is a question how far their attitudes represented those of the rest of the population. It is even difficult to penetrate to the deepest beliefs and opinions of the literate, because so much medieval writing was conventionally woven around the ideas, and even the language, of the Bible, the classics, and the church fathers. Some medieval works are scarcely more than a string of allusions. We may assume, however, that attitudes repeatedly expressed in a number of different ways by a variety of writers and artists have a general currency. Further, it is possible to penetrate beneath the explicit. Since people believe it unnecessary to express those things that seem most obvious and self-evident to them, it is the assumptions that are only implicit in their writing that are often the most fundamental.

Certain attitudes largely derived from Christianity not only had wide currency among the literate but commanded deep conviction even among the uneducated throughout the early Middle Ages. A sacred, rather than a profane, view of the world was generally assumed. Everything was created by God, and, as God was manifest in the world, everything was an expression of God. Yet the dualism inherent in Christianity, as well as simple observation of nature and of human nature, required that the world be mistrusted. Not all of the things in the world reflected the goodness of God. Some things were clearly evil. How could the creation of a perfect and good God include such imperfections? The answers to these questions were to be found in the doctrine of original sin. Since the fall of Adam and Eve, not only humanity, but nature itself, was corrupt.

Poets often used beautiful images derived from nature, but the images were expected to be understood metaphorically. For example, in a poem by Alcuin, a bird who has flown away from his home and lost his way is a symbol of a scholar who has gone out to study and not yet returned to his home monastery; or, on another level of meaning, the soul that has not yet found its way home to God. Nature as well as literature was interpreted on several levels, and it was not forgotten that this world was a temporary stage on our journey to the other.

The ideal of *peregrinatio* prevailed, therefore, with all its implications. The concerns of this world are vanity of vanities, and the proper attitude toward them is disengagement and contempt. Greatness was therefore measured differently in medieval society from the way it is measured in ours. It was not the person who changed the world who was great, but the one who in his or her proper place contributed to its order, or the one who learned how to rise above it. At first glance, there seems to the modern mind to be a paucity of great men and women in the Middle Ages, individuals whose characters and peculiarities are as well known to us as those of Alexander, Caesar, or Napoleon. Medieval people did not glorify leaders who desired to change the world, or to leave an indelible stamp on the course of human history. People found the deeds of obscure saints more worthy of admiration. Men and women who worked for order in the world by filling well their assigned place in society, like Gregory VII or Louis IX, received their due. But equally often it was the man of prophecy, the obscure ascetic or the mystic, who was considered great. There was no virtue in fame or worldly power. Artists, writers, architects, and sculptors often refrained from signing their work, which was offered in praise of God, not for the applause of the world. Medieval writers delighted in describing great kings or bishops whose wealth and power were suddenly brought to nothing by the hand of God; how, for example, on the death of William the Conqueror his supporters deserted him to seek out the new king, and his servants stripped the bed linen out from under the royal corpse. In the Middle Ages, holiness, rather than fame or wealth, was the way to obtain status, not only with the clerical writers who preserved the history of this period, but with a lay populace that delighted in stories of holy saints and divine miracles.

Early Christian society did not encourage ambitious world-changers or individual heroics. Human society was considered static, and political and legal systems were supposed to reflect the unchanging divine order of things. There was an absolute divine moral law, which the human mind could find both in revelation and in the rational principles of right reason (natural law). Rulers believed that they did not *make* law; they *discovered* it. Their task was to construct human legislation and administration in accordance with divine law. When human laws conformed to divine law, they were considered "just"; when they did not, they were considered "unjust" and consequently null and void. In practice, of course, laws were introduced and changed to meet new conditions. But these changes were never thought of as progressive, but rather as a return to pristine purity. For example, Henry II of England, who made sweeping innovations in the administrative and legal systems of his country, always maintained (and possibly believed) that he was simply returning to the good old laws of his grandfather, Henry I, who had declared that he was restoring those of the early Saxon king, Edward the Confessor.

Early medieval respect for order was reinforced by excessive reverence for the past. There was little sense of progress. The culmination of the world would be the Second Coming and Last Judgment, but these would be cosmic, not historical, events. Augustine had elaborated a theory of time and of history that provided for the idea of progress, but this proved uncongenial to all but a very few sophisticated historians, such as St. Bede. For the most part, medieval people ignored the idea that human events were leading anywhere and preferred the venerable and almost universally held tradition of the ancients that the Golden Age lay in the past. For the medieval mind there were two manifestations of the Golden Age: the primitive, apostolic church, golden in its purity; and classical Rome, golden in its splendor and intellectual achievements. The writings of the fathers of the church on the one hand, and of the classical philosophers and poets on the other, were credited with enormous authority. As Bernard of Chartres respectfully remarked, "We are but ants on the shoulders of giants." Disputes in theology were referred to the church fathers, and disputes in medicine to Galen. Men who wanted their writing taken seriously indulged in a kind of reverse plagiarism and passed it off as a newly discovered work of one of the ancients.

The Greek conception of an orderly cosmos prevailed in the Middle Ages. It was a universe immeasurably simpler than ours: a stationary round earth, around which revolved the concentric spheres of moon, sun, planets, and stars. Everything in the universe, according to the Aristotelian doctrine followed in the Middle Ages, had its proper and appointed place. On earth, everything seeks its own place by moving, unless inhibited, in a straight line. Fire is the lightest element and strives always to rise; if one picks up a stone, holds it aloft, and then drops it, it will seek to return to its proper place as quickly as it can.

Human society was as static and orderly as the cosmos, and numerous writers (for example, Pseudo-Dionysius the Areopagite, a sixth-century monk) wrote treatises comparing the earthly hierarchy with the heavenly. In fact there were three basic social hierarchies, the feudal-manorial, the urban, and the ecclesiastical. Within this ordered society, every institution and every person had *libertas*. The meaning of *libertas* was quite different from the meaning of "liberty" now. It meant the right—and the duty—of an individual to occupy his or her proper place in society. A carpenter ought not to try to become a knight; on the other hand, no one ought to deprive him of his proper status as carpenter. And a knight ought certainly not to be a carpenter! In practice, of course, people did change professions and gained or lost status; but theory, reinforced by the practical demands of existing social systems, did much to inhibit social mobility. Curiously, it was within the church, the institution most devoted to hierarchy and order, that a man might most easily improve his lot. Bishops often gave scholarships to poor boys of intelligence, and only within the church could a son of a serf or a penniless freeman rise to prominence and power. Even when most conservative, the church remembered Christ's admonition that it was what was within a man, rather than his outward appearance, that was important. Opportunities for women remained severely limited, but a woman could escape the role of wife and mother if she wished by entering a monastery. In an age when childbirth was a life-threatening experience, a monastic vocation, with its expectation of chastity, was an attractive option for many women.

The assumptions of Christianity appear everywhere in medieval thought and culture, but they had competition.

The practical demands of the agricultural economy and of military organization had created a feudal mentality with a code of ethics known as chivalry. The ideas of chivalry did not directly contradict the values of Christianity, but they tended to emphasize different virtues and vices. For example, the fundamental vice in Christian thought is pride, but, since feudalism depended upon loyalty to one's lord, treachery was the worst thing imaginable to the feudal mind. Gradually these ideas colored Christian values. Christ was frequently depicted as a feudal seigneur. Our duty is to remain personally loyal to him as if in fulfillment of a feudal contract; if we break that contract, we take the consequences bravely and go to hell. In much Christian thought it is Satan's treachery to his lord, God, that is particularly evil, and in the *Divine Comedy* it is traitors who share with him the lowest depths of hell: Brutus, Cassius, and Judas Iscariot.

Among the peasants, Christianity was limited by many traditional values derived from paganism and from ancient agricultural traditions. In the later Middle Ages, the expansion of commerce, rise of the towns, and consequent emergence of a class of merchants and industrialists promoted the rise of an ethic based upon worldly material success and respectability; and one of the more curious episodes in the history of morality is the coloration by this worldly, bourgeois ethic of a Christianity whose spirit was originally otherworldly and revolutionary.

The establishment of an officially Christian society promoted and enforced the spread of Christian values within society; but at the same time it encouraged the adjustment of these values to those arising from other sources of society.

The Song of Roland, written in French near the end of the eleventh century, illustrates the mingling of non-Christian with Christian attitudes in a poem that is at first sight wholly Christian. The story is well known: after a lengthy, but inconclusive, military campaign, Charlemagne wishes to convert the Muslims of Spain to Christianity by peaceful means. But he sends to the court of the Muslim king, Marsila, a treacherous ambassador named Ganelon. Ganelon deliberately misrepresents Charlemagne's proposals to Marsila, saying that the Franks' real purpose is to turn half of Spain into a fief for Count Roland. Ganelon is motivated by his violent hatred for Roland, Charlemagne's favorite adviser and comrade-in-arms. Roland is Ganelon's stepson, and they have had long and bitter disputes over family and property. Encouraged by Ganelon, who agrees to see to it that part of the Christian host is betrayed to them, the Muslims deceive Charlemagne by feigning acceptance of his terms. If Charlemagne will return to France, declare the Muslims, Marsila will arrive in a month's time, convert to Christianity, and become Charlemagne's vassal. Charlemagne is delighted by the news, and the Frankish army begins to return northward across the Pyrenees. By Ganelon's contrivance, Charlemagne leaves a rear guard at the Pass of Roncesvalles under the command of Count Roland to cover his retreat; this rear guard is set upon by a vast army of Muslims who, completely outnumbering them, defeat and kill them all. Charlemagne appears at the scene of the battle too late to save Roland but in time to destroy the Muslim army and avenge the death of his comrade.

On the surface, the poem looks like a call to crusade. The Muslims are described as idolaters and devil-worshippers; they practice black magic; and some of them are twisted and demonic in appearance. The war is a war for Christianity against Islam, of good against evil, of light against darkness. Yet in that war the Christian hero was slain; and even after his final victory, Charlemagne complained, "'How toilsome is my life!' / And wept, and tore in sorrow his white beard."

Christian values have really little place in the poem. The only man of the cloth among the characters is Archbishop Turpin, who is too zestfully occupied with warfare to concern himself with mercy and charity. "A curse on him who smites not rudely now!" he calls out in battle; and he has little time for blessings, even for those who lie dying. The characters perfunctorily observe the Christian externals: Charlemagne goes to Mass, and Roland confesses before he dies. But by no stretch of the imagination is this a deeply Christian poem. The dead Roland is borne directly up to heaven by the archangels Michael and Gabriel, in the manner not of a penitent Christian, but of a pagan hero borne off by the Valkyries to Valhalla.

For a poem calling for a Christian crusade against Islam, the Muslims are often admirable. They appear less often as heathen idolaters than as noble warriors worthy of their opponents' steel. Here the influence of classical humanism is evident: the author of the poem has in mind the *Iliad* or at least the second book of the *Aeneid.* The battle scenes, in which personal struggles between one brave warrior and another are featured seriatim, and the name Priam improbably borne by one of the Muslim nobles, indicate that the author was thinking of the war between the Greeks and the Trojans. He draws many parallels between the two sides: the Muslim king, Marsila, is a just, honorable, and dignified ruler, like Charlemagne, and like Charlemagne he surrounds himself with a council of advisers. The Muslims fight for "fair Spain," the Franks for "France the sweet." The war is brought on by the evil counsel and treachery of the traitorous Ganelon. The poem is charged, like a Greek tragedy, with the sense of brooding and ineluctable fate. Charlemagne has a dream warning him of the evil consequences of the expedition, nor does he trust the traitor Ganelon; yet he is powerless to stop the fatal train of events. Roland, affected by the classical tragic flaw of overweening pride, refuses to blow his horn for rescue until it is too late, and Nemesis pursues him to his inevitable death.

The poem is also deeply chivalric. The great virtues are to fight well and to die well. Cowardice brings dishonor, and to yield in battle is worse than death. The great sin is treachery, and for that sin Ganelon dies a hideous death. Charles first orders that he be hanged like Judas on an accursed tree; but the judges demand that he be tied to four horses who, when they are driven apart, pull his body asunder. Even Ganelon's defense before the king's court is feudal: he argues that because he openly threw down the gauntlet of defiance, he was entitled to pursue his feud with Roland to the death.

Even as feudal values permeate the supposedly Christian epic of Roland, they also permeated the entire structure of the church, from the papacy down to the smallest parish. The rulers protected and patronized the church because of their desire for order in society and their need of well-trained administrators; they were not as a whole indifferent to spiritual values, but they insisted that these take second place to the practical needs of society. Church and state did not represent separate institutions in medieval society; the duties of church officers covered both the sacred and profane.

The Christian church was, of course, a product of historical development. Christianity spread through the regions of western Europe at an awkward time. Beginning in the mid-fourth century, this portion of the western Roman Empire was transforming itself dramatically. The Roman imperial bureaucracy was slowly collapsing. By the early fifth century, members of powerful Roman senatorial families living in fortified country villas defended by private armies contended with Germanic warlords for authority over fragments of the previously united empire. It was within this volatile environment that Christianity began to spread rapidly in the West.

When Constantine became the sole ruler of the Roman Empire in the early fourth century, he began placing Christian bishops at the heads of the various dioceses—the local seats of Roman bureaucratic administration. In the West, when other elements of Roman culture were fading away, these bishops represented a connection to the emperor in faraway Constantinople and the continued presence of Roman civilization, especially to the Germanic newcomers to the region. By the end of the fifth century, a large part of the population of Gaul consisted of Germanic immigrants who had migrated from beyond the borders of the Roman Empire. The most important of these immigrants were the Franks, who, after the conquests of Clovis in the late fifth and early sixth centuries, politically dominated Northern Gaul. Like all of the Germanic peoples on the Roman frontier, the Franks wanted to be Romans. They had no desire to overthrow Rome, or to destroy it; instead, they were greatly attracted to the sophisticated culture, the wealth, the security, and the majestic grandeur of the Roman Empire. The newcomers wanted a piece of this action. They wanted to share in the glory of Rome. But the Frankish population of Gaul understood Roman culture within the context of its own Germanic worldview. Part of becoming Roman meant abandoning traditional deities and appeasing the powerful god of the Romans. To learn about this god and how to please him, the German newcomers in Gaul turned to the bishops and other institutional leaders of the Christian church. But were these church leaders up to the task?

In Gaul, the purity of Christian belief and practice tended to vary greatly according to the spiritual leadership qualities of local church officials. This leadership was not always strong. Since the reign of Constantine, Christian bishops held not only spiritual responsibilities as the shepherds of the Christian flock, but secular responsibilities as the local representatives of imperial Roman rule. Bishops were chosen, as often as not, for their political and administrative acumen, and their secular duties often left little time for spiritual guidance. Nominally, the bishops of Gaul fell under the authority of the emperor, but by the end of the fifth century, the emperor had only a minimal presence in the West. The bishops of Gaul were more likely to acknowledge the spiritual authority of the pope in Rome, but the pope's influence outside his own Roman diocese was remote and indirect at best. It was not until Pope Stephen crossed the Alps to personally seal his agreements with Pepin in the middle of the eighth century that a pope found himself with the time and ability to travel outside the environs of Rome itself. In reality, authority within Christian Gaul was decentralized to a great degree. Bishops oversaw Christian practice in their local regions with virtually no outside supervision. Many bishops, of course, were capable spiritual leaders. Anselm of Milan at the end of the fourth century, Augustine of Hippo around the year 400, and Gregory I of Rome in about 600 are just a few obvious examples of bishops who combined exceptional secular leadership with inspired spiritual guidance. But many other bishops were not so capable, or even interested in spiritual matters. Increasingly, local secular rulers came to control the appointment of bishops, often selecting men who were personally loyal rather than spiritually able. After the fourth century, the spiritual leadership of bishops in Gaul, with notable exceptions, tended to be poor.

Under inconsistent leadership, Christianity among the Germanic communities in the West tended to be an odd blend of old and new practices—a veneer of Roman Christian rituals over pagan German custom. It was common, for example, for peasants to recite Christian prayers over magic amulets in order to heal their cows, or to ensure a bountiful harvest. The kings of the Franks, beginning with Clovis at the end of the fifth century, perceived Christianity primarily as the worship of the god who had made the Romans strong. The members of Frankish war bands offered up prayers, sacrifices, and oaths to this god as if he were a divine warlord; in return, they expected strength, security, and victory over their enemies. In contrast, the Christianity practiced in and near the city of Rome was a much more traditional form of worship. The Franks greatly respected Rome, which they regarded as a holy city and the center of the Christian priesthood. And even though Rome was far away—too far away to exert any direct influence over the churches of Gaul—both kings and popes preserved the relationship of mutual dependence established by Pepin and Popes Zachary and Stephen.

From the mid-eighth century, the welfare of the papacy depended upon the protection of Frankish rulers. But by the end of the ninth century, these rulers were nearly powerless. After the death of the Carolingian emperor in 899, the imperial designation was not renewed. In 936, however, a strong ruler, Otto the Great, became king of the eastern Franks. Over the next 25 years, Otto solidified his authority over his rivals; by 951, he controlled most of the lands east of the Rhine and north of the Alps. In 955, Otto greatly increased his prestige by defeating a large raiding party of Magyars at the Battle of Lechfeld. Otto had proven himself to be the most able western ruler since Charlemagne, and in 962, Otto duplicated the achievement of Charlemagne by traveling to Rome and receiving an imperial coronation from Pope John XII. And as Charlemagne had sat in judgment upon Pope Leo III, Otto the Great sat in judgment upon Pope John, accused by his enemies—with much justification—of heresy and paganism as well as of immorality. Otto at first declared John innocent but, after John had broken several political promises to the emperor, finally deposed him. This was the first deposition of a pope by an emperor since Martin I had been removed by the Byzantine emperor in the seventh century.

With the blessing of the papacy, Otto effectively controlled the papal lands of Northern Italy. Later, his son conquered Burgundy, and for centuries the kings of Germany simultaneously possessed the titles of king of Italy and king of Burgundy. But the kings of Germany were much occupied north of the Alps; and with the Italian political situation being so extremely complex, particularly in the cities of Lombardy, they could not often guarantee the stability of Rome. As a result, the papacy was commonly at the disposal of the Roman nobility, which selected popes on political and venal grounds. Many of the popes of the tenth century were monsters of depravity that exceeded the brutality of the least admirable popes of the Renaissance. It was said that one pontiff turned the papal palace into a brothel and that pilgrims ceased visiting the shrine of St. Peter lest they be ravished by his successor.

The bishops were integrated into the feudal political system in a variety of ways, all of which interfered with their spiritual functions. In the first place, they continued to serve as administrators for the state. Kings relied upon bishops and archbishops for advice at meetings of the royal council; and they employed bishops as chancellors or other officials in the central government. Further, much local authority was entrusted to the bishops. The Carolingians had established as local governors the counts (with jurisdiction over civil affairs), the dukes (with largely military jurisdiction), and the bishops (sometimes with both). In France, for example, Reims, Laon, Langres, and Noyon were completely under the control and jurisdiction of bishops; and in other cities throughout Europe the bishops either had complete power or shared power with lay lords. This civil responsibility of the bishops was a direct continuation of that which they had acquired during the decline of the old Roman Empire. A society in which political authority was weak and decentralized needed the support of whatever institutions commanded any kind of respect or obedience. The kings came to rely upon the bishops more than upon any other single institution for the maintenance of public order; and for precisely this reason, they had to make sure that only bishops whom they could trust were elected.

There were other reasons why the kings needed to control the bishops. In the same way that the popes were building the patrimony of

St. Peter, each bishop was building up the personal possessions of his own see. Technically such possessions did not belong to the individual bishop or even to the bishopric, but to the patron saint of the diocese. At Liège in Belgium, for example, episcopal possessions were known as the patrimony of St. Lambert, and, there as elsewhere, the patron saint laid up many treasures on earth.

There were several sources of these possessions: (1) Many wealthy people tried to buy their way out of sin by giving gifts of money or land to a church, either during their lifetime or as a bequest. These gifts were sometimes given in the form of "divine service," by which the saint was to hold the land as long as certain spiritual services were rendered the donor (for example, he might ask that Mass be said for him weekly or daily); or the gifts might take the form of "free alms"—land given, again for pious purposes, with no duties whatever attached. (2) The bishop had sources of revenue that often rendered him wealthy, and he might use these moneys to add to the patrimony by purchase. Most bishops came from the leading families of medieval Europe, the same families that produced dukes, counts, and other secular leaders. (3) More rarely, land could be occupied by brute force, or confiscated as a result of a legal judgment in court.

The patrimony was held free and clear by the church and owed no military or monetary service to the king. So much land passed to the church that at some periods as much as a quarter of western Europe was in its hands. The kings were therefore obliged to confiscate church property, as did Charles Mattel; to order that no more land be given the church, as did Edward I (1272–1307) in his Statute of Mortmain; or at least to make doubly sure that bishops were men they could trust.

But the patrimony was by no means all of the land held by a bishop, and often it was not the most important part. The bishop frequently held territories in feudal tenure. That is to say, he was granted lands, just like a lay lord, in return for the execution of feudal duties, including military service. A bishop holding such land was obliged, every bit as much as a count or a baron, to come when called to the royal army and to provide the king with the number of warriors requisite to the amount of land he held. Usually the bishops sent their troops without going into battle themselves, but Archbishop Turpin in the *Song of Roland* is not an unlikely figure. St. Boniface had to reprimand a bishop for slicing off the head of a family enemy; Bishop Odo of Bayeux was a bloody and unscrupulous fighter; and the bishops of Liège not infrequently appeared in the imperial army.

As administrators, as the possessors of enormous church properties, and as feudal lords, therefore, the bishops had so much wealth and power that the kings could not afford to let them remain outside of his control. The German kings depended upon the support of the bishops more than upon any other single group, except perhaps the towns. The French kings gradually, through the eleventh and twelfth century, added to the number of sees to which they might directly appoint. The system was self-perpetuating: the more power and wealth the bishops had, the more the kings needed to appoint loyal men; but to secure and preserve the loyalty of such men, the kings had to bestow upon them further power and wealth. It is no wonder that many bishops kept their eyes more attentively upon the throne than upon the cross.

The diocese of Liège is a good example of the enormous temporal complications of a powerful bishopric. Liège was a village until the eighth century, when, owing to certain disputes, the bishop of Tongres moved his see there. The bishop gathered clergy round him, tradesmen and artisans came to serve the clergy, and the population grew. The location proved to be a good one, near the land route between the Rhine and Flanders, and by the early tenth century the city was of some economic and political consequence.

Liège is located in Wallonie, the French-speaking part of modern Belgium, but in the Middle Ages Wallonie was part of the kingdom of Germany. Ecclesiastically, Liège was part of the province of Cologne, whose archbishop was the immediate ecclesiastical superior of the bishop of Liège. Politically, Liège lay in that part of Germany known as Lower Lorraine. But the duke of Lorraine was never very powerful, and his duchy was divided into numerous little counties and baronies, all relatively independent. Lorraine was a rich province, and the king of Germany wanted to control it securely, yet he was puzzled as to the means of doing so. The dukes were weak and often hostile, and the lesser nobility too disunited. If he were to control the area at all, the king had to rely upon the bishops.

In Lower Lorraine the two most important sees for political purposes were those of Cologne and Liège. Otto the Great appointed his younger brother Bruno as archbishop of Cologne (953–965), and Bruno proved a loyal and effective viceroy, extending his influence even into France. But the kings did not have enough brothers to staff every diocese in the kingdom, and they were obliged to secure other support. In 972–1008, the diocese of Liège was under the rule of a brilliant bishop, Notger. Notger undertook public works to improve the city, erected fortifications, cleared the countryside of robbers, improved the order and discipline of his churches, and founded an episcopal school that began to attract scholars from all over Europe. By the end of the century, Liège was one of the great intellectual and artistic centers of northern Europe.

Notger and his successors also took pains to increase the patrimony of St. Lambert and to improve their political situation. They entered readily into an alliance with the king. The deal was simple: The bishop of Liège would act as the king's supporter and administrator; in return, the king would protect and support the bishop of Liège and give him grants of land and money. The king wanted the petty nobility of the province brought into order; the bishop wanted to annex their territories. The policy recommending itself was simple: the king would support the bishop's conquest of his neighbors.

By conquest and by purchase, then, the power of the bishops was extended up and down the Meuse River and its tributaries. The count of Liège gradually lost his powers and was eliminated; the county of Huy was annexed; and dozens of smaller fiefs shared the same fate. Nor were the purchases of property more edifying: when Bishop Otbert (1091–1119) bought the castle of Bouillon from Count Godfrey, he raised the money from his parish priests, who had to sell their churches' ornaments and squeeze the rest out of their parishioners. In the meantime, Liège became the firmest ally of the kings. It was at Liège that the Emperor Henry IV, pursued by a victorious and vengeful alliance consisting of his own son, the barons, and the pope, found final refuge; it was there, in the last loyal city in his kingdom, that he died in 1106. Liège retained its political independence till the French Revolution; and a great monument on the Meuse still honors the wars not of Belgium, but of Liège—from 1105, when the Liègeois repulsed the old emperor's enemies at the Battle of Visé, to the Second World War.

The worldly preoccupations of the bishop of Liège were enormous. He was the spiritual director of the diocese of Liège and, as such, the head of a complicated diocesan administration. The diocese was divided into archdeaconries, each archdeacon having spiritual jurisdiction over the parishes in his archdeaconry. At the city of Liège itself sat the bishop at his cathedral. There also was the "great archdeacon," who controlled the financial matters of the diocese, and the cathedral chapter, which consisted of the priests living at the cathedral and occupying themselves with the administration of the diocese. The chapter was headed by a dean, and both dean and archdeacon often proved rivals to the bishop for authority. Throughout the diocese stretched a complicated system of ecclesiastical law courts and church schools.

But in addition to being spiritual head of a diocese, the bishop was also prince of his temporal possessions, including the patrimony and his feudal holdings. These were scattered throughout the diocese, making up about a fourth to a third of its territory, the rest being still in the hands of the lay nobility. As prince, the bishop was the head of a complicated civil administration, with its own officers and law courts. This administration was parallel to, but independent of, the ecclesiastical structure. As prince, the bishop was responsible not only for internal administration but for the fulfillment of his feudal duties to his overlord, the king of Germany. The bishop was obliged, exactly like any lay lord, to send troops to the king for his campaigns. When Bishop Wazo failed to send military aid to King Henry III during a campaign against the rebellious count of Holland, the king summoned him to court and reprimanded him publicly. Wazo's plea that his spiritual duties had prevented him from participating in the campaign did not visibly impress the king, and his suggestion that a bishop's spiritual functions were more important than his temporal was greeted with disbelief and, one may suppose, astonishment.

Under these circumstances, the interference of temporal with spiritual concerns was massive. Nor was such interference limited to the bishops. The monasteries, which also possessed wealth and wide lands, were also a tempting plum for the kings, many of whom simply caused themselves to be elected abbots. King Hugh Capet of France (987–996), for example, was abbot of the rich monastery of Saint-Denis, north of Paris.

The ideal of a Christian society was transformed, and not subtly, by worldly concerns. The desire of the spirit of order was not to withdraw from or to spurn the world, but to convert it. Now in order to convert society, a church must to some extent meet society on society's terms. The balance between aloofness from the world to the point of seeing it as irrelevant and mixing with the world to the point of compromise is always difficult to maintain, and inevitably a certain coarseness crept into a church that had to deal with a coarse society.

There were monasteries that drifted away from observance of the rule, allowing the monks to wander about at will. Among the bishops the most common sin was simony, the buying and selling of ecclesiastical offices. All too often a king would give a diocese to a man who promised a lump sum, a share of the revenues, or at least loyal political support; and the new bishop would recoup his losses by selling attractive parishes to the highest bidders or by otherwise extracting money from the faithful. Things were no better in the villages, where lay feudal lords often obtained possession of parish churches—churches of their manors, churches they had built, or churches given them by another feudal lord or by the king. These laymen were known as "lay proprietors," and they had much the same kind of control over the parish priests that the king had over the bishops. They selected the priests themselves and either sold them the parishes or else hired them at a small percentage of the parish revenues. Like the simoniac bishops, these priests had to recover their outlay, and in violation of the canon law, they frequently sold the sacraments (another variety of simony), refusing to bury or baptize without pay. Such priests were often illiterate, lived openly with women, frequented taverns, and otherwise lived lives that not only did not inspire but sometimes revolted their parishioners.

The decline of the liturgy was a most important element in this disaffection. The liturgy was the public worship of the Christian people, and from the time of the earliest church it was centered upon the Mass. The Mass was the gathering of the people of Christ in brotherhood around the table of the Lord, where the sacrifice of Calvary was reproduced and where the bread and wine, having been transformed into the body and blood of Christ, were received by the people in Holy Communion. The Mass was the occasion of the offering up of the self to God in the form of the unconsecrated bread and wine and the receiving back of the consecrated bread and wine now become Christ. It was a sacrament that was simple, understandable to the people, and reverent. It was a service of the community gathered together, uniting them in love and fellowship.

In the earliest church, the Mass was in Greek; but as early as the fourth century, the language was changed to Latin throughout western Europe, in order that the people might understand it. But by the end of the seventh century, ordinary uneducated people no longer understood Latin, and the ignorance of many priests was such that they were unable not only to understand but even to recite the words properly. As a result, the Mass was presented to the people not as the life-giving word of God, but as an unintelligible mumbling. In effect, the priests preserved the forms of Christian worship without the content. Further, the growing wealth and prestige of the clergy persuaded them to emphasize the separation between them and the people, and churches consequently became larger and more formal. The table of the Lord was removed from the center of the congregation and placed at one end of the church, where the priest said Mass with his back to the people. In large churches, a choir and even a choir screen separated the congregation from the altar, rendering the service sometimes invisible as well as unintelligible. An altar rail emphasized the separation of the people from the Lord's table. The congregation ceased to make the responses to the priest, this function being taken over by altar boys, who, like the priests, usually mumbled incomprehensibly. The processions ceased in which the people had come forward to offer their gifts, and free gifts were replaced by compulsory tithes. In the earliest days of the church, the community that gathered for Mass prefigured the Christian community that would enter into the Kingdom of God at the end of history. As the Mass developed into an elaborate formulized ritual, it came to represent instead the authority of the institutional church. Attendance at Mass was probably quite low, and Communion, originally weekly for everyone, became so infrequent that councils were obliged to set forth the rule that one must go to Communion at least once a year under pain of sin. As the Mass lost much of its meaning to most ordinary Christians, the religious life of the church was diverted more and more into private devotions, peripheral cults, and externals. Genuflections, the rosary, private prayers, or the veneration of saints filled the needs of a people deprived of more substantial spiritual fare.

It is of course easy to exaggerate the corruption of the church. The priests and monks who were living orderly and decent lives did not attract attention. It is equally clear, however, that the corruption was neither isolated nor atypical. The effect upon the morale and the morality of the Christian people may be imagined. It is scarcely surprising that disaffection from the church was not uncommon. But an age or an institution is not to be judged by its failures, or everything would be worthy of condemnation. Judgment is better made in terms of the vigor of the institution in taking measures to combat and to overcome those failures. Even in the darkest moments of the church, when the attempt to achieve order had degenerated into disorder, the spirits both of true order and of prophecy demanded reform. Against the superstition and the corruption, the voice of a purer Christian spirit was never silent.

Chapter Seven

Reform

The popular perception of the medieval church today is one of uncompromising order. Outside of scholarly works focused specifically on the subject, the church of the Middle Ages is likely to be portrayed as a monolithic, oppressive institution that promoted ignorance by deliberately propagating self-serving superstition and that stifled independent thought by burning alive anyone who disagreed with its dogmatic theology. Certainly, there were those in Christian society then (as now) who resisted—sometimes violently—any idea that they believed to be threatening to universal order as they perceived it. Historical evidence, however, offers little to support such an extreme position regarding the medieval church as a whole. In fact, the medieval church is characterized by continual efforts to revise and perfect its institutions and practices, efforts that originated and found support within both the laity and the clergy, the congregation and church leadership alike. The instinct for self-examination and self-regulation is, contrary to the popular stereotype, perhaps the most distinctive feature of the medieval church, whose leaders continually proved to be remarkably responsive to the needs and desires of its membership. When faced with problems and weaknesses in its institutions, church leadership typically responded with thoughts of reform, defined by Gerhart Ladner in his monumental work, *The Idea of Reform*, as "The idea of free, intentional and ever perfectible, multiple, prolonged and ever repeated efforts by man to reassert and augment values pre-existent in the spiritual-material compound of the world." In other words, when church leaders wished to improve their institutions and practices, they looked back in time to the perceived pristine purity of the primitive church community. They sought to regain perfection by eliminating the corruption that had crept in through time.

But medieval reform was not wholly a matter of recapturing a mythical golden age. While reformers kept one eye on the past for models of structure and behavior, they also kept one eye firmly fixed on the way ahead, which they knew with great certitude was leading to a foreseeable, desirable destination. Augustine had emphasized the teleological nature of the Christian perception of history. As far as early medieval Christians were concerned, history was defined principally by its end, and the goal of Christian society was to prepare for this desired outcome. In addition, Christian thought is fundamentally apocalyptic, that is, it anticipates the *imminent* end of history, which will give way to an eternal state of holy ecstasy. According to the Gospel of Mark, the first public declaration by Jesus was that "The time is fulfilled and the Kingdom of God is at hand." As time passed with no sign of the coming Kingdom, one of the most important questions in the Christian community became how to live in *this* world while preparing for its inevitable, though long-delayed, end. The ever-present prophetic voice within the church continually reiterates the first declaration of Jesus: repent, for the end of time is near. The spirit of order seeks to maintain the church community in a state of readiness for the Kingdom, whenever it might come. Thus, medieval reformers participated in both the spirit of order and the spirit of prophecy by seeking to emulate the perfection of the past in order to prepare for the perhaps imminent, but certainly inevitable ecstatic experience at the end of time.

The monastic reform movements that took place in Burgundy and Lorraine at the beginning of the tenth century illustrate the backward- and forward-looking nature of medieval reform. These reform movements had their roots in the social and political turmoil of the late Roman Empire.

The Christian communities in the West were not unaware of the inconsistent quality of its episcopal leadership. The Christians of Gaul and Germany, desiring qualified spiritual leadership, were ripe for an alternative authority. They did not have to look far. Although bishops traditionally represented the highest effective authority in the Christian community, they were not the only religious leaders in the West. By the end of the sixth century, monastic houses filled with monks engaged in divine communion were becoming a common sight in Gaul and Germany. To the Christians of these regions, especially those dissatisfied with the lukewarm religious leadership of their local bishops and the rustic ignorance of their local priests, the monastic houses seemed like islands of divine knowledge, spiritual peace, and sanctuaries of holiness in an otherwise spiritually empty and hostile world. Over the course of the sixth century, members of the Christian laity began to be attracted more and more to the aura of holiness emanating from the increasing numbers of monastic houses. Feeling unfulfilled by the spirit of order represented by the network of bishops, lay Christians sought out the prophetic spirit of the monks.

Monasteries offered more than spirituality to the Christian community, however. They were perceived to be strong fortresses against the forces of a very real enemy. Christians believed that the prayers of monks would protect the entire community from the powers of Satan. In addition, each monastery was built around one or more relics, that is, the body parts or intimate personal belongings of saints, who were known to dwell with Christ in heaven. It was believed that the local saint would sanctify and protect the community that kept its relic safe. As much as anything, the holy monks functioned as special guardians of the relics of the saint. They served as intermediaries between the community and the saint, who, in turn, served as an intermediary between the community and Christ. The saint would not only protect the surrounding community from evil spiritual forces, such as demons, but from natural phenomena, such as floods and drought, and from physical opponents, such as raiders and invading soldiers. If the saint failed to provide protection, the monks would ceremoniously expose the relic of the saint and publicly flay it with reeds or leather thongs. This procedure was known as the humiliation of the saint, and was meant to regain the saint's attention so that he or she would perform his or her proper protective function. The guardians of the saint were expected to be worthy. They were themselves expected to lead saintly lives, to be humble, holy, and righteous. Lay Christians developed a great deal of respect for the virtuous men and women in the monastic houses, for the abbots and abbesses who governed the monasteries, and for monasticism as a holy institution. Ironically, this great respect proved to be an obstacle to the goals of the monasteries and the monastic ideal.

After the sixth century, many monasteries became rich and worldly. This development occurred gradually, accidentally, and as the result of good intentions. Secular lords donated land to monasteries, and in return the monks prayed for the salvation of their benefactors. One should not be overly cynical when regarding this practice. Lords and ladies gave gifts to monastic houses because they believed that the monks were truly holy and that their prayers offered effective protection against evil, as well as sure entry into heaven. The monks prayed for their benefactors because they believed that anyone aiding a divine institution with needed support was demonstrating his or her faith, and should be brought to God's attention. But individuals who have invested a great deal of wealth in an institution often expect some measure of control in order to insure a return on their investment. Prominent benefactors began to influence, or even control certain monastic functions. A lord who had donated a great deal of his wealth wanted to ensure, for example, that the monks were fighting effectively for his salvation. How many monks were praying for his soul? How often? Was the lord's name prominently featured in the Mass, or was it lost among many other names? Would a private Mass on behalf of the lord be more appropriate? In extreme cases, companies of monks found themselves required to pray continually for the soul of an especially powerful and generous benefactor. Sometimes they worked in shifts so that the benefactor's name would be constantly brought before God, twenty-four hours a day, seven days a week. To a great many prominent lords and ladies, the holy monastic houses seemed like gateways to heaven, and they were eager to take advantage. Many of these powerful men and women came to control the elections of abbots and abbesses, or to simply assume the offices themselves.

It must be noted that monks themselves came primarily from noble families. Frankish kings and nobles from the sixth century onward frequently used monasteries to make provision for excess sons who could not be adequately set up in land, and for daughters who could not be suitably married off. Monasteries also provided a new home for noble widows. Monastic houses were places of great dignity and esteem, worthy to house the most noble of men and women. In many cases, noble parents gave up their children to a monastery, often with an endowment of land to provide for their support. As time passed, many monasteries began to restrict their enrollment to the members of only a few privileged noble families. In extreme cases, monasteries became "country clubs" for society's elite. The monastic life was often perceived by the nobility as a convenient career choice rather than a spiritual vocation. By the eighth century, the institution of monasticism, a victim of its own success, was in some danger of losing its reputation as a holy authority.

Monasteries were originally intended to be havens from the cares of the world, but over time, many prominent monastic houses found themselves in the center of thriving settlements. Because of the respect given to the monastic ideal, monasticism became the one institution of the church that most directly touched the lives of the common people. People wanted to reside in the proximity of a reputable monastery in order to participate in its holiness and receive its maximum protection. As a result, monasteries became the focal points for large secular communities and played a prominent role in the development of towns and cities. Outsiders came to these new urban centers to visit the monastery and leave donations. They also spent money in the towns for goods and shelter. As monasteries became vital economic centers in these communities, their focus tended to become more and more worldly. Gradually, the worldly values that church institutions shared with secular ones began to be perceived as real problems.

Christianity was such an important social element in early medieval society that it is accurate to state that the "church," in the sense of the *ecclesia* or community of believers, and "society" were virtually synonymous terms. But *some* social functions that were seen as normal and healthy among the laity were perceived by many to be inappropriate for the clergy, especially the regular clergy. For example, new bishops and abbots were often required to pay a fee to a lord in return for their appointment. Paying a fee in return for some sort of official appointment was a standard procedure in the world of the laity, but when a church official paid a similar fee, many people interpreted this act as simony, defined as the buying and selling of spiritual offices. Simony was considered by most Christians to be a terrible crime. The name comes from the story of Simon Magus, who tradition maintains attempted to purchase the gift of the Holy Spirit from the Apostle Peter. By the end of the ninth century, simony was routinely interpreted as a highly visible symptom of the growing secularization of spiritual institutions.

Another problem developed because nobles often were not willing to give up their secular lifestyles after becoming monks. Many continued to surround themselves with luxurious furnishings and to wear expensive stylish clothing. Many noble monks took mistresses, and in extreme cases, lived openly with wives or concubines. Any violation of a clerical vow of chastity was referred to euphemistically as "clerical marriage," and was deemed inappropriate for one who was supposed to dedicate his life to prayer, mediation with the divine, and the guardianship of holy relics. It would be a mistake to conclude that monasteries in general were corrupt. Still, a few highly visible tenth-century monasteries were well known to be primarily secular communities where noblemen lived depraved lives of luxury and self-indulgence. Such places were not tolerated, either by the laity or the leaders of the church; none escaped repeated attempts at purification and reform.

Problems such as simony and clerical marriage were not accepted in any degree by the majority of Christians, lay or clerical. At the beginning of the tenth century, several scattered independent efforts were undertaken more or less simultaneously to reform the institution of monasticism. These reform efforts were tremendously successful. They resulted in a widespread reform effort that eventually reached the papacy, leading to a papal movement known as the Gregorian Reform. The tenth-century monastic reforms changed the course of western history.

There were two kinds of reform in the Christian community, usually cooperating with each other and often unaware of the differences between them in their attack upon the common enemy, yet quite distinct. One was reform based upon the precepts of order. The reformers of this variety argued that the trouble was found in the disorder of the church and that disorder could be cured by means of discipline. This discipline was to be achieved by strengthening the authority of the leadership of the church and bolstering the power and efficiency of those in charge of the Christian society. Reformers of order might support the pope or the bishops as the most proper authorities to lead Christian society; or they might equally well support the emperor or the kings; but they were all agreed that what was needed was the obedience of the Christian people to just and proper authority. The arguments of order dominated political as well as theological theory. One historian of medieval political thought, Walter Ullmann, calls their point of view the "descending theory" of authority: God delegates his authority to an earthly vicar (the emperor or the pope, depending upon one's point of view), who in turn delegates it to his officers, secular authority to temporal lords and spiritual authority to ecclesiastical lords. In order to be in conformity with God's will, one has only to obey one's superiors. If by chance the leaders should err, they bear the responsibility for their error, but their inferiors are not to reason why.

The other kind of reform sprang from the prophetic spirit. To the prophet, order was of subsidiary importance or even a positive evil. The law of God is written in the hearts of people, and the need for an earthly authority is minimal. As the Kingdom of God is not of this world, our chief concern should be not to improve the world, but to rise above it.

The prophetic spirit was fond of citing from the Gospels the story of Mary and Martha. When Jesus visited the sisters, Martha busied herself about the house, cleaning up and cooking dinner, while Mary sat at Jesus' feet listening. At last Martha grew annoyed and asked her sister to help, but Jesus replied, "Martha, Martha, you are troubled and busy with many things, but one thing is needful: and Mary has chosen that good part." In other words, though good works in the world are desirable, the higher vocation is meditation upon the world of God. The prophetic spirit looked with indifference upon the struggles of pope and emperor for the control of Christian society and was unimpressed by the papalists' argument that the root of evil was lay influence in the ecclesiastical order. The ecclesiastical order itself was superfluous; the Holy Spirit within was to guide a person's life. The prophetic variety of reform was always the voice of a small minority that flourished among monks, mystics, and heretics; yet, oddly, many of the prophets commanded great respect in a society that, however much concerned with the things of this world, never wholly forgot the other.

There were three major sources of reform in the years between Boniface's mission and the papal revolution that began about 1050: the kings, the monasteries, and the laity.

Royal leadership of reform was of course concerned with the creation of order, and within the context of order, it was perfectly natural. There was the long tradition of imperial control of the church that stretched back to Constantine. There was the practical consideration that only kings had the wealth and the power to enforce reform. And ordinarily the kings had proper intentions. Most of them were sincere Christians; and they recognized the value of the church for education and administration. There were plenty of opportunities for exploitation of the church: for example, simony, the confiscation of church properties, or the diversion of church revenues. But most rulers wished to build and maintain an upright church, so long as their own control of it was retained. When the papalists later argued that corruption was the result of lay interference in the church, they forgot that lay interference had also produced most of the reform.

Among the Franks, the reform traditions of Boniface were continued by Pepin the Short, his son Charlemagne, and his grandson Louis the

Pious (814–840). Convinced by Alcuin and other advisors that the Frankish state could revive the vigor and glory of the Roman Empire, Charlemagne set about to make his capital, Aachen, an intellectual center and the Frankish church a model of efficiency and purity. The zeal that led Charlemagne to attack the Avars, Saxons, and Spanish Muslims was religious as well as political and military in motivation, and he and his advisers were as determined to continue the internal improvement of the church as to extend the geographical boundaries of Christendom.

Charlemagne and his son Louis the Pious strove to restore discipline to the monasteries by reestablishing the rule of St. Benedict. Charlemagne died with this dream still unrealized, but Louis brought the plan to fruition. He collaborated with another Benedict, St. Benedict of Aniane, a champion of reform. Together, they succeeded in forcing lapsed Benedictine monasteries back to strict obedience to the rule and bringing under the rule houses that had not yet accepted it. By a decree of the council of Aachen in 816, only the Benedictine rule was to be recognized in the kingdom of the Franks. The efforts of Louis and Benedict produced a triumph of regularity not only in the Frankish kingdom, but owing to the vast prestige of the Franks, throughout western Europe.

When after 870 the kingdom was divided, generally speaking, into a kingdom of the West Franks (later France) and a kingdom of the East Franks (later Germany), the rulers of those countries continued to support reform as long as they were powerful enough to do so. In Germany, Otto the Great and his successors held a series of national councils in which the church supported royal policy in return for strong royal efforts for reform. Otto III (983–1002), the grandson of Otto I, had as tutors some of the great reforming monks of his day. The young king demonstrated what he had learned by elevating one of these tutors, Gerbert of Aurillac, to the papacy. Gerbert, a monk, reformer, and the greatest scholar of his time, reigned as Sylvester II from 999 to 1003, and proved to be one of the few worthy popes of the period. Subsequent kings of the East Franks continued to advance the cause of reform: the efforts of Henry II (1002–1024) and Henry III (1039–1056) on behalf of the church were so great that both of them were canonized.

The kings of the Franks continued to support educational as well as moral advance. The West Frankish court of Charles the Bald (843–877) was almost as brilliant as that of Charlemagne itself; and in Germany the Ottos and their successors encouraged intellectual activity at court, in the episcopal schools such as that of Liège, and in monasteries such as

Fulda, founded by Boniface, which became in the tenth century one of the intellectual centers of Germany.

The kings of England were even more attached to reform than were their Frankish counterparts. Alfred the Great (871–899) developed his own intellectual court; one of the few early medieval monarchs who could read, he himself translated from Latin into English the *Dialogues* of Gregory the Great, the *Consolation of Philosophy* by Boethius, and other works. His successors, notably Edgar the Peaceful (959–975), strongly supported the monastic reforms of St. Dunstan and made efforts to appoint competent and moral bishops.

But royal reform, no matter how sincere, was postulated upon the demands of public order. The reforms centered in the monasteries were at once more prophetic, more vigorous, and often less enduring. Monastic reform at first was part of the royal program: witness the support of Charlemagne and Louis the Pious for the Benedictine order. But in the latter part of the ninth century, royal power was shattered and as incapable of promoting reform as it was of doing anything else. Accordingly, independent and spontaneous movements sprang up in the monasteries themselves.

Reforming monasteries arose all over Europe, but there were three chief centers of activity: the Low Countries and the Rhineland; Burgundy; and northern Italy. Why these areas should have been the centers of reform is not certain, but there is probably a correlation with the fact that they were important centers of both economic and intellectual activity.

Monastic reform was itself based in part upon order and in part upon prophecy. The reformers wished to restore the *libertas* of the monasteries, that is, their proper place in the Christian order. To this end they sought to eliminate lay abbots and to remove the influence of lay proprietors and even of bishops. Accordingly they aligned themselves with the papacy, placing themselves directly under the authority of distant Rome in order to escape closer and more effective authorities. The result was, for better or for worse, to make the great abbots almost independent. But the more important goal of monastic reform was the restoration of the spiritual life. It was for this purpose that St. Gerard of Brogue (d. 959), for example, withdrew from the world and founded an ascetic monastery on his wealthy father's estate in the diocese of Cambrai. It was for this reason that at Camaldoli and at Fonte Avellana in Italy, monks withdrew into eremitical isolation. To St. Guthlac, alone and filthy on his island in the East Anglian fens, or to St. Romuald who emerged from the marshes of Italy with a green color induced by swamp gases, only direct communication between the individual and his God seemed to fulfill the injunctions of the Gospel to leave all one has and follow Christ.

But the curse of the church is that nothing fails like success. Those monasteries that achieved the greatest influence and spread reform most broadly were themselves most subject to decline. The two most successful centers of monastic reform were Cluny in Burgundy and Gorze in Lorraine, each of which became the model and center of a large organization of daughter houses. Gorze, founded about 933 by St. John of Gorze with the help of Bishop Adalbero of Metz, exercised its influence upon over a hundred houses in Germany, Austria, and northern Italy. Cluny was as spectacular in the south, and it serves as a good example of both the success and the difficulties of monastic reform.

With the help of Duke William the Pious of Aquitaine, St. Berno, the wealthy son of a noble, withdrew from the world and in 909 founded the abbey of Cluny in Burgundy, restoring there the strict observance of the Rule of St. Benedict. The reaction of the secular nobility to this foundation indicates that among even the wealthy laity who had most profited from the corruption of the church, respect for the spirit was strong. Though Cluny was located on his property, Duke William relinquished all authority over the monastery, allowing the monks to choose their own abbots and to control their own affairs. Large donations of money and land flowed in, knights and great nobles came to make retreats at Cluny and to seek spiritual advice from its monks; and monks themselves were attracted in great numbers to the pure life. Under Abbot Odo (926–942), Berno's successor, the pope granted Cluny immunity from the authority of the bishops and placed it directly under the protection of Rome. Odo continued to cultivate the support of the wealthy and influential, and many lay proprietors of monasteries turned their powers over to him. By the time of Odo's death seventeen houses, including the influential monastery of Fleury, were under the authority of Cluny.

Under Abbot Maieul (954–994) and Abbot Odilo (994–1048), the number of such houses rose past a hundred, and a complex organization had to be set up for their administration. The abbot of Cluny retained authority over all the houses, each one of which had a prior in charge who was responsible to the abbot and subject to visitation by the abbot or his representatives. Cluny itself remained exempt from all outside authorities except the pope—and even papal authority was more nominal than real. In the meantime gifts from the wealthy flowed in and an enormous and elaborate abbey was erected; and the abbot of Cluny, now next to popes and kings the most influential man in Europe, received in splendor the great and the powerful from all over Europe. At the height of its magnificence at the end of the eleventh century, the monastery at Cluny was the head of a huge monastic empire containing many hundreds of dependencies and associated houses throughout Europe. By imperceptible stages, Cluny began to drift away from the strict observance of the rule and to prefer power and wealth to humility and poverty. In the twelfth century, it was itself the target for a new generation of reformers. St. Bernard, remarking with disgust the splendors of their sumptuous church, warned the Cluniacs that they bedecked their walls with gold and jewels at the expense of the spiritual needs of the poor.

By the mid-eleventh century, in fact, monasticism was entering a most serious crisis, against which the policies of even an uncorrupted Cluny would be insufficient. Since the sixth century, the monasteries had been one of the most important pillars of Christian order. They were centers of calm and tranquillity. They were agriculturally productive. They were far and away the most important centers of education, producing scholars, artists, and administrators, as well as monks, for all of Europe. But by 1050 society was undergoing profound changes. The long economic depression that had begun in the third century had come to an end, and a new age of rapidly expanding population, growing towns, and flourishing industry and commerce began. The eleventh through the thirteenth centuries are a period of population and economic growth absolutely unparalleled in the history of the West until the nineteenth and twentieth centuries. Rapid population growth provoked rapid social changes. Political order was more secure than it had been since the age of the Antonines in the second century, the growth of towns and cities was revolutionizing the economy, and governments were rapidly expanding their powers and services.

The rise of the towns and of the merchant and artisan classes created new educational requirements: the sons and daughters of merchants needed to be trained at least to keep accounts. Growing wealth provided leisure and the inclination to pursue other things than food and war; and among these distractions, as well as games, hunting, and sex, were philosophy and the arts. The episcopal schools, located in the flourishing towns, now outstripped the bucolic monasteries in numbers, size, and importance. To the great cities flocked scholars from different lands; and with the exchange of ideas, new questions were formulated and new intellectual attitudes developed. Even the other social services of the monasteries—aid to the poor, the lodging of travelers, the care of widows and orphans, and the treatment of disease—were taken over by others. A growing economy provided more jobs and reduced the proportion of the needy and consequently the need for alms-giving. Widows, orphans, and the disabled were often provided for by guilds or by other voluntary religious organizations. With the growth of commerce, inns sprang up along the roads and rivers, providing lodging often jollier than that offered by the monasteries. Medicine was now taught in the schools, and professional physicians, however incompetent by our standards, proved preferable to the care most monasteries could offer.

The effect of these social changes was greatly to reduce the social utility of the monasteries. The result was a crisis in monasticism and a subsequent reorientation of the monastic life. From the ninth to the end of the eleventh century, the only rule permitted in the West had been that of St. Benedict; now it was replaced by a number of others. More importantly, the fading of the monastic contribution to order opened the way for a revival in the monasteries of the spirit of prophecy. A new wave of monastic reform swept over Europe. The less devoted found more congenial occupations in the growing cities or elsewhere; those who remained were no longer charged with so many social responsibilities; and the monasteries turned back to asceticism, meditation, and contemplative spirituality.

From the eighth to the eleventh centuries, however, the spirit of prophecy, often uncongenial to a church seeking order, was frequently driven into dissent. There were no great movements of religious dissent until the twelfth century, but the earlier period produced numerous deviations of individuals and small groups. A strict theological definition of heresy is a "doctrine tenaciously held against the doctrine of the church," but dissent went far beyond theological heresy. The practice of strange rites and superstitious cults was equally a sign of disaffection. The chief distinction between medieval and ancient dissent is that whereas the heresies of the early church were chiefly concerned with points, sometimes fine points, of theology, those of the medieval church were chiefly concerned with moral questions. The heresies of the early church were debated by priests and bishops in schools and synods; those of the Middle Ages were often propounded by laymen in the fields and marketplaces.

The nature of dissent reflected the state of society. The chief concerns of the church in the years 700–1050 were corruption and reform. The dissenters were themselves either immoderately corrupt and ignorant or else overzealous adherents of reform. The former were the Eccentric heretics; the latter were the Reformists. One of the most striking Eccentrics of the early Middle Ages was Aldebert, a fanatic whom St. Boniface had difficulty in controlling. Aldebert claimed that he had been filled with grace while still in his mother's womb and that, a saint of God's election, he was born in a miraculous fashion. A charismatic personality, he preached to growing crowds of peasants and passed out his fingernail-parings and hair-cuttings as holy relics. He argued that his authority to preach derived from a letter which was written to him personally by Jesus and delivered by an angel. Boniface was not the man to take such disruptions of public order lightly, and he used every means at his disposal to combat them, including a number of synods and appeals to the pope for assistance. At last Aldebert disappeared, apparently less because of ecclesiastical pressures than because the people had tired of him.

Reformist dissenters were those who subscribed wholeheartedly to the reform of the church but who, exposed to the ignorance and intolerance of the parish clergy, grew impatient and eventually radical in their demands. They perceived the contrast between the purity and simplicity of the apostolic church and the decay of that of their own time, and they were impatient of any hesitation in returning to the Golden Age. Reformists had appeared in the eighth and ninth centuries—Claudius of Turin in Italy is an example—but they became more common and numerous in the eleventh, in response to the growing sentiment for reform throughout the church. In 1025 a large band of Reformists was arrested and tried for heresy at Liège; Reformists were executed at Orleans in 1022; and from the 1020's on, there were numerous incidents throughout Europe, particularly in France, Germany, and the Low Countries.

Typically, Reformists began by attacking the immorality of the clergy. When improvement was slow in coming, they proceeded to attack the institution of the clergy in its entirety, arguing that men did not need mediators between themselves and God, that the true church was invisible and consisted of those whom the Holy Spirit had illuminated. Their only authorities were the Bible and the inner light, and they rejected all that did not correspond to what the Holy Spirit told them was the interpretation of the Scriptures.

Exaggerations breed exaggerations; extremism on one side usually provokes extremism on the other. Both the established church, in its search for order, and the Reformists, in their expression of prophecy, had exceeded moderation and upset the stability of the church, which depended upon a salutary balance. The coldness and self-satisfaction of the established church drove the Reformists into opposition; but opposition was precisely what was intolerable to the church of order, which accordingly grew ever less tolerant of dissent. No one was executed for heresy in the western church between the sixth and the eleventh centuries, but beginning with the burning at Orleans in 1022, a new era of bloody intolerance began. Ironically, it was the desire to reform the church that produced both the prophetic heresy and the orderly repression. The human tragedy of the situation was clearly demonstrated in a case at Cambrai in 1077. There a man named Ramihrd was arrested for preaching against the corruption of the clergy. The mob seized him from the bishop, took him out to the end of town, and burned him to death. Ramihrd's guilt consisted in preaching to an ignorant and conservative clergy at Cambrai the very moral doctrines then being advocated by the reforming pope in Rome.

Education and intellectual achievement were among the most important and durable programs of the reform movements. The efforts of Charlemagne, Charles the Bald, Alfred the Great, and the Ottos, combined with those of the monasteries, contributed to the growth of literacy and learning among both the clergy and the laity. The kings obtained much success in their program of education for social utility. Under Charlemagne, for example, the monks developed a style of writing called the Caroline minuscule, which was more legible than previous styles and became the model for our present lower-case letters. At the palace school, Alcuin formally established the seven arts of Boethius as the basis of education, dividing them into the trivium (grammar, rhetoric, and dialectic) and the quadrivium (arithmetic, geometry, music, and astronomy). The trivium and the quadrivium continued to be the core of undergraduate education throughout the Middle Ages and into the Renaissance, and they were the basis for the later development of more advanced subjects: the quadrivium promoted the study of mathematics and science; from grammar proceeded the humanistic study of literature; from rhetoric developed legal studies; and from dialectic came scholastic philosophy.

Yet in the period 700–1050 there were few original thinkers. The intellectual level of the seventh century was too low a base from which to start, and scholars had perforce to devote themselves to elementary education. Neither royal concern with social utility nor the excessive medieval reverence for the past promoted nonconformity. Carolingian culture was an attempt to revive and to combine the wisdom and glory of early Christianity, classical Rome, and royal Jerusalem. Charlemagne and his court even affected antique names: Charlemagne was David, Alcuin was Horace, and Theodulf, the poet and architect, was Pindar. As society and culture as a whole became more settled in the later tenth and early eleventh century, utilitarianism yielded enough to permit the rise of humanism, the study of the classics for their own sake. But this promoted pedantic imitation rather than originality.

The two most original thinkers of the period were Bede (673–735) and John Scotus Eriugena (c. 810–877). Bede was a monk at the abbey of Jarrow on the barren coast of Northumbria; and though he never journeyed more than a few miles from his birthplace, his genius made him the greatest scientist of the early Middle Ages and the greatest historian since Augustine. He wrote on astronomy and cosmology, he calculated the tides for different latitudes and for different coastal configurations, and he popularized the dating from the birth of Christ that is now in use all over the world. But his most impressive work was his *History of the English Nation.*

This book is remarkable because it was the most critical and thoroughly investigated work of history since Thucydides. Although he himself remained at Jarrow, Bede interviewed visitors to the abbey, obtained whatever books were pertinent to his subject, and even sent out research assistants throughout England and as far as Rome to copy materials otherwise unavailable. Rising above the narrow parochialism of an era in which local churches or abbeys were the most usual subjects for the historian's pen and in which the English kingdoms were still politically disunited, he treated the history of the English people as a whole. Avoiding the rambling and logically inconsequent style of the chroniclers, Bede's history is tightly organized and structured on a theme: the gradual conversion of the English from paganism and from Irish Christianity to Roman Catholicism, which was to be the focus for the unity of the island. Bede is the only historian of the early Middle Ages who seems to have comprehended the great historical implications of Augustine's thought and who has worked out a story illustrating the meaningful and providentially purposive development of events. For Bede, history is not a jumbled box of moral maxims, but a dynamic development guided by the hand of God. Like Augustine, Bede used his great intellect to discern and to explicate the order both in the natural world and in human affairs.

Eriugena, an Irishman who settled at the court of Charles the Bald, where he taught and wrote philosophy, was strongly influenced by the mystical thought of Augustine, of the Neoplatonists, and of the Syrian monk Pseudo-Dionysius. For Eriugena, the true order of the universe is eternally veiled from humanity. "We do not know what God is... because He is infinite and therefore objectively unknowable. God Himself does not know what He is because He is not anything. Therefore, nothing can be predicated of God literally or affirmatively. Literally, God is not, because He transcends being." This is not atheism; on the contrary, it is an affirmation that God's greatness transcends all human categories, even those of being and knowing. At the end of the world, "God, who is in Himself incomprehensible, will be somehow comprehended in the creature."

Bede and Eriugena were exceptional thinkers during this period. More typical was Alcuin, a great admirer of Bede and the intellectual leader of Charlemagne's court. Arriving in Aachen from York in the 780s at Charlemagne's invitation, Alcuin brought the vital tradition of Northumbrian scholarship to Charlemagne's court. He established himself as the head of a court school, and among his students was Charlemagne himself. A lifelong educator, Alcuin used education as a means of reforming and regulating the clergy. He founded many new schools, wrote texts on grammar, and composed the first treatises on rhetoric and dialectics since Boethius. Setting up a scriptorium, Alcuin assigned an unprecedented number of scribes to the task of preserving classic and patristic manuscripts. These efforts typified the direction of Alcuin's thought. Believing that the advent of Christ represented the culmination of all true knowledge, Alcuin emphasized the authority of the fathers of the church over new or original thought. Alcuin authored numerous commentaries on Scripture, always following in the tradition of the patristics and carefully avoiding innovation. Nevertheless, in the very act of establishing the boundaries for discussions of doctrine, Alcuin contributed to a lasting theological framework for Christian discourse. Under the influence of Alcuin, theological questions were necessarily solved through reference to precedent, especially the precedents established by the writings of the church fathers and the findings of the ecumenical councils of the fourth and fifth centuries. Not until the twelfth century did Christian intellectuals begin to venture beyond the authorities established by Alcuin and the members of his circle.

The way of Alcuin is the way of reform, of identifying problems as the corruption resulting from unwanted changes, and of finding solutions in the examples of the past. To this day the principal means of responding to issues of church belief and practice is to investigate the earliest history of the church for answers. But no reform movement ever succeeds in actually recreating the past—conditions change, societies develop, and the past is irrevocably past. Attempts at reform inevitably lead to changes and developments that defy prediction. The reform spirit of the Carolingian court established the lasting authority of the patristics, but it also led to unforeseen events that introduced revolutionary changes to the western world, changes that established many of the identifying characteristics of medieval society.

Chapter Eight

Revolution

Clerical reformers practiced two varieties of reform in the Middle Ages, one motivated by prophecy and the other by order. The reform of order led to a program of political revolution in the eleventh and twelfth centuries that created a tightly knit ecclesiastical corporation under the leadership of the papacy. This revolution transformed the nature of the church into a papal monarchy, and it made the papacy from 1050 to 1300 the single most important authority in western Europe.

The growth in the eleventh century of a more complex society made this revolution possible: expansion of the population and of economic productivity, extension of communications and increasing contacts with the world outside the West, the rise of the towns and of new urban social structures, the achievement of political stability, the increased size and efficiency of governments. In a simpler society, order could be maintained with a less rigid structure; now the diverse thrusts to non-conformity provoked from the forces of order a new and far more ambitious offensive. It was in the period after 1050 that the transformation of the church from a community to a corporation was achieved.

The papalists used two primary arguments to justify the creation of a tightly organized church under papal monarchy. The first emphasized the continuity between papalist reform and the earlier reform movements. Moral reform, the argument went, can only be accomplished when the influence of the laity is removed from the church; and the influence of the laity can be removed only when the church obtains enough political power to enforce its independence. The second argument was derived from natural law. It is necessary that human law be established in accordance with the principle of justice, that it be in accordance with the will of God. Any human law that is unjust must either be changed or considered null and void. Any ruler who does not rule according to the principles of justice must be corrected or deposed. But how are the Christian people to judge whether a law or a ruler is just? If everyone decides for themselves on the basis of their own conscience which laws they should obey, the result is anarchy. Some objective authority is needed to which to refer, and for the papalists that logical authority is the vicar of Peter, to whom Christ entrusted the leadership of his flock.

In practice, assertion of these papalist principles required a double program: tighter and more efficient organization of the church under papal leadership, and exercise of papal authority over temporal affairs. Both sides of the program were revolutionary.

The internal constitution of the church had been from the second century traditionally episcopal. It was ruled by a coalition of bishops that represented the community of the apostles and that wielded as a body the authority granted the apostles by Christ. The coalition was, however, never a formally constituted body, except when it met as an ecumenical council. The great patriarchs gradually increased their power over that of the other bishops. Because of their political importance, Rome and Constantinople had emerged by the fifth century as the two most influential sees. This state of affairs was confirmed in the seventh century, when the other patriarchal sees—Alexandria, Antioch, and Jerusalem—all fell into the hands of the Muslims. From a very early period, the bishops in the West tended to grant, at least nominally, a great deal of authority to the bishop of Rome. Over time, aided by the increasing weakness and isolation of the Byzantine emperor and by the support of the English and the French, the papacy extended its power throughout the West. In the meanwhile, it continued to exercise influence in the East as well, and even at Constantinople the pope was recognized as occupying an especially honored position among the bishops.

The papal position, which had made such great strides in the eighth century only to suffer from generally weak leadership in the ninth and tenth centuries, advanced rapidly in the period from the eleventh through the thirteenth, when the old tradition of a community of bishops was replaced by the idea of papal monarchy. The authority of Christ, instead of being delegated to the apostles as a whole, was now deemed to have been delegated to Peter, who then in turn delegated it to his apostolic colleagues. Hence the pope was the vicar of Christ on earth (this title now replaced that of "vicar of Peter"), and the bishops derived their authority from him. The result was the creation of a strongly organized church under the monarchy of the pope, where the discipline and doctrine of the papacy could be everywhere enforced. As in the early church the Mystical Body of Christ had been identified with the Christian community *(ecclesia)* and the Christian community with the institutional church, so now the church was identified with the *ecclesia romana.* The pope was the representative of, and the ultimate authority over, the entire Christian community. This was itself a revolutionary program.

But the papalists' attitude toward the temporal power was even more revolutionary. There were three broad theories of the relationship of the temporal to the spiritual power current in the Middle Ages. All assumed, as almost all societies have until recent times, that there was no distinction between church and state. Indeed, such a distinction would have appeared meaningless. The church, like the state, was responsible for the order of society; the state, like the church, was responsible for promoting the salvation of its members. Each was a manifestation of a united Christian society. Of the three fundamental ways in which authority over Christian society could be conceived, the first placed the emperor at its head, with authority passing from God to the emperor, who delegated temporal authority to the kings and princes and spiritual authority to the pope and bishops. The second theory argued parallelism: Christ granted spiritual authority directly to the pope and temporal authority directly to the emperor. Parallelism was a compromise that proved uncongenial to the medieval desire for a simple cosmos. In the third theory the pope was at the head and, receiving his powers directly from Christ, delegated spiritual authority to bishops, councils, and abbots and temporal authority to the emperor and kings.

From the time of Constantine through that of Henry III of Germany (1039–1056), who deposed three popes, the imperial theory generally prevailed in practice, for the simple reason that imperial power was usually much greater than papal power. On occasion a strong pope such as Nicholas I (858–867) would assert the superiority of the spiritual to the temporal, but until 1048 such papal boldness was exceptional.

After the election of Leo IX in 1048, the papal position grew rapidly more powerful until, following a long conflict with the temporal rulers, the popes emerged victorious. From about 1125 to about 1300 it was the papalist theory of Christian society that generally prevailed over the imperial. An enormous revolution had been accomplished. The papal revolution was what sociologists call "norm-oriented": that is, it accepted traditional assumptions about society, simply replacing one supreme ruler of that society—the emperor—with another—the pope. It was not "value-oriented": it did not challenge the fundamental structure of society. The analogy is closer to the American among modern revolutions than to the French or Russian. There was enough corruption in the eleventh-century church, and enough enthusiasm for more sweeping reforms, that in retrospect a more fundamental revolution would seem to have been possible, like the one that eventually did occur with the Protestant Reformation in the sixteenth century. But medieval society was too conservative and not yet complex enough socially to support such a violent change. Furthermore, the papacy proved successful in capturing the reform movement by setting itself at its head. In the history of the Catholic Church there have been three periods of acute crisis: the eleventh century, the sixteenth, and the twentieth. In the sixteenth century the papacy failed to align itself with the forces of reform until it was too late; the result was the Protestant Reformation. As a new century approaches, it is not yet clear whether the current papacy is able or willing to meet the challenge of reform; the twenty-first century, like the sixteenth, may be a time of significant changes in the Catholic Church. But in the eleventh century a succession of able and devoted popes, by assuming the leadership of reform themselves, diverted the currents of revolution from radical into essentially moderate channels.

The dispute providing the focus for revolution concerned investitures. The investiture controversy concerned the propriety of a lay ruler's bestowing upon a bishop the symbols of his spiritual rule. Investiture was the feudal ceremony in which a lord gave his vassal a kernel of wheat, a clod of earth, or some other symbol of the fief that the vassal was receiving in return for his homage. Since so many bishops in the eleventh century were themselves feudal vassals, they received investiture for their fiefs from their lords, usually the kings. The kings, who were accustomed to appoint the bishops, acquired the additional habit not only of investing them with the symbols of their secular power, but also of bestowing upon them the episcopal ring and crozier (pastoral staff), symbols of their spiritual authority. To the papal reformers, there could be no clearer symbol of what they considered the fundamental difficulty with the church: lay influence.

But the issue of lay investiture was for the most part only symbolic. Directly underlying it was a more important issue: who had the right to appoint the bishop? In the early church, bishops were elected by the united acclamation of the clergy and people. In the more formalized church of the Middle Ages, such spontaneity was exceptional, and it became general practice for the cathedral chapter to act as representatives of the clergy and people of the diocese in the election of a bishop. As royal intervention increased, it became even more common for the kings simply to appoint the candidate. Bishops usually controlled a great deal of land and wielded significant political authority; kings, therefore, were anxious to see men they could trust in that high office. Election did not permit a bishop to enter immediately upon his duties; he had first to be consecrated—to receive the laying on of hands by other bishops—before he was considered to have the gift of apostolic succession. But this presented little difficulty to the kings, who could always procure from among their loyal episcopal supporters the three bishops requisite for consecration. It was this royally appointed episcopate with its temporal loyalties that the papal reformers were most interested in suppressing and replacing with bishops nominated by the papacy. It seems to have seldom occurred to the reformers that it was hopeless to try to remove lay interference in the church as long as the church wielded political influence.

Underlying the dispute over episcopal elections was a deeper struggle that some historians have classified as a warfare between church and state. This classification is insufficient. In the first place, few people at the time would have understood the distinction between church and state, and it is always tricky to argue that people are really fighting for something different from what they believe they are fighting for. In the second place, the phrase "church against state" conjures up a picture in which popes, monks, and bishops on the one side confront emperors, kings, and nobles on the other. Nothing could be further from the truth. At the height of the war between the Emperor Henry IV and Pope Gregory VII, the majority of the German bishops, as was quite natural for royal appointees, supported the emperor. On the other hand, the chief allies of the pope were many of the German nobility, who for their own political purposes wished to weaken the imperial position. Many of the monks were prophetically indifferent to the question of who should dominate the Christian order; they were, on the whole, inclined to accept the royal domination of the church and to regard papalism as unnecessary and irrelevant to the true spiritual demands of Christianity. The situation by 1080, when Gregory VII had chosen a king of his own and Henry IV his own pope, demonstrates the inadequacy of the "church against state" interpretation. On one side was a pope, a king aspiring to be emperor, bishops, abbots, princes, knights, and townspeople; on the other side was an emperor, a pope, bishops, abbots, princes, knights, and townspeople. The struggle is therefore best understood as a vast civil war affecting all segments of a united and indivisible Christian society. The revolution consisted in the success of the popes in substituting themselves for the emperor as the supreme authority in that society.

The papal revolution began in 1048 with the election of Leo IX, but, like most revolutions, it had been prepared for by the previous development of a revolutionary theory. The papalists claimed Petrine texts of the Gospels as the source of their position, contending that Christ's commission to Peter is nowhere matched by any corresponding commission to Caesar or any secular power. They referred also to the words of Gelasius I to the Emperor Anastasius I in 494: "There are two chief powers ruling this world: the holy authority of the popes *[auctoritas]* and the royal power *[potestas]. The* spiritual power is more important than the temporal because it is responsible to God for the kings themselves." Gelasius' meaning was not clear, but the papalists chose the interpretation pleasing to them, that *auctoritas* is superior to *potestas* and that the kings are responsible to the spiritual power.

In the eighth and ninth centuries, papalist arguments were advanced by the Donation of Constantine and by other forgeries. In the first half of the ninth century a number of documents were forged in the episcopal chanceries of northern France. Claiming to be collections of early papal and conciliar decrees, the forgeries were a clever mingling of real and spurious materials, with the aim of showing that in the ancient tradition of the church the kings did not intervene in its affairs. These false decretals, as they were called, built up the prestige of the bishops and, incidentally, that of the pope, whom, as a more distant authority, they preferred to the king. The great Pope Nicholas I (858–867), taking advantage of temporary royal weakness, further advanced papalist theory. In the first place, Nicholas argued, the papacy receives its rights directly from God, and the "foremost see is therefore to be judged by no one." Bishops, councils, kings and emperors, all these derive their powers from the pope, who is the protector of the whole Christian people in matters of discipline and doctrine.

In the tenth and eleventh centuries, two great prelates from Liège, ironically one of the centers of reform theory as well as one of the strongholds of imperial politics, urged the superiority of the spiritual to the temporal power. Rather (d. 974), bishop of Liège and then of Verona, argued the supremacy of the episcopacy in general, without special reference to the pope. "Bishops," Rather declared in one of his less temperate moods, "are gods, lords, messiahs, angels, patriarchs, prophets, apostles, martyrs, anointed kings, princes, judges ...." Wazo, bishop of Liège from 1042 to 1048, defied the Emperor Henry III (1039—1056) on three occasions, declaring: "...to you we owe fidelity; but to the pope we owe obedience. To you, O king, we must answer for worldly things; to the pope, however, we must answer for everything concerning God's service."

With these ideas current, particularly in northern Italy and Lorraine, only the opportunity was needed in order to launch a revolutionary program. That opportunity was provided by Henry III at the synod of Sutri (1046). Henry III was a pious emperor, who believed that it was the emperor's duty to control the church and to direct it toward morality and Christian purity. He believed that his authority entitled him to depose and appoint popes according to his best judgment; and he was the last emperor effectively to exercise this power. In 1046 there were three claimants to the papal throne: Benedict IX, whom the chroniclers describe as "bestial," the representative of one noble Roman family; Sylvester III, the almost equally reprehensible candidate of another family; and Gregory VI, a generally reputable and moral man who, however, was guilty of simony in purchasing the papacy from Benedict IX. To straighten out a situation that was spiritually unedifying and conducive to political instability, Henry III intervened, and at two synods in December 1046 (Sutri, December 20, and Rome, December 23), he secured the resignation of, or deposed, all three candidates. Gregory VI went north to Lorraine in exile, accompanied by his relative Hildebrand. Henry proceeded to appoint as pope two German bishops in succession, Clement II (1046–1047) and Damasus II (1048), both of whom pursued policies of reform under imperial patronage. On the death of Damasus, Henry appointed yet another German bishop, Bruno of Toul, whom he confidently expected to continue the policies of his predecessors.

Bruno, who took the throne name of Leo IX (1048–1054), did not disappoint Henry in his devotion to the cause of reform; but he was from Lorraine and had learned the papalist rhetoric of that region. When he came down to Rome as pope he brought with him a brain trust of papalist Lorrainers: Humbert, whom Leo made cardinal bishop of Silva Candida; Frederick, the brother of Duke Godfrey of Lorraine; Hugh the White; and Hildebrand, who, though an Italian, had spent two years in the north with Gregory VI. Leo was unwilling to make a radical break with the emperor, whose good will he desired and upon whom he relied for support against the Normans of southern Italy; but he did undertake an unprecedented tour of France and Germany, calling reform synods, visiting dioceses, and building up in northern Europe a more direct consciousness of the presence and prerogatives of Rome, with the hope of bringing the bishops under papal rather than imperial control.

Leo's successor was Victor II (1054–1057), who worked closely with the emperor, but imperial influence was badly shaken by the death of Henry III in 1056. Henry was succeeded by his six-year-old son, Henry IV, under the regency of his wife, the Empress Agnes, a pious and trusting but by no means politically astute woman. The next year, Victor II died and was succeeded by Frederick of Lorraine, who took the title Stephen IX (1057–1058). Stephen's family was violently anti-imperial, and the new pope not only neglected to notify the regent of his election, but even entertained the idea of placing his own brother, Duke Godfrey, on the imperial throne. The erosion of the imperial position vis-à-vis the papacy now became marked. It was the result not so much of any weakening of imperialist theory, but of the practical disadvantages of a weak and indecisive regency.

It was under these conditions that Humbert of Silva Candida was encouraged to publish a work that he had completed earlier but had feared to publish while Henry III was still alive. This was the *Three Books against the Simoniacs,* the opening shot in a long battle of the books between papalist and imperialist theoreticians. Humbert's position was that the root of evil was lay influence in the church and that there could be no effective reform unless this were wholly rooted out. The entire function of the temporal power was to act as the arm of the church, of which the pope was the head: the emperor and the kings existed for the sole purpose of protecting the clergy and of executing their orders. The Mystical Body of Christ is identified with the bishop of Rome and his cardinals: the pope is to society as the sun is to the universe; the emperor is like the pale moon, shining only with reflected light. These ideas, the most radical statement to date of the papalist position, were put into practice by subsequent popes.

After a short interlude following the death of Stephen IX, the revolution passed out of the hands of the Lorrainers into the hands of Italian reformers who were no less radical. Gerard, the archbishop of Florence, who became Nicholas II (1059–1061), launched two effective attacks upon the lay power. In 1059 at a great synod in Rome at the Lateran palace, where the medieval popes dwelt, Nicholas issued the first formal prohibition of lay investiture and the first formal regulation concerning the election of the pope. Henceforth, in order to prevent further imperial interference, the pope was to be elected by the cardinals of the Roman church, and all lay interference was strictly forbidden. Later, at the Council of Lyon in 1274, it was decreed that the cardinals meet in conclave *(conclave:* locked up "with a key") so as to preserve absolute secrecy and freedom from attempts to influence the election from outside.

All the reform popes till now had had short reigns, and only the debility of the empress's politics had enabled them to get away with so much. But Nicholas II was followed by two popes in succession, both Italians, both as vigorous as any of their predecessors, and both enjoying long tenure in office: Alexander II (1061–1073) and Hildebrand, who took the throne name of Gregory VII (1073–1085). It was under these two popes that the theories of papal supremacy were first put into wide practice; the reign of Gregory VII, in particular, made it clear that the struggle for the control of Christian society was joined to the death. Hildebrand was born in Italy, was for a short time a monk, and then, as a relative and friend of Pope Gregory VI, learned something of papal politics, including their disappointments. After accompanying Gregory into exile, he returned to Rome with Leo IX as a member of the brain trust and rose rapidly in the ranks of the hierarchy as subdeacon, legate, and eventually (1059) archdeacon. As archdeacon, he exercised almost as much power as the pope himself; and the monk Peter Damian, whose prophetic spirit did not allow him to be impressed with the claims of spiritual order, cynically suggested that "if you want to live in Rome, you have to declare loudly that you follow the pope's lord more than the lord pope." In 1073, he was finally elected pope in violation of the Lateran Decree of 1059, by acclamation of the people. Called by his German friends Hellbrand ("Bright Flame") and by his enemies Höllebrand ("Hellfire"), Gregory's life is proof that a burning spirit can dwell within a breast committed to order. He was convinced that he had a divine mission to reform society and that his power over society was, under God, unlimited. No longer merely the vicar of Peter but now the vicar of Christ, the pope has, he argued, the duty of exercising his authority over all the earth.

Three conditions prepared the way for the implementation of Gregory's program: the weakness of the empire, the tradition, now twenty-five years old, of the revolutionary papacy, and the development of canon law. It was from a perusal of the old decrees of canon law, both legitimate and forged, that the famous *Dictatus Papae* ("dictates of the pope") was compiled. This curious document, which was placed in the official register about 1075, is an unorganized list of the titles of a collection of real or suppositious canons from the past, compiled by Gregory or one of his supporters in support of papalism. It contains some memorable statements: only the Roman pontiff is rightly called universal; he alone can depose or reestablish bishops; he alone can use imperial insignia; all princes must kiss his feet; he is entitled to depose kings. Whether anyone outside the papal court ever saw this document until much later is problematic—the *Dictatus Papae* at the very least provides the theoretical blueprint for Gregory's policies. Gregory himself never achieved such the lofty level of authority proposed by the *Dictatus Papae*—in fact, he ended his life in exile believing himself, with some justification, to have failed in his larger aims. But the program of papal authority outlined by this document continued to serve as a list of goals for future popes, and many of these goals were later achieved.

The practical program of Alexander II and Gregory VII was almost as impressive as their theoretical statements: to reform and reorganize the church, to establish papal authority in the eastern church, to reclaim Spain for Christianity, and in all this to enlist the support and obedience of the kings of the West.

The papal policy in regard to the internal organization of the church resulted in its being transformed into a papal monarchy. The means used were these. First, papal government at Rome was strengthened and expanded. The *curia,* the equivalent of the *consilium* (administrative and advisory council) of the kings, grew larger and complex. The curia was dominated by the cardinals, who, together with the pope, formed the *ecclesia romana,* which was in turn identified with the whole Christian community. Cardinals originally existed in many dioceses and were so called because they were "hinges" *(cardines)* between two churches: a cardinal priest would have a parish but also be invited to serve as an administrator in the cathedral. Gradually, particularly in Rome, where the task of administration was great, the cardinals gradually lost all but a nominal connection with their original parishes. Certain parishes in Rome came to be established as cardinals' parishes with only nominal duties, and to these the popes would appoint those whom they wished to have as administrators. Certain deaconries in Rome and certain tiny dioceses around Rome were also set aside for administrative purposes, so that there were cardinal-bishops and cardinal-deacons as well as cardinal-priests. The power of the cardinals in the administration has been so great that they have ever since been under attack.

With the growth of the papal administration came an enormous increase in the volume of papal correspondence: regulating jurisdictional disputes and protecting legitimate bishops and monasteries against usurpers, admonishing recalcitrant bishops, upbraiding meddlesome rulers, and urging bishops and synods to take stronger measures for reform. Another means of papal control was the summoning of councils and the encouragement of local councils or synods. No ecumenical council had been called since the ninth century, for the imperial power was weak, and the papacy did not yet feel itself in a strong enough position to dominate one. But from the time of Nicholas II the popes called frequent and ever-larger synods, until in 1123 the First Lateran Council began a series of ecumenical assemblies summoned by the popes and directed to enact papal policies.

Among the popes' most effective weapons were the legates. A legate was an officer sent out to a locality by the papal court with full jurisdiction over a particular problem just as if he were pope. For example, Alexander II sent Peter Damian with full papal powers as a legate to Germany in 1069 to persuade the young King Henry IV not to divorce his wife. But under Gregory VII and his successors, such temporary legatine missions were often supplemented by sending out legates with long terms of office and with jurisdiction over wide areas. For example, Gregory sent Hugh of Die to France with the authority to act throughout that kingdom exactly as if he were the pope himself. Hugh was fanatically loyal to Rome and, more Catholic than the pope, he believed wholeheartedly that only unbending adherence to papal decrees could be tolerated and that harshness was the only way to keep the church in line. Wherever he went, he took precedence over the local bishops and archbishops; he visited dioceses and parishes demanding moral reform; he called synods and councils on his own authority; and he even deposed bishops—including, in 1080, the powerful Manasses of Reims, who had with some asperity refused to attend a council to which he was summoned by the legate.

In consequence of these extensions of papal power, the authority of bishops and local synods gradually deteriorated. From a loosely organized Christian community, the church became a papal monarchy. One result was that the lay authorities were now confronted with a church that was more tightly organized than ever and more difficult for them to control. Far from relinquishing its political power in the name of reform, the church acquired more, and the need of the kings to dominate it was therefore increased rather than diluted. Under these conditions, conflict became highly likely.

The struggle of the papacy with the empire was not limited to the western empire. As early as the reign of Leo IX, the reform popes were determined to restore their authority in the East, which had been deteriorating for centuries as the doctrines and practices of the two halves of the Christian church drifted slowly apart. In 1054, Leo sent the two firebrands Frederick of Lorraine and Humbert of Silva Candida to Constantinople to work out an agreement with Emperor Constantine IX. Constantine was willing, but the patriarch of Constantinople, Michael Kerullarios, who matched Humbert in intolerance and rashness, deliberately humiliated the papal legates and provoked the mob to outrages against churches of the Latin rite. Kerullarios was determined to end papal influence at Constantinople once and for all, and he succeeded in provoking the legates to take actions that equaled his own rashness: they formally laid upon the high altar of the Cathedral of Hagia Sophia a bull excommunicating the patriarch. The emperor tried in vain to bring the antagonists to a conference table. Kerullarios publicly burned the papal bull, and the legates went home to urge a policy of harshness and coercion against the East. The events of 1054 are the most dramatic in the long process of division between the Roman Catholic and the Eastern Orthodox churches, and they were confirmed by the bloody wars of the western crusaders in the East. Particularly damaging was the crusade in 1204, when western warriors ravaged the city of Constantinople itself. Only in the second half of the twentieth century has any progress been made in restoring relations. If the 1965 meeting in Jerusalem between Pope Paul VI and the Patriarch Athenagoras of Constantinople, and the formal lifting of the excommunication of Michael Kerullarios that same year did not shake the world with their daring, they at least symbolized a spirit of compromise that was lacking for nine hundred years.

The papal zeal for the assimilation of the eastern church extended to the conversion of Jews, heretics, and Muslims as well, and it was Gregory VII who first contemplated calling Christians to arms to liberate the Holy Land. This crusading ideal, which would be further developed by the popes of the twelfth and thirteenth centuries, seems an ironic manifestation of a religion founded by the Prince of Peace. Yet it was a logical—if not a reasonable—corollary of papalist theory. If the pope was indeed the vicegerent of Christ over Christian society and consequently over the world, he had a true authority to enforce on the world the demands of Christian morality and the edicts of Christian law. Enforcement of law logically entails, and has historically always included, the use of force. Hence the pressures put on the eastern church, hence the increased prosecution of heretics, hence the growing intolerance of Jews, hence the crusading spirit and the eventual foundation of military-oriented religious orders like the Templars, and hence the approval of civil war and rebellion as measures against the disobedient kings and emperors of the West.

Because the papacy was situated in the West, it was in the West that the conflict with the temporal powers was most violent. The papalist attitude toward the kings of France and England was often as severe as that toward the western emperor, but because it was the emperor in whose domains Rome lay and because it was the emperor who, like the pope, claimed authority over all Christian society, it was against the empire that the papacy exerted its most vigorous efforts.

In 1066 Henry IV (1056–1106), having reached the age of sixteen, began his personal rule. The young king inherited the determination and political skill but not the favorable political circumstances of his father, for the ten-year regency of his mother had reduced royal power in relation both to the church and to the nobility. Henry immediately turned his energies toward restoring it to its former heights. Since the bishops still possessed great political influence, it was absolutely necessary to control them if political order was to be reestablished. In 1073 Gregory VII came to the papal throne, possessed of determination and energy equal to Henry's, and equally resolved to control the bishops.

From 1073 to 1076 an uneasy peace prevailed between the two men: they wrote letters expressing their mutual esteem, and Gregory supported Henry in his successful repression of a major rebellion in Saxony from 1073 to 1075. But the *Dictatus Papae* of 1075 already indicated that Gregory would not tolerate the reestablishment of imperial domination of the church, and in the same year the pope issued a formal decree against the investiture of bishops by laymen. When early in 1076 dispute over the succession to the archdiocese of Milan made it clear that emperor and pope were going to press irreconcilable claims to name bishops, the battle was joined. By the end of February, 1076, each had threatened the other with deposition. By autumn, events in Germany gave the advantage to the pope. The nobles of southern Germany rebelled against the king, whose growing power they feared, and they met at Tribur in October to seek an alliance with the pope.

In order to avert what would have been a deadly combination Henry crossed the Alps and in January, 1077, waited for the pope for three days outside the castle of Canossa, where Gregory was in residence, begging him for forgiveness. It was a humiliation from which Henry reaped considerable short-term advantages. Gregory, reluctantly weighing the duties of Christian charity more heavily than those of political expedience, granted absolution to the king in return for Henry's promise that he would allow the pope to judge between him and the rebellious nobles. The nobility went ahead and at Forchheim in 1077 declared the king deposed, electing Rudolf of Swabia in his place. Gregory, abiding by the agreement of Canossa, refused to sanction this action on the grounds that Henry would remain the rightful ruler until he was properly judged by the pope. Thus Henry shrewdly and at the cost only of temporary humiliation broke the papal alliance with the nobles. He returned to Germany and waged successful war against his opponents, while Gregory kept his own counsel and declared for neither side. In 1080, at last convinced of Henry's bad faith, Gregory declared the king deposed "for his insolence, disobedience and deceit" and recognized Rudolf as the rightful ruler. It was a dramatic moment in the history of the church: on several occasions emperors had deposed popes, but never before had a pope presumed to depose an emperor. But it was too late. In the same year Henry called his own synod to depose Gregory as a false monk, sorcerer, fornicator, and plotter of murder. Rudolf died in the fall, and though another pretender was elected, Gregory's German allies were in disorder and shortly ended effective resistance. With his military supremacy, Henry was able to capture Rome by 1084, install his own pope, and drive Gregory to die in exile in 1085.

In the meanwhile, the conflict of theories was as violent as that of armies. The manifestos of Humbert and his colleagues elicited response from imperialist writers. Sigebert of Gembloux accused the papacy of fostering Reformist heresy by pressing its program of reform. The accusation was justified, for once an institution encourages a spirit of reform and change, there will inevitably be those who are disappointed that change is not proceeding fast enough and who move from moderate to radical discontent. But it is also true that without persistent reform, an institution will cease to respond to the needs of society and ultimately wither away. The imperialists argued, correctly, that they were conserving the ancient tradition of the church and that the papalists were innovators, a charge that in the conservative Middle Ages the papacy was concerned to deny. But had innovations not been made, there would have occurred either a violent revolution like the sixteenth-century Reformation or else a gradual dissolution and decay of Christianity such as has taken place in the twentieth century.

As the papalist theoreticians advanced their position, and as the political power of the emperor weakened, the imperialist theoreticians faltered. Peter Crassus, a lawyer from Ravenna and a friend both of Henry IV and of the antipope set up by the king, wrote a treatise *In Defense of King Henry*. He used the precedents of Roman law to deny the pope's right to excommunicate the king and to revive the argument that the king had the right to order all aspects of society in his kingdom. But Peter's arguments betray an unintentional retreat from the imperialist argument that there must be a unified Christian society under the rule of the emperor. Peter speaks of two orders of men, one bound by canon law and the other by secular law, implying parallelism rather than imperial supremacy. What had happened was this: before the eleventh century, the imperial theory of Christian society was dominant, so that often the anti-imperialists, such as Wazo of Liège, merely demanded parallelism. But when the papalist position hardened and claimed supremacy for itself, the imperialists retreated defensively into parallelism. Another ambivalence of Peter is that he seems to be defending not the rights of one emperor over all society, but the rights of each king in his own kingdom, a step toward the recognition of a political and ecclesiastical pluralism previously unheard of in the Middle Ages.

A writer known as the Norman Anonymous pursued these royalist arguments deliberately. Accepting the unity of Christian society, he nevertheless argued that its leadership was in the hands of the kings. Christ, he said, appears in the Gospels more as a king than as a priest; therefore it is the kings who most directly represent Christ. As for ecclesiastical government itself, papalism is a fraud, for apostolic authority lies with the bishops as a whole, not with the successor of Peter.

Thus the anti-papalist writers moved insensibly away from imperialism toward new positions which would be developed further in the later Middle Ages. The most important of these are political pluralism, the first intimations of nationalism; and conciliarism, resistance to papal monarchy in the name of episcopal collegiality.

The papalist writers of the twelfth century also made some interesting departures from the hierocratic ideas of the past. Honorius of Canterbury argued that the pope had direct authority over the clergy and indirect authority over the kings. But he equated neither clergy nor kings with the *ecclesia,* which was, rather, the "people of God," the Christian church as a whole. John of Salisbury (1110–1180) pressed the identification of *populus* (people) and *ecclesia* even further. The king must rule in accordance with justice; if he does not, he becomes a "tyrant," and the people may disobey his laws, depose him, or even kill him. John is still a papalist, and he insists that the pope must approve such action to make it legitimate, but the principle that all policies must be judged by their effects upon the welfare of the people and that the people are at least in part the judge of these policies was a departure from tradition in the direction of popular authority. In the fourteenth century Marsilius of Padua would further develop this notion of popular authority and social contract, and from there the theory would grow until it reached Locke, Rousseau, and Jefferson. Without fully understanding the implications of their arguments, both the papalist and the imperialist writers were encouraging the growth of the "ascending theory" of sovereignty, which argues that God does not delegate his authority downwards through pope or emperor but upwards through the people. Kings, popes, bishops, and emperors then possess their authority as a trust from the people whose representatives they are. But this notion was far from explicit, let alone prevalent, in the conflicts of the late eleventh and early twelfth centuries, when "descending" theories, either papal or imperial, still held sway.

Those conflicts were not resolved until after the end of the eleventh century. The victory of Henry IV over Gregory VII was not conclusive. Urban II (1088–1099) and Paschal II (1099–1118) continued the war against Henry and his antipope, and by 1104 the papacy had again built a powerful coalition of German nobles, led by Henry's son (soon to be Henry V) against the old emperor. These events did not escape the attention of the chroniclers as a perfect text for the vanity of vanities and the contempt of the world. Even as Henry IV and his antipope, Clement III, had driven Gregory VII to die in exile, so now Henry V and Paschal II drove Henry IV to die in Liège, the last city in his dominions to remain loyal to him.

If Paschal hoped that Henry V (1106–1125) would be more agreeable to papal claims than his father had been, he was mistaken. No vigorous emperor could afford to tolerate papal domination of his clergy. The new king resumed royal efforts to control the bishops; Paschal renewed the excommunication of anyone granting lay investiture; and after an inconclusive interview between the two in 1111, the emperor seized the pope and threw him into a dungeon. There he remained without food until he acquiesced in the imperial demands, which he of course denounced once he was well free of Henry's grasp. Under Paschal and Calixtus II (1119–1124), a number of agreements were worked out with the kings of France, Germany, and England regarding investitures. The kings agreed to invest the bishops only with the symbols of their temporal possessions and to leave the investment with the ring and crozier to the ecclesiastical authorities. But the kings were to invest with the temporals *before* consecration. On the one hand, this arrangement left the king with a veto over the election of the bishop; therefore no bishop could take office without his approval. On the other hand, the king had no direct control over the election of the bishop, since he had no legal power to invest the bishop with the symbols of his office. A powerful ruler could still enforce the selection of the bishop of his choice, but less powerful rulers could be forced into a position of passive acceptance. These compromises lessened the tensions between opposing parties, but did little to resolve the struggle.

The ultimate victory of the papacy in Germany was achieved not by negotiations nor by the triumph of a theory, but by a shift in dynastic politics. Henry V died in 1125 leaving no direct heir, and the title passed to his distant cousin Lothar II of Saxony (1125–1137). Lothar was a member of the Welf dynasty, one of the princely families that had long supported the papacy against the emperor. This tradition, in addition to the more important fact that Lothar's weak and disputed claim to the throne obliged him to make concessions to the church in order to secure its support, meant the end of effective imperial opposition to the papacy. The increasing weakness of the German monarchy now allowed the papacy to press in wherever the empire retreated. The bishops drifted away from imperial control, either to return to their old independence or to support the papacy. Papal appointments to episcopal sees now became common for the first time.

The papal revolution was well under way by the 1130s. The popes had been successful in establishing hierarchical order within the church and in dislodging imperialist claims to supremacy over Christian society in favor of their own. From that time until 1300 would be the only period in medieval history in which the papacy really dominated society. It remained for the popes of the twelfth and thirteenth centuries to develop and expand their position. Yet already, by the beginning of the twelfth century, the seeds of future discontents were visible to a discerning eye. The decline of imperial power and the growth, both in practice and in theory, of political pluralism presaged the rise of the national monarchies, which would after 1300 bring down both papacy and empire, and shatter the ideal of the unified Christian society. And the prophetic elements in the church were increasingly dissatisfied with a church that the principles of order were making more rigid, more temporally involved, and less responsive to the expression of the direct religious experience.

Chapter Nine

The Thrust of the Prophetic Spirit

Enthusiasm for reform in the eleventh and twelfth centuries encouraged the prophetic spirit as well as the spirit of order. Indeed, the more the forces of order transformed the church into a formalized and corporate organization, the more religiously enthusiastic people sought elsewhere for fulfillment. The powerful thrust of the prophetic spirit is thus the result not only of popular enthusiasm for reform in general but of rebellion against the spirit of order. This rebellion expressed itself in movements of popular piety, in new monastic orders, in contemplative spirituality, and in new movements of heresy.

The formalization of the Christian liturgy and sacraments, which had been well underway by the eighth century, continued into the eleventh. The western church had always been more legalistic than the eastern, and the conflict over investiture only heightened this trend. With the development of canon law and the vast extension of ecclesiastical organization under the papacy, with its councils, its decrees, its legates, and its curia and cardinals, legalism developed even further. As the institutions of the church centralized into a corporate body, the ceremonies of the church began to seem more sterile in some ways. The Mass still lacked meaning for most people, and the sacraments were often received, as the laws of the church were accepted, without real understanding. Participation in religion was often limited to formal and external observances that engendered little emotional response.

In the face of this developing formalism came the great upsurge of religious enthusiasm in the eleventh and twelfth centuries, an upsurge attributable in part to the continuation and maturation of the earlier reform movements. Other social and economic changes contributed to this new wave of religious enthusiasm, as well. During this period, medieval European society was experiencing rapid growth due to a number of factors. The invasions of western Europe that characterized the ninth and tenth centuries had come to an end. Climatic conditions improved, leading to higher agricultural yields and fewer crop failures.

The population of western Europe grew at a rate that was not exceeded until the modern era. New lands were cleared, and towns and cities experienced a sudden revival. More people were living closer together and enjoying greater prosperity than at any time since the decline of Roman civilization. Traditional ways of participating in religious life did not always offer spiritual fulfillment in the context of the new social and economic conditions of eleventh- and twelfth-century Europe.

Great numbers of people from all social and economic orders wished to express their religious enthusiasm in ways that seemed more personally satisfying than those provided by the formalized institutional church. The result was the growth of pious practices whose purpose was to bring the individual into a more direct religious experience. Anything was embraced that rendered the spiritual sphere closer and more attainable: hence the fervent practice of the cult of the saints, especially veneration for their relics and for places physically connected with them. It was thought that the physical remains of a holy person retained some of his or her sacred power, and every church institution strove to acquire a skull, a tooth, or at least a fragment of a venerable thighbone. These relics were sometimes placed under the cornerstone of the altar and sometimes set into ornaments of exquisite design known as reliquaries. The relic was often the focal point for visitors to the church institution, who made their vows and gave their gifts to the saint in return for, or in hope of, services rendered.

Certain shrines, renowned for the special piety of their saints or the miraculous circumstances surrounding their origins, became centers of long pilgrimages. The alleged burial place in Spain of the Apostle James, revealed to a monk by a miraculous star, became the shrine of Santiago de Compostella, visited by pilgrims from all over the West. The shrine of Our Lady of Chartres, that of St. Thomas Becket at Canterbury, that of St. Peter at Rome, and, most important, that of the Holy Sepulchre in Jerusalem, the traditional tomb of Christ, were visited by pilgrims whose numbers and enthusiasm increased throughout the eleventh and succeeding centuries. In April, when the weather began to warm, wrote Chaucer, "thanne longen folk to goon on pilgrimages,/ and palmeres for to seken straunge strondes,/ to ferne halwes, kowthe in sondry londes. . . ." ("Then people long to go on pilgrimages, and palmers to seek strange shores and distant shrines known in many lands"). The pilgrimage was often a long and difficult task, but it could be undertaken by individuals as an act of deeply felt devotion. That men and women, many of them wealthy people of substance, should undertake journeys under the most uncomfortable traveling conditions that often endured for months or even years is proof of the fervent spirit of the time.

Of the saints, the most popular was the Blessed Virgin. The cult of the Virgin, though ancient in its origins, took a central place in Catholic worship only during this period. The Virgin was venerated in the first centuries of the church but apparently to no greater degree than the most important apostles or church fathers. The highly emotional defense of her title as Mother of God against the Nestorians in the fourth century suggests that by then she was already the center of special veneration—a veneration encouraged by the iconography of the Nativity, which invariably showed the baby God protected by his Mother. The cult of the Virgin was strongest in the East, but by the ninth century it was already deep-seated in the West, as well. By that period Mary was already the mediator between humanity and God, praying mercifully to her Son for the sinner. As Christ was the new Adam, so Mary was the new Eve, who brought forth salvation on the earth as the old Eve had brought forth ruin. Born without sin, ever virgin, and sinless in her life, she was at once the ideal of maidenly purity and maternal devotion.

By the twelfth century the popular veneration of the Virgin had exceeded all previous limits and surpassed the boundaries of ecclesiastically approved doctrine. In a rough society that did little to protect its members, the individual turned to this mother-sister figure with fervent devotion. Everywhere the Virgin worked miracles; everywhere she succored the poor, the sick, and the lonely. To anyone who showed her special devotion, she extended her special protection, and she more than once rescued a murderer from the gallows because he had showed himself her special man. Popular devotion to Mary often descended into sentimentality, as in the famous tale of the "Juggler of Our Lady," where the little monk who is unable to write or paint or sing goes before the statue of the Virgin at night when all the other brothers are in bed and wins her favor by juggling for her.

The doctrine of the church ordinarily grows out of the meditations of theologians or the decisions of councils, but the veneration of Mary was assimilated into Christian doctrine from popular devotion. It is often wrongly assumed today that the stern and inflexible leaders of the medieval church dictated an unchanging doctrine to a passive populace, and that the Christian community simply accepted what they were given without contributing to the thought of the church. On the contrary, Christian doctrine has always incorporated the changing trends and beliefs of contemporary society, even if reluctantly. The cult of the

Virgin was a manifestation of a larger trend to humanize Christian expressions, a trend that transformed the representations of Christ in sculpture and painting from the stiff and hieratic judge of the universe to the suffering and wholly human victim, rejected and unjustly condemned by humanity. Mary was a kind and loving mother; she knew what it was like to feel bereavement and loss, and she could sympathize with the sufferings of poor mortals. The greatest hymn to the Virgin is perhaps the "Stabat Mater," written in the thirteenth century, which dwells upon her share in the tears of humanity:

Stabat mater dolorosa
Iuxta crucem lachrymosa
Dum pendebat filius;
Cuius animam gementem
Contristantem et dolentem
Pertransivit gladius.

(Weeping, the sorrowful Mother stood by the Cross while her Son hung dying. A sword had pierced her mourning and grieving soul that suffered with her Son.)

The wide extent of the Virgin's cult is reflected in the fact that of the cathedrals and churches erected in the twelfth and thirteenth centuries, an enormous proportion were dedicated to her. Most of the great cathedrals of France, for example, are cathedrals of Notre Dame: Notre Dame de Paris, Notre Dame de Chartres, Notre Dame d'Amiens, and so on. The erection of cathedrals all over Europe is in itself a manifestation of popular spiritual enthusiasm, for the enormous cost in money and in time was met in large part by the free donation of skills by artisans, architects, sculptors, and glaziers, and of hard labor or money by the population as a whole.

Cathedrals, the seats of the bishops, had dominated the major cities of early medieval Europe, but these cities were scarce and undeveloped. Beginning in the eleventh century, however, cities began to grow and new towns and cities began to dot the western European landscape. Whereas cities had previously served as administrative and cultural centers, the new cities became the focus for renewed trade and new manufacturing. The elite citizens of the newly emerging bourgeois order accumulated a great deal of wealth. But church doctrine did not regard material wealth with approval. The Sermon on the Mount in the Gospel of Matthew, for example, cautioned believers to store their treasures in Heaven rather than here on earth. Wealthy townspeople needed an acceptable outlet for their excess wealth; spending money on church buildings represented a very acceptable outlet indeed. As a result, the revival of towns and cities resulted in a wave of cathedral building that started in France and spread throughout the cities of western Europe.

Cathedrals represented a manifestation of a town's religious faith. The cathedral towers rose above every other structure in the city, demonstrating the majesty and glory of God. But cathedrals were built for practical economic reasons, as well. A cathedral could put a town on the map. It attracted pilgrims, who contributed tourist dollars to the town coffers. It also attracted new businesses by showcasing a town's wealth and economic stability (today, we build sports arenas and convention centers for the same reason). Cathedrals were the residences and offices of bishops, and thus became the homes of the increasingly sophisticated church bureaucracies that were developing at the time. As episcopal bureaucracies expanded, new clerks and church officials came to reside and work in the cathedral towns, adding to the population and economic stability. Clerical leaders did not force townspeople to build cathedrals; cathedrals were an enormous source of pride for the people of the towns and cities. Throughout the eleventh and twelfth centuries, the towns and cities of medieval Europe vied with each other to build ever larger and larger cathedrals, until the massive structures began to collapse under their own weight. More than simply the result and source of increasing wealth, cathedrals represented the growing civic pride and increasing religious enthusiasm of the High Middle Ages.

Popular enthusiasm also created a number of semimonastic movements, such as the Beghards and Beguines, laymen and women who lived a communal life dedicated to simplicity, poverty, and meditation. A similar enthusiasm brought about a revival of monasticism. The old reformed monasteries such as those of the orders of Cluny and Gorze had themselves suffered corruption, and by the end of the eleventh century new reforms were perceived to be necessary. But these new reforms were of a different nature than the old. The Benedictine order had ceased to be the center of educational, medical, and charitable activities. A more complex society demanded more advanced and specialized training in medicine and law, as well as philosophy and theology, and this new training was best provided in the cities by the episcopal schools in the cathedrals, and later by the universities that arose from these schools. The kind of education demanded for their administrators by ecclesiastical and secular governments, or by young merchants in the cities, was not being provided by the monasteries. Both secular governments and the new tightly organized church government established by the papacy had developed other means of establishing and keeping public order and no longer relied upon the monasteries for that purpose.

Before 1100 a number of monastic reform movements had begun, and these movements encouraged not only moral reform and purification but also an altogether new approach to monasticism. This new approach aimed not toward public utility and order, but toward prophecy. The new monk was to withdraw from the world and to practice asceticism and contemplative spirituality in order to achieve a deeper religious experience. The new monk was not to be a pillar of societal values, yet he was to have a commitment to society greater than before. His duty was to stand outside the normal values of Christian society and to preach its utter transformation in the manner of the prophets of Israel and of Christ himself. For the new monk, attempts to reform society through moderate, progressive measures were futile: what was needed was a radical revolution that would prepare the hearts of humanity for the Kingdom of God, which is not of this world.

The success of these new monastic movements in attracting large numbers of enthusiastic converts to their way of life and even of enlisting the support of kings, nobles, and ordinary people who chose to remain in the world, was amazing. Like that of the monasticism of the third and fourth centuries, this success is partly explicable as a reaction against the advance of ecclesiastical order.

Presages of the new monastic spirit were visible by the mid-eleventh century in men such as Peter Damian, who had no use for either imperial or papal order. But toward the end of the century, the new spirit became at once both more radical and more popular. The old Benedictine order could not contain it; and for the first time since the ninth century, new orders were founded, though all were deeply influenced by the Rule of St. Benedict. In broad terms, there were two varieties of the new monasticism, one devoted primarily to ascetic withdrawal and contemplation, and the other dedicated to preaching the spirit of prophecy to the world. The two most important orders were the Carthusian and the Cistercian. The Carthusians, founded in 1084 by St. Bruno of Cologne, practiced an almost eremitical life of silence and self-abnegation. The monks spent most of their lives isolated in their cells, coming together only once each evening for Vespers and for a common meal on Sundays. Of all orders they kept themselves the most free of corruption, but the very rigors that made this purity possible limited their popularity.

It was the Cistercian order that had the widest influence. About 1075, Robert, a Benedictine abbot, organized a strict community at Molesme. But in 1097 or 1098, Molesme itself seemed to Robert to be growing lax, so he moved to Citeaux to found a new monastery. With the help of Stephen Harding, Robert there restored the Rule of St. Benedict in all its original rigor. Later, in 1119, Stephen Harding wrote the "Charter of Love" (*Carta Caritatis*), which was accepted as the new rule of the order, now called the Cistercian. Rejecting pomp and luxury, the Cistercians banned private property altogether, ate only black bread and water with a few stewed vegetables, emphasized manual labor in place of study and scholarship, slept on rude beds with no other covering than their day clothes in dormitories unheated even in the dead of winter, and refrained from all unnecessary speech. That such a severe life could prove attractive to thousands of people, including men of substance, in a period of general prosperity, is a tribute to the power of the prophetic spirit.

For after an initial period of difficulties the Cistercians began to enjoy a phenomenal success, a success for which St. Bernard of Clairvaux (1091–1153) was more responsible than any other person. The little community at Citeaux had almost wasted away owing to desertions and disease when, in the winter of 1112, St. Bernard arrived with thirty other novices. Although Bernard had been born into a wealthy family at Fontaines in Burgundy and would have inherited considerable estates, his conscience informed him that Christ had counseled the young rich man to go and sell all that he had and follow him; and at the age of twenty-one Bernard sought out Citeaux as the strictest monastery he could find. In 1115 he left Citeaux to found another house obedient to the Cistercian practice in the Vale of Wormwood, a desolate spot that he renamed Clairvaux. By the time of his death he had founded sixty-five Cistercian monasteries and attracted multitudes to join the order.

The vigor and charisma of this man were such that it was said that mothers shut up their sons and wives their husbands when he passed by,

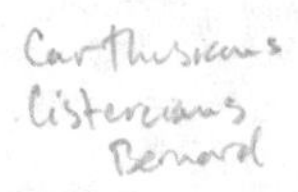

for fear that he would lure them away to the monastery. His asceticism was so severe that he declared that mirth was a step on the road to hell, and he was never seen to laugh or to make a joke himself. He practiced mortifications of the flesh beyond those which he enjoined upon others; and when they complained of their hardships, he suggested the whip as remedy. He had no hesitation in reprimanding the great and powerful for their follies. He wrote letters of admonition to the holy Abbot Suger of Saint-Denis, one of the chief counselors of the kings of France, telling him that his way of life was a disgrace. He led the prosecution of Abelard as a heretic and drove him into seclusion. He used his personal charisma to overturn the legitimate election of a pope in 1130 and to persuade the kings of Europe to accept the candidate he considered the more moral, Innocent II, a former Cistercian monk. Bernard's energy was not the product of mental disturbance, harshness, or unkindness. Rather, he was possessed by a love of God so great and consuming that it did not permit him to allow rest either to himself or to others. He gained, and used, his wide political and spiritual influence not for personal aggrandizement, but to preach as a prophet the transformation of the world. He was the closest medieval equivalent to the prophets of the Old Testament.

The second group of new orders was that whose first purpose was preaching and for which the ascetic and monastic life was a way to reach the growing numbers of people, particularly in the towns, whom social change and dislocation had to some extent alienated from the faith of their parents. This task had first been undertaken by the "regular canons." The clergy of the cathedral chapter, who lived together with the bishop, were known as canons. As early as the eighth century, disciplinary efforts had been made to place these canons under a rule. There were also canons living in the so-called collegiate churches, that is, parish churches in which a number of priests dwelt together. By the beginning of the twelfth century, it was evident that earlier efforts to establish discipline among the canons had not been wholly successful, and this fact, in addition to the recognition of the need for more effective preaching, prompted the foundation of a number of orders of regular canons—secular priests whose commitment was to the world rather than to the cloister, but who adopted a monastic rule for the purposes of strict discipline and whose vigorous preaching was in the prophetic spirit.

There were several of these orders, the Victorines, the Augustinians, and the Premonstratensians, who were the most influential. The Premonstratensians were founded by St. Norbert, a canon of the cathedral chapter of Xanten in the Netherlands, who until the age of about thirty-five lived an easy, even luxurious, life. In 1115 he was caught up by the prophetic spirit and withdrew into a hermitage for three years. Then, recognizing his obligation to teach the transformation of the heart to the world, he began to wander up and down the Rhine preaching. Norbert was at first condemned for preaching without permission, but Pope Calixtus II recognized the utility of such enthusiasm and permitted him to found an order of regular canons with headquarters at Prémontré, a deserted field near Laon in northern France. Like the fully monastic orders, the Premonstratensians practiced fasting and silence as well as other monastic virtues, but they placed a special emphasis upon learning and teaching, so as to prepare themselves to bring the Gospel to the people. Eventually more than two hundred Premonstratensian houses were founded.

By the end of the twelfth century, the Premonstratensian and other canons settled down to a more sedate life, exchanging itinerant preaching for the training of younger preachers in seminaries. The Cistercians had become corrupt, and Cistercians sent to southern France to preach against the Albigensian heretics only encouraged converts to the heresy by means of their bad conduct. A new movement of reform was necessary.

This new religious reform occurred toward the end of the twelfth century. A young Spanish priest named Dominic, who had come to southern France with his bishop in order to join in the moral struggle against the Albigensians, decided to devote his life to the improvement of both the morality and the intellectual quality of preachers. In 1215, with the approval of Pope Innocent III, he founded the Order of Preachers (Dominicans). The Dominicans and their contemporaries the Franciscans were known as friars (*frères*, "brothers"); both orders of friars continued the work of the regular canons in preaching and teaching to the world. After meeting Francis of Assisi (see below), Dominic guided his order to a life of asceticism. Known as mendicants, because they vowed absolute poverty and lived at first by begging, the friars wandered about Europe preaching wherever the needs of the community demanded. The Dominicans engaged heretical leaders in public debates, where they defended the Roman church with great force and skill. Austere and intimidating, the Dominicans became renowned as the "watchdogs of the lord," a phrase that was a pun on their name (*domini canes*, "dogs of the lord"). Then with their emphasis upon learning and teaching, the Dominicans gained great influence in the newly emerging

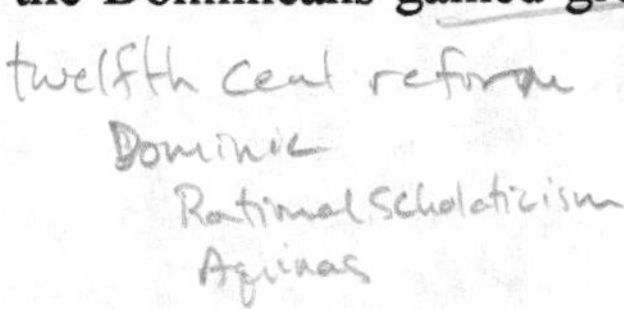

universities. Rational scholasticism was dominated by great Dominican teachers such as Albertus Magnus (1206–1280), the teacher of Thomas Aquinas, and Aquinas himself (1226–1274).

The other chief mendicant order of friars was the Order of Little Brothers (Franciscans), founded by St. Francis of Assisi (1181–1226), and approved by Pope Innocent III in 1209. Francis was born John Bernardone, the son of Pietro Bernardone, a wealthy cloth merchant in the northern Italian hill town of Assisi. As a boy, John earned the nickname "Francis" ("Frenchy") because of his love of French songs and poetry. Destined by his father to raise the family status by becoming a knight, Francis took part in one military campaign during which he was captured and imprisoned. It was perhaps while he lay sick of fever in prison, meditating upon the meaning of his life, that he determined to turn from the world and to go out and preach a life of morality. This decision was confirmed soon afterwards, when, meeting a leper in the road, he felt compelled by the love of Christ to dismount and to embrace him. The particular virtue of St. Francis is that his love of God after his conversion drew upon the strength of his earlier powerful and joyful love of the world. As a young man he had written beautiful lyric poetry in praise of women; after his conversion his poetry was equally intense in praise of God and God's creatures:

> Praise be my Lord God with all His creatures, and especially our brother the sun, who brings us the day and who brings us the light; fair is he and shines with very great splendor; O Lord, he signifies to us Thee. ("The Song of the Creatures, " translated by Matthew Arnold.)

Francis concieved of the world as wholly sacred: he recognized the personality of God in his fellow humans, in animals, in inanimate objects or even in impersonal forces. He spoke to the birds; he walked out of his way to avoid treading on a worm; and in the agonies of his deathbed he addressed the cauterizing iron as "Brother Fire" and the last bright angel as "Brother Death." Francis was the perfect manifestation of the prophetic spirit, who loved the world with a burning intensity and devotion that compelled him to go out and bring it to a recognition of its true nature. In this world that he loved, Francis saw beneath the external appearances to the reality of God's spirit within, and his life was a manifestation of that inner light to others. St. Francis was one of the simplest, and one of the most completely devoted, of Christian contemplatives.

Franciscans

After leaving his father, who renounced him as an ungrateful madman, Francis withdrew into solitude as a hermit and lived by begging his bread. Having given up his rich clothes, he donned the rough garb and rope belt of a scarecrow, the origin of the brown Franciscan habit. He began to preach to the people and soon attracted disciples from every walk of life. At last he founded an order dedicated to preaching, to teaching, and particularly to holy poverty: "I strictly command all the brothers," he said, "never to receive coin or money either directly or through an intermediary." Like the Dominicans, their concern for the teaching of the faith led the Franciscans into education and into the universities, where they pursued experimental science and contemplative spirituality—subjects derived from experience—more frequently than logic and metaphysics, the more usual domain of the Dominicans.

Like many previous reform movements, the Franciscan order was victimized by the extent of its success. Francis rejected hierarchy and strict organization within his new order, but as the order grew, a certain amount of organization became necessary to prevent the order from dissipating. The order began "using" donated goods, services, and buildings in order to maintain its existence. For years, Francis resisted demands to write a rule for his order, and so one was written in his name. As the rapid growth of the Franciscans resulted in more and more compromises on his original ideal, Francis abandoned his order to its own devices. In his life, Francis spurned institutional structures. Upon his death, his order had a large basilica built over his grave.

Popular heresy, like popular devotion, monasticism, and contemplative spirituality, was a product of both the reform movement in general and of revulsion against ecclesiastical order in particular. Medieval heresy in the West was always primarily moral rather than theological and popular rather than sacerdotal. From the eighth century, numerous religious dissenters had appeared, most of them Reformists, whose zeal for the reform of the church carried them beyond the limits of orthodox restraint. Such representatives of the prophetic spirit were often admirable for their refusal to compromise the religious spirit in the name of order; often, however, rebellion led them into eccentric, sometimes insane, doctrines. The pogroms against the Jews and the slaughter of heretics and infidels by the crusading mobs sprang from the same source of unbridled and undisciplined popular zeal.

The tradition of dissent, with its emphasis upon Reformism, remained unchanged until about the mid-twelfth century, but by the eleventh century it had begun to attract both more adherents and more adverse attention from the authorities. Prophetic Reformism continued to be the chief expression of religious dissatisfaction, and between orthodox and heretical prophecy was a thin and often arbitrary line drawn by the authorities. For example, Valdes, a merchant of Lyon, began in the 1170s to wander about the countryside with his followers preaching poverty and a return to apostolic simplicity in terms very similar to those used only a few years later by St. Francis and St. Dominic. But unlike the two saints, Valdes encountered the strong opposition of his bishop, and when he went to Rome to appeal his case, had had the misfortune to be out-talked and humiliated before a papal synod by the smooth, fast-talking, and unsympathetic English prelate and social critic, Walter Map. He also mistimed his journey to coincide with the Third Lateran Council, which was called specifically to deal with heresies. Pope Alexander III had little time to deal with Valdes and his ragtag band of followers, and simply referred the matter back to the bishop of Lyon. Valdes returned to Lyon feeling neglected by the pope and with the laughter of the council ringing in his ears. He continued to preach in defiance of his bishop, drifted into more and more extreme condemnations of ecclesiastical order, and was finally branded as a heretic. Between Valdes with his "poor men of Lyon" and Francis with his "little brothers" devoted to poverty, there was little distinction beyond that of their reception, yet one was considered a heretic and the other a saint. Ironically, however, the Waldensians, Valdes's followers, remained loyal to his principles in spite of frequent condemnations and persecution, while the followers of St. Francis, protected and encouraged by the authorities, quickly abandoned his stricter admonitions. Again, religion seems to have benefited less from the approval than from the rejection of society.

In the 1140s a new heresy appeared in western Europe. The new heretics called themselves "Cathars," which means "pure ones." Because they were associated early on with the southern French city of Albi, they were also widely known as the Albigensians. Catharism was a semi-Christian religion of dualism brought to Italy and southern France by Bulgarian missionaries who were members of the Bogomil sect, itself ultimately derived from Middle Eastern Gnosticism. Like the ancient dualist Gnostics, the Cathars believed in an ever-present cosmic war between the god of Good and the god of Evil. The god of Evil was inferior to that of Good, but it had successfully revolted, and eons would elapse before Good finally triumphed. Good is spirit, and Evil is matter. In its cosmic revolt the god of Evil created the universe in order to entrap pure spirits in the prison house of matter. The Old Testament, therefore, is the work of Evil, since it reveres the wicked Creator. Since matter is evil, flesh is evil, and indeed the human body is hideous filth conceived by demons in order to imprison the human spirit. Sexual activity, especially that which might lead to the production of a child, is therefore highly undesirable, for no sin can be worse than to cooperate with the god of Evil in forcing yet another spirit into the flesh. Christ is the messenger sent by the god of Good to teach us how to extract our souls from the flesh; being holy, he did not really take on flesh, and, his body being an illusion, he did not really suffer on the Cross. Crucifixes and images, which dignify the body, are therefore inventions of the god of Evil and his minions.

The Cathars absolutely rejected the Roman Christian church, its priesthood, and its sacraments. Their own sacrament was the "consolation" (*consolamentum*), which was administered to those believers (*credentes*) who had shown themselves capable of leading a pure life, and which absolved them from all past sin. Those who had received the consolation were called "perfect ones" (*perfecti*), and they were obliged to abstain from sin entirely, on pain of damnation, since the consolation could not be repeated. For the same reason, some who had received the consolation starved themselves to death afterwards so as to escape the flesh more quickly, before they succumbed to temptation. Since the consolation was supposed to wipe out all previous sin, many of the simple and less devoted believers put it off till the end of their lives and in the meantime allowed themselves all manner of physical and material pleasures. But the Cathars were sincere enough to make such quantities of converts that by the end of the twelfth century the religion had spread all over northern Europe, particularly in the Low Countries and the Rhineland. In southern France and in northern Italy, they made up such a large portion of the population of all classes that in 1208 Innocent III felt compelled to preach a crusade against them.

The rapid success of Catharism has a number of causes but only one fundamental explanation: the previous existence of a strong tradition of Reformist dissent. The Reformists, in their ascetic extremism, emphasized the dualist elements latent in the orthodox Christian tradition to the degree that they were ready and willing to accept the stricter dualism of the Cathars. Documents from the Rhineland show the process at work at Cologne: at first there is a report of a Reformist sect; the next report tells of a group within the Reformist sect that is preaching a new and more radical doctrine; and the final document portrays a group completely dominated by Catharism—the whole process having taken only a few years. Catharism, though the most radical heresy that western Christianity ever faced, owed its success to the demands of the Christian prophetic spirit.

Catharism, as well as much else in southern France, was almost wiped out by the Albigensian Crusade of 1208–1223, after which it gradually dwindled and disappeared. But that hostility to orthodoxy remained at least covertly in southern France can be seen by comparing a map showing the centers of thirteenth-century Catharism with one  showing those of sixteenth-century Calvinism: the correspondence is far too striking to be merely coincidental. Meanwhile, the Reformist variety of heresy, which had never been wholly supplanted by Catharism, continued among the Waldensians and appeared in new forms throughout the Middle Ages, finally achieving wide success in the Protestant Reformation.

Chapter 10

The Offensive of the Papacy

The growth of the prophetic spirit in the twelfth and thirteenth centuries was matched by the advance of order in Christian society under the leadership of the papacy. From the end of the eleventh century the popes continued to implement their policies by means of crusades, councils, and canon law. The spirit of reform was perhaps never higher among all sections of the population than it was in the late eleventh and early twelfth centuries; but the two kinds of reform, order and prophecy, were often at variance. These differences of opinion within the church were brought into relief by the increasing complexity of society: the growth of royal power and of the scope of royal government raised new political difficulties for religion; the centralization of ecclesiastical institutions under papal authority brought the pope's spiritual integrity into question; and the rise of the cities and of the new urban orders made it more difficult to reach the Christian people with an ecclesiastical organization and attitudes designed for a feudal and agricultural society. Finally, the rise of the universities and of scholasticism demanded a complete intellectual reevaluation of the theology of the church.

One of the developments of scholastic thought did much to enhance the theoretical position of the papacy. This was the growth of the structure of canon law. Canon law is the law of the church stated in the decrees of popes and councils from the earliest church to the present. It is distinguished from civil law, which derived either from Roman law (as in most of southern Europe) or from customary Germanic law (as in much of northern Europe, especially England). Church courts were usually separate from civil courts and had jurisdiction *in persona*—over clergy (including university students, who were considered clerics)—and *in re*—over offenses deemed spiritual in nature, such as blasphemy or divorce. The rights of clerics to be tried for all crimes in church courts, where punishments were lighter than in civil courts, was known as "benefit of clergy." In the beginning of the twelfth century, in imitation of the civil lawyers who were beginning at that time to restudy and reclassify Roman law according to rational organizational principles, canon lawyers drew up comprehensive codes of canon law. The most important of these canonists of the early twelfth century were Yvo of Chartres, who helped work out the compromises on investitures, and Gratian, who in 1140 published his *Decretum,* or "Concord of Discordant Canons." Gratian not only collected vast numbers of legal texts and organized them systematically but, observing that the laws were often contradictory, undertook to resolve the contradictions by reason. His resolutions and commentary led to debate, discussion, and reflection upon the nature of the law, which in turn aided the development of political theory.

The free-swinging arguments of the eleventh-century "battle of the books" now yielded to more complex and carefully worked-out structures of thought. These were at first developed mainly by papalists and so were turned to the support of papal theory. Later they were used by conciliarists concerned with limiting that theory. Many of the greatest popes of the twelfth and thirteenth centuries, such as Alexander III (1159–1181), Innocent III (1198–1216), Gregory IX (1227–1241), and Innocent IV (1243–1254) were trained in canon law and used it effectively to advance their position. For example, they elaborated the theory of "plenitude of power," according to which the pope as vicar of Christ has full power over all worldly affairs and, therefore, the right to rule temporal as well as spiritual affairs directly. The extensive interference of Innocent III and other popes in secular matters was a reflection of this theory derived from canon law.

The practical implementation of papal policies was an extension of the Gregorian program, which advocated strong papal authority in order to maintain moral reform. Urban II and his successors revived the institution of the permanent legates, they increased wherever they could the number of episcopal sees subject to papal appointment, and they encouraged monastic immunities from the bishops and kings so that the monasteries might be more directly under papal influence.

Urban II undertook a number of policies that materially advanced the papal position. According to the strict dictates of canon law, those bishops consecrated by imperially appointed antipopes did not have proper authority, and therefore ordinations of priests and the sacraments bestowed by those priests were invalid. If the letter of the law had been enforced, there would have been an enormous number of people throughout Europe with invalid orders, invalid baptisms, and invalid marriages. Urban mercifully decided to "dispense from" the canons and to declare these orders and sacraments valid. The dispensation from the canons when generally established was another weapon of papal power, for it permitted the pope to set precedents that would modify or even change tradition.

Urban demonstrated the jurisdiction of papal power throughout society when at the Council of Clermont (1095) he reaffirmed the Truce of God (originated at the beginning of the eleventh century), which outlawed war during certain seasons of the year and on certain days of the week. In the twelfth century the popes also promoted the Peace of God, which protected clergy and other noncombatants at all times. The potentiality for good of a Christian order in society is nowhere clearer than is this systematic attempt to limit war. But then as now, these efforts were unavailing against the arguments of politicians that "realism" demands the pursuit of their policies at whatever cost of ruin and agony. Political "realism" is usually the justification of actions unrealistic by any definitions of humanity or sanity broader than the narrow assumptions of those who argue them.

Under Urban II the papacy for the first time felt secure enough to call an ecumenical council under its presidency. In 1095, Urban held two large councils for the purpose of securing reform and of building papal prestige within the church and against the temporal powers. One of these was at Piacenza in Italy and the other at Clermont in southern France. Both councils were devoted to attacks upon simony, clerical concubinage, and other vices within the church and against lay interference in ecclesiastical affairs. Though they themselves did not bear the title ecumenical, they set the stage for the six ecumenical councils of the Middle Ages: I Lateran (1123), II Lateran (1139), III Lateran (1179), IV Lateran (1215), I Lyon (1245), and II Lyon (1274). These medieval councils were characterized by papal domination. They were all summoned by the popes and used to advance the order and reform of the church under papal leadership. The decline of papal power after 1300 is visible in the fact that the first ecumenical council called after that date (Vienne, 1311) was dominated by King Philip IV of France, evidence that both empire and papacy were yielding to the new nationalism.

At the Council of Clermont in 1095, Urban launched the First Crusade, a holy war to liberate holy places from the Muslims. The surprising spectacle of the vicar of the Prince of Peace preaching conquest and blood can be understood only in the context of the growing rigidity and exclusiveness of medieval Christianity, which was turned not only against Islam but against heresy, Judaism, and Eastern Orthodoxy. The Christian community could no longer tolerate rivals.

Until the eleventh century, heretics had been treated with mildness and restraint, suffering no more than reprimands or harassment. Now murders of heretics by mobs like the one that killed Ramihrd in 1077 became more common. Initially, it was not the leaders of church institutions, but rather the laity that reacted most energetically against the threats of heresy. Executions by kings and other secular princes began when in 1022 King Robert the Pious of France burned some heretics at Orléans. In the eleventh and twelfth centuries, the secular authorities increased their vigor in detecting the heretics and their severity in punishing them. Frederick II of Germany and Sicily, for example, made death by burning a mandatory sentence for heresy in 1231. The church, in recognition of Christian mercy, never executed anyone for heresy: it conducted the investigations, arraigned and tried the dissenters, and, if they were found guilty, turned them over to the secular arm for "proper attention" *(animadversione debita),* which meant hanging or the stake.

In 1184 the prosecution of heretics was formalized by the Council of Verona under Lucius III, who ordered every bishop to conduct an inquisition in his own diocese. In its origins, the inquisitions were neither horrible nor unusual: they were variations of the "inquests" made by medieval monarchs or their representatives. These inquests or investigations might consist of surveys for the purpose of taxation, like Domesday Book, or investigations by a grand jury for crimes in their area of jurisdiction. In another respect, an episcopal inquisition was an extension of the bishop's powers of visitation, under which he had the duty to tour the parishes of his diocese making sure that proper discipline was kept. By the decree of Verona he was now simply expected to pay particular attention to the maintenance of doctrinal orthodoxy. These inquisitions were launched independently of each other by local authorities: there was no unified Inquisition. Inquisitions for a variety of purposes could be initiated by clerical and secular leaders alike, and inquisitorial procedures varied accordingly. Though many inquisitions were characterized by invasive investigations, horrible tortures, and cruel penalties, the scope and severity of medieval inquisitions have been exaggerated to some degree over time.

In 1231 a papal inquisition was established at Rome by Pope Gregory IX, with powers to investigate heresy throughout the church. In 1233 he made the Dominican order particularly responsible for the extirpation of heresy. The papal inquisition later became a permanent institution, named the Holy Office, for the repression of dissent. The papal inquisition was only one of many inquisitions. It was nothing like, or as vicious as, the later Spanish inquisition, and the horrors even of that body have been exaggerated by novelists and propagandists. But the practices of the papal inquisition were distasteful enough. In accordance with principles of Roman law and of traditional Germanic law, the defendant was held to be guilty unless he could prove himself innocent—which was difficult because the identity of his accusers and sometimes even the specific charges were withheld from the accused in order to protect informers from revenge. Heresy was deemed such a terrible offense that no one could be convicted unless he confessed, and so efforts to secure confessions became steadily more zealous, the use of torture being formally permitted by the canon lawyer Pope Innocent IV in his bull *Ad extirpanda* (1252). When the confession was elicited, the victim was handed over to the secular arm for due attention. Sometimes, of course, the accused was acquitted; or if the offense was his first and he repented, he was allowed to go after being given a certain penance, sometimes a whipping or the wearing in public of distinctive clothing.

The inquisitors have been considered sadists or thieves, depending upon whether one's attention is beguiled more by the spectacle of torture or by the confiscation of the heretics' property. Both accusations, while doubtless justly levied at a few individuals, are unhelpful as generalizations. The inquisitors considered heresy a pernicious disease affecting the soul and therefore a worse danger than any physical plague. No mercy could be shown the heretics' bodies lest they corrupt the immortal souls of others. It was with complete sincerity, and often with great reluctance, that the inquisitors followed their profession. When the logic of the spirit of order and authority within the church went unchecked by mercy or common sense, it permitted Christians to torture and kill other Christians with good will and a sense of piety. The attitude of the papal legate Arnold Amalric at the siege of Carcassonne, during the Albigensian Crusade, is illustrative. He ordered the entire city to be put to the torch. When an attendant suggested that there were orthodox Christians as well as heretics within its walls, he replied, "Go ahead and burn it, for God will know his own." The innocent would go to their heavenly reward, and as for the guilty, flames were their proper environment.

Why should the attitude of the church, so patient with heretics for centuries, have changed in the eleventh century, when the spirit of reform was at its height? Partly because the heretics were somewhat more numerous and more radical than before. Partly because heretical sects were better organized and because, from the twelfth century, they were often tied in with movements of social and economic unrest and were therefore more socially dangerous. But most important, precisely *because* the reform spirit was at its height. The same widespread and fervent breath of reform that made people long to go on pilgrimages, to enter ascetic monasteries, and to become mystics also impelled them to attack and murder heretics and Jews and to undertake holy wars against the Muslims. Religious zeal is a powerful force for love and humanity and purity. When it is willing to sacrifice even one human being to theory and ideology, it can be an equally powerful force for inhumanity. This inhumanity was encouraged by the growing rigidity and exclusiveness of the church. Identifying the Mystical Body of Christ with membership in the visible church, canon lawyers defined the church as those who were in communion with the bishop of Rome. Those who were disobedient to Rome were cut off from the Body of Christ; they were limbs of Satan, damned, and unworthy of consideration as human beings. This tendency to regard one's enemies as less than human is one with which we are not unfamiliar today.

The same arguments that were applied to heretics were also applied to Jews, and the same transition from tolerance to persecution occurred in the course of the reform movement of the eleventh and twelfth centuries. In the diaspora, especially following the sack of Jerusalem in A.D. 70, the Jews had fled Palestine to settle in the cities of the Mediterranean and western Europe, particularly in Spain, where they were called Sephardic Jews and where they built an illustrious culture. In most of the cities in which they settled, they chose to live together in ghettos in order to preserve their identity in the midst of a population at first pagan and then Christian. The Jewish community was tightly organized around the synagogue under the leadership of the rabbi, and it had its own schools, where Hebrew was taught, its own laws and law courts, and its own taxes and tax collection.

This state of affairs was by and large perfectly tolerated by the Christians. Religious arguments were often heated in a period when more Christians and Jews took their religion more seriously than they do now, but these arguments generally remained on a theoretical level, and there were Christian converts to Judaism as well as Jewish converts to Christianity. Christian scholars valued the Hebrew scholarship of the rabbis, and a Christian king like Louis the Pious valued their literacy and employed many Jews in his administration. Jews could also provide certain services that were illegal for Christians to provide, but that were nonetheless beneficial. For example, Christians were prohibited from selling used clothing, which had no justifiable price and was to be given away to the needy. Less well-to-do Christians, however, who could not afford to buy new clothes and possessed too much pride to accept charitable hand-me-downs, could purchase good quality used clothing from the Jewish "ragmen," who, since they were going to hell anyway, were not affected by Christian business restrictions. In this and similar other ways, Jews played valuable roles in medieval towns and cities. On the rare occasions when there were popular outbreaks against the Jews, as in Palermo at the end of the sixth century when the synagogue was plundered and burned, the authorities intervened and enforced strict restitution to the injured. The discrimination of the Visigothic law code against Jews was unusual and should be seen in the context of the more frequent discriminations in law of Arian against Catholic or Catholic against Arian, Christians all. As late as the twelfth century, the Christian citizens of Sens could view with equanimity the erection of a synagogue steeple higher than that of the cathedral.

But already under Louis the Pious the first signs of future distress were visible. Evidently irked by royal patronage of the Jews, Archbishop Agobard of Lyon wrote the first violent anti-Jewish tract of the Middle Ages. Then, from the ninth century onwards, increasing order in society as a whole worked to the general disadvantage of the Jews. The feudal relationship, which demanded the use of a Christian oath in the ceremony of investiture, drove Jews off the land into the growing cities, where they engaged in commerce and in the crafts. But in the eleventh and twelfth centuries the rise of artisans' guilds, each organized around the cult of a particular saint, drove the Jews out of the crafts. They were left with banking, moneychanging, and moneylending, as well as other activities condemned as unfit for (though often clandestinely pursued by) Christians. At this time, a fatal motive of economic envy was added to basic religious antagonism and to the Christian irritation at the Jews' deliberate isolation of themselves from the Christian community. Little pity was shown to the many Jews who grew poor because they were excluded from the crafts, but much envy was directed against the few who grew wealthy at banking and lending. In an age when all commercial ventures were adventures in the original sense of the word, moneylending was particularly risky, and as a consequence interest rates had to be high. The effect, not the cause, attracted the reproach and bitterness of the Christians.

Then in the eleventh century came a wave of popular religious zeal combined with a legalism that excluded Jews more strictly than before from any participation in the general community. The same urge that sent tens of thousands of peasants from western Europe to Constantinople to crusade against the Muslims impelled them to stop along the way to kill infidels closer to home. In one city after another, particularly along the Rhine, the crusaders stopped and looted and burned the Jewish ghettos, putting to death those who would not accept baptism. The pogrom was now invented; it was to continue, first in western and then in eastern Europe, down to the final holocaust under the Nazis. Popular beliefs concerning the Jews grew wilder, and in obedience to an unpleasant psychological regularity, they took forms similar to the Romans' beliefs about the Christians or, later, certain Protestants' beliefs about the Catholics. According to these beliefs, the Jews kidnapped Christian children and killed them in a ritual murder that was an inherent part of the Jewish religion. The Jews poisoned wells. The Jews practiced cannibalism and magic. Most absurdly of all, the Jews, who were hated for their denial of the Christian sacraments, were accused of stealing the Eucharist from churches and profaning it. Their favorite game, apparently, was to take the Eucharist and stab it with a knife; occasionally the villains would be found out by a just miracle, for the wounded Eucharist would bleed unquenchably until the blood, flowing out of the door, attracted the attention of the righteous Christian people.

The attitude of ecclesiastical authorities toward these absurd beliefs and the outrageous persecutions they provoked was at first adequately severe. The bishops of the Rhenish cities whose Jews were attacked by the mobs took great pains, sometimes at the risk of their own lives, to hide or otherwise protect them. St. Bernard declared the persecutors of the Jews heretics, and Pope Gregory X officially refuted the charges of ritual murder as nonsense. But gradually the official position hardened, particularly in regard to converted Jews who relapsed into Judaism, and Innocent III went so far as to demand that the Jews (along with the Saracens) wear distinctive clothing, and that they be prohibited from appearing in public from Good Friday through Easter Sunday lest they profane the sacred holiday. For the most part, the ecclesiastical authorities refrained from official persecutions, but more frequently than not they remained silent in the face of popular outrages or the repressive policies of the Christian kings.

It was not the ecclesiastical leaders, but the Christian princes who were the most persistent, if not the bloodiest, in their persecutions of Jews, and here the motive was plainly money. The Lombards and the Templars, both of whom had amassed wealth by banking and lending, were treated with as much violence as the Jews, though the Jews were often subjected to peculiar humiliations. An English law of 1222 ordered every Jew above the age of six to wear a distinctive yellow badge upon his clothing, an ultimate antecedent of the yellow star of David imposed by the Nazis. Philip IV of France (1285–1314), Edward I of England (1272–1307), Ferdinand and Isabella of Spain (1479–1504), and other rulers used religious arguments as an excuse to confiscate the property of the Jews and expel them from their domains.

The hostility of western Christendom to the heretics and the Jews extended to the Muslims and, to a lesser degree, the Byzantine Christians. This hostility took the form of the crusade or holy war. The idea of holy war was an old one, the Byzantine Emperor Heraclius having preached it when the Muslims first conquered the Holy Land in 637. Charlemagne crusaded against the Muslims in Spain and extended the concept of holy war to the pagans when he converted the Saxons by force. The idea of the Crusades was to rescue Christian people and to regain Christian territories (or to add to them) from the unbelievers. The symbol of the crusaders' purpose came to be the holy places, particularly the Holy Sepulchre (the church built over what is supposed to be the tomb of Christ) in Jerusalem.

The era of concentrated Crusades began in 1095 when Urban II preached the First Crusade at Clermont. The conventional numbering of the Crusades is not particularly helpful, for they were not clearly separated or defined. What is significant is that from 1095 there were frequent expeditions of western Christians (called Franks by the easterners) to the East. Some of these expeditions were led by kings and some by noblemen and knights; some were mere mobs of peasants; some were equipped by Italian cities as ventures for profit; one consisted entirely of children; and one was wholly peaceful—that of Frederick II of Germany in 1227–1229. That emperor, whose devotion to Christianity was openly doubted by his enemies, spent his time in the Holy Land exchanging entertainment, theological debate, and commercial concessions with his Muslim hosts. From 1099 until 1291, the Franks maintained states on the eastern shore of the Mediterranean, but even after these were destroyed, the struggle continued. The war against the Muslims continued in Spain, from which the Moors (Moroccan Muslims) were finally completely expelled in 1492; in the islands and along the coasts of the eastern Mediterranean and North Africa; and eventually in the Balkans against the Ottoman Turks. The holy war was also extended against other enemies: the pagans of the eastern Baltic, whom the Teutonic Knights (a Germanic military-religious order) conquered, and the Albigensian heretics of southern France, subdued in a bloody war lasting from 1208 to 1223. Eventually the crusading ideal lost some of its focus, and popes began to call crusades against purely political enemies. The crusading movement certainly reached its nadir in 1294 when Pope Boniface VIII called for a crusade against the Colonnas, a local Roman family that rivaled Boniface's own in the petty political and economic affairs of Rome.

Many causes of the Crusades have been adduced. They were a manifestation of the age-old struggle between East and West. They were part of a long tradition of Christian holy war, or a righteous effort to regain territories seized from Christendom by force. They were a cynical effort to obtain land and wealth. They were part of the commercial expansion of western Europe, or mass movements symptomatic of social unrest and discontent at home. They were a program to enhance the prestige of the papacy. They were the product of superstitious fanaticism. All of these interpretations are partly true, but an examination of the religious and social environment of the precise time in which they were generated yields explanations similar to those for the persecution of heretics and Jews. The Crusades, whatever else they were, were an expression of the reforming zeal of the period, taking the form of popular fanaticism on the one hand, and of papal legalism and exclusivism on the other.

The results of the Crusades are impressive mainly for their destructiveness. To begin with, there was the enormous expenditure of blood and suffering on all sides. Of the peasant mobs that set out for the Holy Land in 1096, none ever reached their destination: either they despaired and went home; or they were murdered by robbers and bandits; or they died of disease or malnutrition; or if they got as far as Asia Minor, they were massacred by the Turks. Many of the children who set out in 1212 for the Holy Land were killed or sold into slavery by Christian slave traders operating in the south of France. The pogroms in

Europe, slaughter of Muslims and Jews in the sack of Jerusalem by the Franks in 1099, and the rape of Constantinople by its Frankish allies in 1204 are only a few illustrations of the savagery meted out by the Christians to their enemies.

In exchange for all this horror, nothing of permanent value was obtained. The Crusader states in the East lasted awhile and then were wiped out, leaving Jerusalem permanently in the hands of the Muslims. The Muslims, heretofore relatively tolerant of the Christians in their domains, now returned violence for violence, and their counter-crusades eventually brought their banners to the walls of Vienna. The schism between the eastern and the western churches was made unbridgeable by the notorious Fourth Crusaders of 1202–1204. Sent by Innocent III to relieve the Christian forces in the Holy Land, they took passage with greedy Venetian shipowners, who persuaded them to champion the cause of a pretender to the Byzantine throne. After they had begun by sacking the Christian port of Zara, the pope tried to call them back, but it was too late. They proceeded to Constantinople, where they imposed their candidate for the throne by force, and then, when he proved unable to pay the tribute they insisted upon in return, they put the city to the sword. The soldiers of Christ looted churches, fired the city, and raped and killed at will. As a result, the Byzantine Empire was temporarily dismantled and permanently debilitated, making its eventual conquest by the Turks in 1453 almost inevitable. The natural distrust of Byzantine leaders for the West was so great that when in 1439 the Emperor John VIII agreed to accept papal supremacy in order to secure western aid against the Turks, they refused to approve, saying that they would rather see the Sultan's turban than a cardinal's hat in Constantinople. Even today, the memory of 1204 has made it more difficult to secure ecumenical cooperation between the eastern and western churches.

One outcome of the Crusades is immensely significant in Christian history because it did not happen: the conversion of the Mongols. Oddly, this was well within the realm of possibility in the thirteenth century. The Mongols and the other tribes of central Asia had been evangelized by Nestorian Christians, and at the time of the Crusades there were several Christian generals, nobles, and even princesses among the Mongol leaders and their people. The Franciscan missionary William of Rubruck found in his journey to the East in 1253–1254 that there were numerous Nestorian churches and practicing Christians throughout central Asia, even in Karakorum, the Mongol capital, and that there was a bishop of the Nestorians at Peking.

It was possible that a vigorous missionary effort could have established the religion of Christ from the Atlantic to the Pacific. The political situation in the late thirteenth century was particularly conducive to such success, for the Mongols were engaged in the conquest of Muslim Persia and Mesopotamia, and they considered the possibility of an alliance with the Christians against their common enemy. Missions were sent by Kublai Khan to the courts of Louis IX in France and of Edward I of England, and a Mongol representative was at the Council of II Lyon in 1274. In 1286 Argun, the Khan of Persia, dispatched an embassy under a Nestorian monk, a close friend of the Nestorian patriarch, to the court of Pope Honorius IV, from which he went on to see Edward I and Philip IV. In 1291, Argun sent a letter to the West proposing a joint attack upon the Muslims in Syria and promising that the Mongols would turn over Jerusalem to the Crusaders.

But to all these opportunities the Christians prove incapable of responding. The kings were occupied with national struggles in the West; the people were tired of the Crusades; and in 1291 the last stronghold in the Crusader states, the fortress of Acre, fell to the Muslims. No Christian forces came to join the Mongol armies in the war, and though the Franciscan missionaries exerted themselves for years in the East under great hardships and with some success, the Mongols as a whole lost interest in Christianity. Christian missions continued to exist in China until the decline of Mongol power in the fourteenth century, when the Chinese nationalists drove out or executed the Christians as another manifestation of the foreign influence they detested. It was not that the energy of the missionaries failed, but that western Christendom proved unable to marshal the energies and resources requisite to the conversion of the East. Effective penetration of the East was left to the merchants, the Polos of the thirteenth century and their successors in the fourteenth, fifteenth, and sixteenth—when the great age of European expansion was undertaken not by the followers of heaven, but by those of this world. Those who sought the triumph of a Christian order had, almost without realizing it, lost one of their greatest opportunities.

The struggle of the papacy with the temporal powers had not come to an end with the accession of Lothar II in 1125. From that moment the preeminence of papacy over empire was assured, but there were many battles yet to wage, not only with the emperor but also with the kings of England and France.

The example of England illustrates the perennial nature of the conflict. In England, royal power over the church had always been extensive, though it had likewise always been exerted in the cause of reform. William the Conqueror had obtained the throne with the blessing of Pope Alexander II, and the new king made it clear that he was going to exercise as full control over spiritual as he did over temporal affairs. As archbishop of Canterbury he appointed the reform abbot of Bec, Lanfranc (1070–1089), and with him carried out a reorganization and purification of the English church. Honor was rendered the pope as the head of Christendom, Peter's pence continued to be paid, and the church in England continued to profess itself a most loyal daughter of Rome. But in practical matters, the king, aided by his archbishop, ruled supreme. He continued to appoint bishops, he reorganized the dioceses, he separated the church from the civil courts, and he declared that his permission was necessary in order to receive a papal letter, to recognize a pope, or to excommunicate any of the king's barons or ministers.

As long as a just king ruled the church, the pope was obliged to consider the situation tolerable, and in 1081 Gregory VII wrote a letter to William indicating that the latter's virtues required that his vices be treated with patience. In his struggles against Henry IV, it was to the Normans that Gregory could most reliably turn for aid. But the death of the Conqueror in 1087 was followed by that of Lanfranc in 1089, and the potentiality for conflict was now realized. William's successor, William II, inherited his father's will to control the church without his interest in reforming it. From 1089 to 1093 William left the see of Canterbury vacant in order to collect its revenues. At last the king was persuaded to accept Anselm, Lanfranc's successor as abbot of Bec, as his successor in the see of Canterbury (1093–1109). But meanwhile, Anselm had been swayed by the radicalism of the papal revolution, and he arrived in England determined to limit the king's power. He demanded the return of the church properties confiscated by the king after the death of Lanfranc, and he defended the monks from the inroads made on their properties by royalist bishops. Anselm was able to win the support of many of the bishops to the cause of reform and to secure, as well, the support of some of the nobility, who welcomed an opportunity to embarrass the king.

There now began that curious alliance between the church and the English nobility against the rising power of the king, an alliance that was to be called into being time and time again until the final triumph of the king during the Protestant Reformation. Now, in spite of opposition, William II succeeded in driving Anselm into exile on the Continent, where he remained until William's brother Henry I (1100–1135) ascended the throne. Henry, more of his father's temperament than of his brother's, recalled Anselm from exile. But in the meanwhile, Anselm, like the course of the revolution itself, had become much more radical and now refused to consecrate bishops who had received lay investiture. Anselm was driven out for the third time in 1105. A compromise on investitures was reached in 1107, which left the king in firm control of the church. When Henry died, however, the succession was disputed between his daughter Matilda and her cousin Stephen, and the church and the nobility were able to win concessions from both sides.

The struggle was resumed under Matilda's son Henry II (1154–1189). An able and vigorous king, Henry was determined to restore the power and prerogatives of the monarch to what they had been at the time of his grandfather Henry I. As his archbishop of Canterbury, he appointed the son of a Norman merchant family of London, a man who had been his drinking, hunting, and wenching companion for years and who had recently served as an able and industrious chancellor with every sign of complete loyalty to his monarch. This was Thomas Becket of Cheapside, whose personality now underwent a striking change. Impressed either by the spiritual responsibility of his new office or by its political power, he undertook as archbishop to assert the independence of the bishops from the king and the prerogatives of the papacy.

Thomas became archbishop in 1161, and by 1163 he and Henry had already quarreled. The issue that provoked the quarrel, though in itself minor, had broad implications. In order to increase the deterrent to crime and thereby to promote law and order, the king wished to take clergymen who had been found guilty of a civil crime in an ecclesiastical court and try them again in a civil court, where they could be given a stiffer penalty. Thomas's refusal to cooperate enraged his old friend; and in 1164 Henry promulgated the Constitutions of Clarendon, which claimed for the king all the rights, and more, that William the Conqueror had enjoyed over the church. Most of the bishops yielded to the king, some venally, some in good faith that the old tradition of royal reform could be retained; but Becket refused and fled to the Continent. From exile he wrote Henry in 1166, "It is certain that kings receive their power from the church, and the church hers from Christ alone." In the hope of reaching an agreement, Thomas returned to England, but neither king nor archbishop was willing to yield what seemed to him a position that was just and right. On December 29, 1170, four knights, convinced rightly or wrongly that they were doing the will of the king, assaulted the archbishop in his cathedral and murdered him before the high altar. The consequences of the murder were hardly satisfactory to Henry. Thomas became a popular martyr, and the general disgust for the assassination all over Europe obliged the king to do penance at Avranches in 1172 and to renounce most of the disputed royal claims.

For the next few decades a working compromise was obtained, during which papal powers over the English church slowly increased. The next crisis came under King John (1199–1216) and Archbishop Stephen Langton (1207–1228). Here again the church and the nobility made common cause against a king who was pursuing a policy that was not only vigorous but unscrupulous and by any standards, feudal or Christian, immoral. In this struggle, which culminated in the Magna Carta (1215), and in which Pope Innocent III (1198–1216) and his legates directly intervened, Stephen Langton tried to work out a compromise that would secure the best interests of the king and the pope, while protecting episcopal independence as much as possible from both. But in the course of the struggle the pope intervened to the extent of placing all England under an interdict (1208) and excommunicating (1209) and deposing (1213) the king. Like Henry IV at Canossa, John hastily yielded in order to secure papal support against his enemies at home. He declared himself the pope's vassal and England a papal fief. Throughout the succeeding century, the pope and his legates attempted to enforce their suzerainty over England. In this they had generally little success, but it was true, nonetheless, that during the thirteenth century the papacy had more influence over English ecclesiastical affairs than at any time before or after.

The policies of Innocent III in regard to John illustrate the enormous temporal power that the papacy had learned to wield. The pope, basing his claim to direct temporal policy on the theory of plenitude of power enunciated by the canon lawyers, could use four weapons against a king: interdict (which by prohibiting all distribution of the sacraments, including baptism and matrimony, throughout the entire realm was designed to stir up popular pressure against the king), excommunication, formal deposition, and the ban (which combined excommunication and deposition). In addition, the enormous political powers of the papacy could be brought to bear. Stalin's question "How many divisions does the pope have?" would not have been asked ironically in the thirteenth century. For example, in his attack upon King John, Innocent III called upon Philip II of France for help; and that king, eager to strike at his old enemy, launched an invasion of the island, which was repulsed after papal approval was withdrawn in reward for John's submission to Rome.

The intervention of Innocent III in imperial politics illustrates papal political power even more clearly. The declining power of the emperors had already contributed to the rise of that of the popes, and now, after the death of the Emperor Henry VI in 1196, occurred a period of disputed succession. The throne was claimed by both Otto of Brunswick and Philip of Swabia, and in the midst of civil war Innocent issued the decretal *Venerabilem,* declaring that he had a right to decide between the two candidates. Eventually both died, and the throne passed to Philip's nephew Frederick II (1212–1250). Frederick, though powerful in Sicily, was never able to control Germany effectively, and after his death there ensued another period of civil war that further weakened imperial authority. Innocent intervened not only in England and Germany but in France, Bulgaria, Norway, Aragon, and many other territories. His temporal authority was further demonstrated by the leadership he exerted in the inception of the Fourth Crusade and the war against the Albigensians.

The exercise of temporal power on the part of Innocent III was not without precedent. It sprang not from any claim to direct temporal rights but from the theory that the pope was charged with the rule of all Christian society as the vicar of Christ, a papalist theory that had been developing from the time of Gelasius I through the reign of Gregory VII and was now culminating. What Innocent had in mind was not a theocracy but a united Christian society, in which the pope had the duty to oblige princes to rule in accordance with the principles of divine justice. Innocent's theories were the strongest expression to that date of the idea that the construction and maintenance of a Christian order depended upon the strength and authority of the pope as the vicar of Christ over all of society. The pope had "not only the universal church but the whole world to govern .... Peter alone assumed the plenitude of power. You see then," Innocent explained in a letter to the archbishop of Ravenna, "who is this servant set over the household, truly the vicar of Jesus Christ, successor of Peter, anointed of the Lord, a God of Pharaoh, set between God and man, lower than God but higher than man, who judges all and is judged by no one."

These papalist theories were given their strongest expression by Benedetto Gaetani, who ascended the papal throne in 1294 as Pope Boniface VIII. The very election of Boniface was a triumph of the spirit of order over the spirit of prophecy. A few months previously, a hermit named Pietro di Murrone had been dragged from his cell and forced to accept the papacy as Pope Celestine V. Celestine used his short period of power to endorse the struggles of the spiritual Franciscans, against the lax majority of the order, to reinstate the original rule of St. Francis. But he was unable to cope successfully with the machinations of the powerful cardinals who wished to use him as a tool, and resigned the papacy, dying shortly after.

The ardent exponent of papalist order, Boniface VIII, was the successor of the unhappy defender of prophecy. Boniface was a man whose natural tendencies to rashness were encouraged by the extreme difficulties under which he was obliged to labor as pope. He was accused by envious detractors of having managed the resignation and even the death of his predecessor, and he never lived down the reputation for unscrupulousness that these rumors—probably unjustly—gave him. He was threatened in central Italy by a combination of hostile cardinals and certain families of the Roman nobility, of whom the most antagonistic was the Colonna family; in southern Italy the Aragonese had taken Sicily away from the papal allies, the Angevins; and he was under pressure to call a crusade to regain the Holy Land, whose last Christian fortress, Acre, had fallen in 1291. Most important, he was challenged by the rising power of the kings of France and England.

While the empire and the kingdom of Germany had lost most of its power to influence papal policies, France and England were becoming yearly more wealthy, more unified, and more determined to establish and to preserve their natural identities. In France Philip IV (1285–1314) and in England Edward I (1272–1307), engaged in expansive foreign policies and in increasing the size and strength of their governments, were faced with a financial crisis and sought new means of raising tax monies. Both hit upon the solution of imposing a regular and fairly high tax upon the clergy. The clergy had on previous specific occasions been asked for aid, as when the kings were planning crusades, but it had become common to ask for such aid in the name of a crusade even when the king had no intention of ever going on one. Now for the first time a tax of the clergy was imposed for general purposes.

The response of Boniface VIII touched off a struggle that eventually dealt papalism a deadly blow. It was an unjudicious, even violent, response, but it was one in the tradition of Gregory VII and Innocent III, whose ideas Boniface was attempting to carry out in his own extreme fashion. His immediate response to the kings' taxation was the bull

Clericis laicos (1296), forbidding such policies. But both kings were under too much fiscal pressure to accept such a judgment. In England, the king attempted to seize church property and was restrained only by the fact that the clergy and nobility made common cause of their grievances against the growing power of the monarchy. In France, the king put an embargo on the export of gold and silver, in effect preventing the clergy from sending taxes to the pope, and in addition pressed policies, like the liability of bishops to trial for treason, aimed at establishing his authority over the pope.

A long series of angry exchanges began, ending in the issuing of the bull *Unam Sanctam* by Boniface in 1302. *Unam Sanctam* is one of the strongest statements of the papalist theory of order ever issued: "Therefore, if the earthly power errs," it stated, "it shall be judged by the spiritual power .... but if the supreme spiritual power errs it can be judged only by God, and not by man .... Therefore we declare, state, define, and pronounce that it is altogether necessary to salvation for every human creature to be subject to the Roman pontiff." Though this was a fulfillment of traditional papalist theory and not the mad ravings of a megalomaniac, as some nineteenth-century historians implied, it was a position that could be successfully countered by the newly powerful kingdoms of the west.

Philip IV replied to *Unam Sanctam* by declaring the pope a usurper and a heretic and threatening to summon a council to depose him and elect a new pope. By August, 1303, Boniface was preparing a bull of excommunication against Philip; and to prevent this, Philip's counselor Guillaume de Nogaret, with the help of Sciarra Colonna, burst into the papal castle of Anagni on September 7, 1303, and seized the pope. Soon afterward Boniface died, and by 1305 Philip had secured not only the election of a more cooperative pope but the removal of the seat of the papacy, for the only time in its history, away from Rome. Arguing that at Rome the popes were too subject to the political influences of the Roman nobility, Philip established the papacy at Avignon in southern France.

For the purpose of securing order in Christian society, the papacy had prosecuted heretics and Jews, preached crusades, and founded the inquisition. In the name of order, too, it had brought down the empire. Now the kings were to bring down the papacy, and with it the ideal of a united Christian society based upon the theological doctrine of the Mystical Body of Christ and the memory of the *imperium romanum*. In the meantime, the search for order was carried on in the realm of the intellect as well as in that of politics.

Chapter Eleven

The Scholastic Order

Scholasticism was a search for order in intellectual life. By its most literal definition, scholasticism was the theology and philosophy taught in the great schools of western Europe from the twelfth through fourteenth centuries. And in one sense its cause was the growth of population that promoted the development of the episcopal schools in the cities, where students and teachers from all over Europe drew together. Paris, Oxford, Bologna, Toulouse, and other great centers of learning offered cathedral schools, which in the twelfth and thirteenth centuries developed into universities, that encouraged the exchange of ideas in a stimulating atmosphere. Within this environment, scholasticism was (by a more precise definition) the creation of a new method to deal with and to assimilate the new philosophical and scientific materials that came into medieval Europe during the mid-twelfth century.

These new materials were mostly very old: works of Aristotle and other ancient Greek philosophers and scientists that had been lost to the West owing to the general ignorance of Greek. They had always been known, though not generally used, in the eastern empire, and in the seventh and eighth centuries the Muslim conquerors of the Near East translated them first into Syriac and then into Arabic. They then went on to use them as the basis for a brilliant culture, with its centers at Baghdad and Córdoba. With the aid of these books, the Arabs thrust far ahead of the West in medicine, mathematics, and astronomy, and Muslim philosophers, including Avicenna (980–1037) and Averroës (1126–1178), grappled with the problems of reconciling Greek learning with Muslim revelation. The same problems were posed to the Jewish philosophers of Spain, such as ibn-Gabirol (c. 1020–1070) and Moses Maimonides (1135–1204).

The Christians remained ignorant of these problems until the mid-eleventh century, relying upon Plato and the Platonically expressed thought of the church fathers and Augustine. Some of Aristotle's works were known and respected, but much of his more advanced logic and almost all of his science had been lost. Then, in Sicily, southern Italy, and Spain, where contacts between Islam and Christianity were common, Christian scholars began, tentatively at first, to make translations of the lost works from the Arabic, the task continuing into the twelfth and thirteenth centuries. Since the original Greek texts had by this time been expanded and elaborated by the commentaries of the Arab philosophers, the result was the importation not only of many unfamiliar Greek ideas, but of Muslim theories based upon exotic doctrines with which early Christianity had come into contact but had never wished to assimilate.

The effect upon twelfth-century Christian philosophers and scientists was radical: suddenly at hand were materials with which their view of the world could be at once rendered more precise and enormously expanded. Theologians—and most of the philosophers of the Middle Ages were theologians—then had to decide whether to condemn the new materials outright or to assimilate them into a new system. Throughout the period, conservatives attempted to eject the new ideas from theology, even attempting to have their study banned at the schools, and it was agreed even by the most progressive that some were indeed irreconcilable with Christianity. But gradually theologians responded to the challenge by creating new systems. The choice was as clear to them as it had been to the Muslim and Jewish theologians: either reconcile the new knowledge with revelation or permit a deep chasm to be formed between faith and reason.

The goal of the scholastics was to work out a synthesis between the old and the new knowledge. The question was how to go about it. After the establishment of schools where ideas could be exchanged, the next requisite was the development of an effective method of assimilation that could be generally accepted by scholars. For almost a millennium, theological, philosophical, and scientific disputes had been referred for solution to the "authorities" of the past: the Bible, the classics, and the church fathers. Following Plato, Paul, and Augustine, the mode of philosophical expression was allusive, allegorical, repetitive. To the modern mind, it often appears to wander far afield before returning to the point.

Now in the course of the twelfth century, a wholly new mode of expression was developed. This method was logically consequent, beginning, like Aristotle and Euclid, from axioms and proceeding from deduction to higher deduction and to lateral corollaries until from one trunk a thousand ramifications had spread, creating a new and coherent system. Even the derivation of the axioms was in part new. They were still largely drawn from the Bible, the fathers, and the classics; but sometimes, in imitation of Aristotle, they were drawn from sense experience. The first of Aquinas's famous five proofs of the existence of God, for example, begins by postulating from sense experience alone that we observe the existence of motion in the universe. From that postulate he draws deduction after deduction until he arrives at a prime mover whom, he says, all men call God. This building of theological systems not on the basis of revelation, but on the basis of natural philosophy was called natural theology, and it proceeded in the same way as the speculative metaphysics of the ancient Greeks. Then, after drawing all they could from the premises of natural theology, philosophers such as Aquinas superimposed revelation upon the structure of natural theology and proceeded to draw from the principles of revelation what deductions they could. This part of the process was called revealed theology. When finished, the process formed a coherent system of the world, leaving out nothing relating to the philosophical understanding of God and his relations with man.

For such systems, reference to precedent and authorities was insufficient. Besides, it was found that the very axioms of tradition differed: for example, one of the church fathers might contradict another. The spirit that sought a perfect order in society and a perfect order in the universe could not tolerate such ambiguities. In order to resolve them and to proceed beyond the frontiers established by the past, a new tool was needed. That tool was reason.

Today, when we take reason for granted and when, under the influence of Marx and Freud and the scientific method, we are often even suspicious of it, it is difficult to imagine the vernal enthusiasm of the philosophers in the twelfth and thirteenth centuries when they discovered this tool. To be sure, humans had used reason ever since they became humans, and the sophisticated use of reason in philosophical speculation was highly developed by the ancient Greeks. The fathers of the church and earlier theologians were aware of Greek rational thought and had applied it to their early theological syntheses. But the excitement of those first efforts by Justin Martyr and of their fullest development by Augustine had long been submerged in exaggerated humility and respect for the past. The ancient innovators had themselves become authorities. Now the scholastics broke the bonds of authority and with zest and excitement determined to apply reason systematically and in logical progression to every aspect of human knowledge. The analogy that springs to mind immediately is the scientific spirit of the nineteenth and twentieth centuries: vigorous, creative, heady, a bit arrogant, confident (until recently) of its ability to probe every dark corner of the universe and to answer all questions. The rational spirit of the twelfth and thirteenth centuries was enthusiastically applied not only to theology and philosophy, but to civil and canon law, to political theory, and to medicine and the other sciences.

The first of the great medieval religious rationalists was St. Anselm (1033–1109), abbot of Bec and then, as archbishop of Canterbury, the opponent of William II and Henry I. As energetic in philosophy as in politics, Anselm wrote a number of theological works, the most important of which are the *Proslogium, the Monologium,* and the tract *Cur Deus Homo* ("Why God Became Man").

In the *Proslogium* Anselm expressed for the first time the ontological argument for the existence of God. Not a proof in the ordinary sense of the word, but a statement that the existence of God is self-evident, the ontological argument has been challenged and reaffirmed by philosophers from Anselm's time to our own. God is defined in such a way, Anselm implied, that he necessarily exists. Anselm's ontological argument legitimized the application of rationality to theological problems by demonstrating that reason, unaided by sensory data or by revelation, could be used to support known theological truths. He set the stage for the use of reason as an authority in and of itself.

In the *Monologium,* Anselm proceeded to offer proofs for the existence of God based upon experience. The ontological argument is an *a priori* proof, of the Platonic and Augustinian variety, in which truth is achieved through introspection; the arguments of the *Monologium* are *a posteriori*, resting upon observation, and these look forward to the Aristotelian method used by Aquinas. The further significance of the *Monologium* is in its manner of proceeding step-by-step in logically consequent fashion. It is this thorough, rational, tightly knit, and logical procedure that caused Anselm to be named the "father of scholasticism."

Anselm taught and wrote at Bec, a monastic school. Another great theologian of the twelfth century was also a monk, the great Cistercian St. Bernard. More even than most great men, Bernard refuses to fit into any category: harsh, yet filled with love; an ascetic recluse, yet a friend of kings and wielder of great political influence; a contemplative and prophet, yet devoted to the spirit of order. Bernard cannot be classified as a scholastic, but his approach to the contemplative life was logical and systematic.

The thrust of ecclesiastical order had brought about a riposte of the prophetic spirit in many forms, including the contemplative live, which from the twelfth through the seventeenth centuries enjoyed a currency throughout Christendom greater than either before or after. But the contemplative life itself was affected by the prevailing urge to intellectual order. In his *Steps of Humility,* St. Bernard developed contemplative theology—the exposition in orderly, consequent fashion of the steps leading to, and away from, the contemplative experience.

Bernard was a man of strong opinions and the chief opponent of another man who made great contributions to the development of scholasticism: Peter Abelard (1079–1142). Unlike the monks Anselm and Bernard, Abelard had his base of operations in the schools of Paris, now emerging as centers of scholastic thought. Trained in dialectic and in theology, Abelard's brilliant and aggressive mind contributed greatly to the development of early scholasticism. He offered a solution to the heated debate over universals, arguing against realists that words or ideas had no independent existence of their own, and against the nominalists that ideas were not simply arbitrary names but possessed a real and useful existence as concepts within the human mind.

Abelard's difficulties arose from the application of his keen logic to theological problems. In his famous *Sic et Non ("Yes* and No"), Abelard assembled a list of 168 theological propositions and then showed how in each of them could be found opinions of the church fathers that were diametrically opposed to one another. The implications were clear: one could cite authorities for any theological position. Therefore, Abelard argued, the reason of the individual must be applied to the solution of theological problems. It was not Abelard's belief in reason in itself that was unusual. Influenced by Greek tradition, Christianity had always placed great stock in reason; and from the end of the eleventh century men such as St. Anselm had replaced the older, rambling theological style with logical, orderly development of their arguments. This indeed was the essence of scholasticism. But Abelard's views seemed to St. Bernard and others to be extreme in their intellectualism. At a time when the humanity of Christ was being increasingly emphasized, Abelard appeared to consider him an abstraction, less the God-man who suffered for us on the Cross than a remote source of ethical teachings whose value could be proved, and whose details could be elicited, by the application of logic.

Bernard challenged the methods of Abelard, and the subsequent clash between these two charismatic giants polarized the major powers of the medieval world. And yet, upon close examination, the theological ideas associated with Bernard and Abelard were not very different and never served as the focus for their conflict. What, then, caused this monumental clash?

We can get a hint of the reasons for the struggle by examining the ideas of a noted contemporary: the educated contemplative, Hugh of St. Victor (1096–1141). Hugh was the master of the monastic school at St. Victor's in Paris; he was widely regarded as one of the most influential theologians of his time. According to Hugh, God created the world for the sake of humanity: "Humanity is set in the midst of creation," he taught. Humanity stood between God and the visible world and had a place in each. The world served humanity; humanity should serve God. Humanity had been given a great freedom: the freedom to choose God. No one could be forced to turn his or her heart or head to God, the highest good. To serve God in freedom meant using the highest gifts of the heart and the head that humanity had received from God: emotion on the one hand, reason on the other. Hugh of St. Victor, then, represented a bridge between what turned out to be two radically opposed methods of understanding the Christian faith. Bernard and Abelard represented the parting of the ways: Bernard advocated the primacy of emotion, of the heart; Abelard fought for the primacy of reason, of the head.

Both Bernard and Abelard are products of the same intellectual tradition. The primary focus of intellectual activity in the High Middle Ages was the relationship between faith (or revelation) and reason. Educated medieval Christians believed that knowledge was acquired by one of these two paths. Throughout the Middle Ages, Christians believed that Truth resided in Scripture, in the writings of the Church Fathers, and in the authority of the Holy Church. But most people, especially people with education or simple curiosity, wanted more than simple faith—they sought to *understand* the Truth. How could Truth not only be known, but comprehended and understood?

Bernard believed that Truth could only be understood through the emotions, the heart. He believed that humanity had been created in the image of God with a "great soul" (*anima magna*). But humanity is bowed low with sin: it has a "bent soul" (*anima curva*), because it has turned away from God in rebellion. The source of humanity's sin is its willfulness—humanity presumed to know more than God. This willfulness was evident to Bernard in people such as Abelard, who were attempting to understand faith through the resources of the head, through reason. Faith to Bernard meant humble submission, the banishment of self-will so that the will was again open to love and illumination through revelation. Loving without reserve, one yearned only for union with God. Humanity's aim, fulfillment, and highest dignity lay in becoming absorbed into God, being caught up wholly into the process of love in which God the Father embraced God the Son, encircled by a blazing nimbus lit by the flames of the Holy Spirit. "Heart speaks to heart," wrote Bernard: the heart of humanity called to the heart of God, and God's heart called to the heart of humanity. But humanity was incapable of loving God without God's grace. "The cause of loving God is God." True understanding, then, is an inner experience. Bernard was one of the first medieval Christian leaders to emphasize the interior life of the believer over external displays of spirituality.

Ironically, Abelard also stressed the importance of the interior over the exterior. Abelard taught that the concept of Good exists both in the mind of humans and in the mind of God. Therefore, morality is a question of inner intent, rather than exterior deeds. "We call intention good which is right in itself," wrote Abelard, "but the action is good, not because it contains within it some good, but because it issues from good intention." Further, he wrote, all acts that proceed from good intentions are good, but dark deeds arise from wrong intention. No amount of penance will pay for a sin if the penance does not arise from good intention. Penance can only be effective if the penitent is truly contrite. How can fallen humanity truly intend to do good? Because Christ's supremely unselfish sacrifice has rekindled in humanity the desire to love. Christ's love permits humanity to love in intent, "so that we do his will from love and not from fear." Because of Christ's inspiring example, which rekindled dormant desires in the heart of humanity, we are capable of grieving for our sins and we are able to seek repentance with a contrite heart.

Both Bernard and Abelard believed that the path to redemption lies in the interior life of the believer. But where Bernard saw the interior life as the emotions of the heart, Abelard saw the intent of the mind. The conflict between the two was between methods of understanding a faith that both shared. Yet, even these methods of understanding were not mutually exclusive—Hugh of St. Victor was able to bridge the gap between the head and the heart. The contest, then, was a battle of wills between two dominant personalities. Neither allowed room for compromise; as a result, the more organic theology of Hugh of St. Victor gave way in the face of a winner-take-all conflict between two opposing camps represented by Bernard and Abelard.

Bernard won his battle against Abelard. He engineered a condemnation of Abelard, along with all his works. Pope Innocent II himself prepared the bonfire in which Abelard's books were burned. But Abelard won the war. He accepted his sentence of excommunication with uncharacteristic humility and silence, and spent his final years in retirement at a daughter house of Cluny under the protection of Peter the Venerable, the greatly respected abbot of Cluny. Once out of the limelight, and especially after his death, Abelard's prestige and status grew. Bernard came to be perceived as the destroyer of a giant intellect, and he could never shake his guilt. When he wanted to condemn the works of another advocate of reason, Gilbert of Porrée, a friend of Abelard's, Bernard was reprimanded by the cardinals of the Roman Curia. It was the methods of Abelard, the primacy of the head, the use of logic and the dialectic, that Bernard opposed, but these methods outlived Bernard. Abelard's strong defense of reason against tradition and his use of the method of opposing authorities and then resolving the opposition by the use of logic were of immense importance in shaping the course of later scholasticism.

The implications of Abelard's method were made most fully explicit by the greatest scholastic philosopher and theologian, Thomas Aquinas (1223–1274). This extraordinary man was destined by his wealthy parents to a high post in the hierarchy, but as a child he had already shown a tendency to scholarship instead of politics. He refused the offices that his father offered to procure for him and went instead to join the mendicant order of St. Dominic. Large and slow-moving, he was nicknamed the Dumb Ox by his teachers and fellow students until he demonstrated in debate that he was able to out-argue his professors. He studied and then taught at the University of Paris, where his piety and brilliance, as well as his noble connections, made him a frequent guest at the court of Louis IX. The author of many tracts on philosophy and political theory as well as of theology, he is said to have kept several secretaries busy at once with his dictation.

The two works that have earned him his reputation as the greatest systematic theologian in history are the *Summa Theologica, a* textbook for advanced students, and the *Summa contra Gentiles* ("Summa against the Unbelievers"), which, being designed to convince Muslims, Jews, heretics, and the ignorant of the truth of the Christian faith, is a more elementary, and consequently a more fully explained, summary of Christian doctrine. In these works Aquinas at once perfected the scholastic method and incorporated into a new synthesis the recently rediscovered Greek thought. The supplanting of Platonic and Augustinian by Aristotelian thought is symbolized in the fact that Thomas commonly referred to Aristotle simply as "the Philosopher."

Thomas's method was to begin with the most fundamental questions of theology, and then to pursue each with all of its implications. The summas are closely knit and organized with Euclidean precision. Following Abelard, Aquinas began each step of his demonstration by raising a question (for example, "Whether God exists?"). He then went on to state the philosophical objections to the existence of God (for example, "It seems that God does not exist; because if one of two contraries be infinite, the other would be altogether destroyed"). After stating, fully and as strongly as possible, all the objections, he then set forth one or more statements from the Bible or the fathers of the church (for example, "On the contrary, it is said in the person of God: 'I am who am' [Exodus, 3:14]"). Finally, he went on to use his own reason to resolve the problem ("I answer that..."; in answer to the problem of God's existence, he propounded his famous five proofs based upon experience).

The scope of the summas includes all that might be asked of God and God's ways with the world: the nature of truth and the way to obtain it, the nature of God, the attributes of God, the action of God in the world, the creation and the nature of the universe and its variety, the eternity of the universe and the nature of time, the problem of the existence and nature of evil, the nature of man, the spirit and the soul, moral good and evil, the immortality of the soul, the place of the angels and of Satan, free will, providence and predestination, salvation. These problems are studied in such complete detail that Thomas's system itself later became established as authoritative in Catholic thought. Even those who no longer find Thomism convincing or useful cannot fail to be impressed by the intellectual beauty and grandeur of the system, so complete and clear is each part, so perfectly orchestrated are all the parts, and so internally balanced and consistent is the whole.

Even Aquinas had difficulty in making his views prevail during his own lifetime, and no sooner was scholasticism firmly established than it began to decline. The thought of Duns Scotus (c. 1270–1308), a Franciscan and the most intricate of all the scholastics, is symptomatic of the causes of decline. So perfectly had Thomas raised and answered the basic questions, that his successors, such as Duns, were obliged to turn to more and more obscure questions or to more and more complex solutions of old ones. Aquinas's proofs of the existence of God are relatively simple and easy to follow, but Duns's are so long and intricate as to be almost opaque to anyone not long-trained in scholastic expression. Duns's followers became even more obscure and unconvincing than their master, and the later Protestant Reformers came to call anyone teaching a tortuous and incomprehensible doctrine a "dunce."

Ultimately, Duns Scotus argued against the use of reason to explain Christian revelation. According to Duns, theologians had shown that the natural world does not teach humanity of its divine destiny. But it was equally true, said Duns, that philosophers had shown that nothing supernatural (for example, the sacraments) is necessary for salvation. Both propositions are equally proven, according to Duns, given the rules for argument within each field of discourse. But these two propositions are contradictory. Therefore, theology and philosophy do not lead to the same truth. The problem, said Duns, was that scholastics had been asking the wrong question, that is, "How can reason be reconciled with revelation?" The question is meaningless, according to Duns, because God does not function as Intellect, but rather as Will. Truth is not subject to reason; truth is a function of the Will of God.

This kind of difficulty appeared even more clearly in the works of Siger of Brabant (c. 1240–1284) and William of Ockham (c. 1300–1349). Siger propounded the doctrine of the two truths, arguing that reason and revelation, though both true, are often mutually contradictory. When they are, it is futile to try to reconcile them. We must accept both truths, each in its compartment, and not try to synthesize them. Ockham argued, in similar fashion, that faith and reason, both necessary to man, could not be brought together. According to Ockham, human reason is capable of drawing conclusions only about things that can be sensed. But everything one can say about God is only an imposition of human constructs. Reason cannot be applied to God, because God is beyond reason. One cannot even argue that God exists, because God is not bound by the human construct of existence. The truth of God's existence is a matter of faith alone, a truth revealed in Scriptures and tradition, but a truth that exists apart from the world of rational thought. Theology, then, according to Ockham, is nothing more than an empty controversy over words. In part of their lives, humans should follow faith, in part of their lives they should follow reason; and one should not be dismayed at contradictions. Thus, at the very time that scholasticism seemed to have succeeded in producing a view of the world at once internally coherent and corresponding to objective reality, some of the most intelligent scholastics were questioning whether this was indeed possible.

Scholasticism continued through the fourteenth and fifteenth centuries; but, lacking conviction in its ability to find the truth, it degenerated more and more into games with words, and it lost the general assent of the community. In the realm of the intellect as well as in that of politics, the search for Christian order was vigorous and brilliant but not wholly successful. And in the intellectual as well as in the political sphere, the fourteenth and fifteenth centuries saw the triumph of prophecy over order.

Chapter Twelve

Christianity in the Autumn of the Middle Ages

The years 1300 to 1500, like those from 250 to 700, mark an important transition period. Depending upon whether one is looking backwards or forwards, the era is either the "autumn of the Middle Ages" or the "Renaissance." All periods are periods of change, but these two centuries saw the beginning of a real departure from the principles of order that had long characterized medieval Christianity. The ideal of a unified Christian society was yielding to royal nationalism in northern Europe and to urban particularism in Italy; in the East, Greek Orthodox Christianity suffered almost total eclipse as a result of the conquest of the Byzantine Empire by the Turks, completed in 1453; the papal monarchy over the institutions of the church was challenged from several sides; people were losing confidence in the ability of reason to build an intellectual order corresponding to objective reality. The reactions generated by the temporary triumph of the spirit of order now gained greater strength as order waned.

Behind these shifts in attitude lay increasingly rapid changes in society as a whole. The growth in power of the towns and their merchants, on the one hand, and of the kings and their governments, on the other, encouraged a rising secularism. A series of famines and plagues in the fourteenth and fifteenth centuries brought about a decline of population that created great dislocations of agricultural society and provoked peasants' revolts and uprisings. Owing to the emergence of more literate leaders and to the growth of a sense of common cause, the free peasants and the city laborers took a more active part both in politics and in the church. In both the ecclesiastical and secular spheres was emerging the idea that the "people" (which usually still meant free men of a certain stature) had a right to be taken into account—partly because of the need of governments whose demands and scope were growing for a wider basis of support; partly because of the rise, for other practical reasons, of representative assemblies in both the cities and the kingdoms; and partly because of the development of political theories like those of Marsilius of Padua.

Marsilius upheld the ascending theory of sovereignty, arguing that God's authority is delegated to the "people" (i.e., the people of responsibility and social stature), who in turn choose their rulers. The rulers—princes or popes—are merely the "ruling part" of the community. They are responsible not only to God *for the* people, but to God *through the* people. They are public servants subject to dismissal, not rulers by divine election.

The papacy in these two centuries gradually lost its position at the center of Christian society. Most of the popes during this period were able and qualified, and they were supported by theoreticians who vigorously defended papal supremacy. But the political, social, and intellectual climate offered other alternatives to centralized papal authority, and circumstances arose that made those alternatives seem plausible.

The first blow to the papacy was the kidnapping of Boniface VIII in 1303, followed by the election of Clement V (1305–1314), who moved the papacy to Avignon and was perceived to be sympathetic to the policies of King Philip IV. Philip's control over the pope must not be exaggerated. Clement did not move his administration in order to be dominated by the French king, but for his own protection. Growing political tensions in Rome had made the pope's position there perilous. The court at Avignon was fortified, it was close enough to Italy to exert a direct influence over Italian affairs, and it was near another estate already controlled by the papacy. The popes remained at Avignon until 1377 in what was called the Babylonian Captivity, after the biblical episode of the Jews' enslavement by the Babylonians in the sixth century B.C. The decadence of the Avignon papacy has, however, been exaggerated until recently by historians. The Avignon popes continued to exercise the power of appointing bishops in wide areas of Europe. The papal administration continued to grow in complexity and power, and a pope such as Benedict XII (1334–1342), who used his influence to effect a general reform of the religious orders, was not atypical either in his piety or in his energy. After Clement V, the Avignon popes were not overtly sympathetic to the policies of the French monarchy; indeed, the papal courts of Avignon tended to identify strongly with the southern French, who tended to resent the dominance of the northern King. There is little evidence that there was any widespread disaffection from the papacy simply because it was established at Avignon. Indeed, the arguments of Philip IV for the salutary effect of the removal of the pope from the intrigues of the Roman nobility had some validity.

Nonetheless, the Avignon papacy fostered a growing perception that the papacy had turned away from its spiritual responsibilities in its efforts to increase its worldly authority. One of the primary goals of the Avignon papacy was to enhance the status of the pope as the spiritual leader of the Christian community. But most Avignon popes chose to demonstrate their exalted status through the display of external pomp. This choice was not the only one available; conceivably, the Avignon popes could have chosen to hold themselves up as examples of moral simplicity, moderate asceticism, and contemplative spirituality. But this choice would have been extremely difficult. The papal curia was by now an advanced bureaucracy and the highest court of appeals in Christendom. And the early fourteenth century followed a period of increasing prosperity. Secular leaders were highly respected for their extravagant displays of wealth. At a time when the papacy was competing with secular rulers for leadership of Christian society, the popes of Avignon chose to engage these rulers on their own terms. The papal palace of Avignon dazzled visitors with its sights and with the hustle and bustle of its daily activities. Crowds of courtiers, petitioners, and bureaucrats rushed through the corridors and halls at all hours. Poets and artists from all over Europe gathered in the streets and met in the public establishments. The papal court of Avignon was recognized as the most sophisticated and civilized court in the land. Papal authorities perceived Avignon as a shining tribute to the glory of God, but some people wondered if God was being properly served by such extravagance. They wondered whether the pope should present himself as a ruling lord when he was supposed to be a spiritual shepherd. They wondered why he lived in a wealthy resort area instead of Rome, where he belonged. In short, the Avignon popes chose the wrong approach in trying to enhance their status as the moral conscience of Christendom. They wanted to establish themselves at the top of Christian society by outshining the kings and princes of Europe. But in gaining temporal status, they lost much of their spiritual prestige.

The worst aspect of the Avignon papacy was in the difficulties it foreshadowed. These difficulties were partly owing to the fact that everyone knew that the papacy belonged at Rome and would eventually return there, so that the election of a Roman pope and a consequent schism was always a possibility, and partly the result of the growth in power of the papal administration itself, the curia. The cardinals who dominated the curia had long been accustomed to thinking of themselves as sharing with the pope the primacy of the *ecclesia romana.* In 1352, inspired by this tradition and perhaps also by the growing power of the kings' councils in the secular states, they issued a document demanding that in future conclaves a papal candidate must bind himself before his election to follow the policies recommended by the cardinals.

Events soon transformed these potential weaknesses into actuality. In 1377 Pope Gregory XI (1370–1378) elected to return to Rome in spite of unsettled conditions there, and in the next year he died. Amidst great confusion in a situation where the papal court had not yet really been transferred back to Rome, a group of cardinals in Rome hastily elected Pope Urban VI (1378–1389), a man of violent temper, who undertook to break the power of the cardinals long before he had the requisite support or influence. Accordingly, some of the cardinals met again and elected Clement VII (1378–1394), who chose to retain the papal seat at Avignon. From 1378 to 1409 there were two popes, one at Avignon and one at Rome, and there was no authority to judge which was legitimate. Kings supported one or the other according to policy: the king of France and his allies backed the Avignonese popes, and the king of England and his allies naturally supported the Romans.

The Christian community could not tolerate two popes, especially when each pope excommunicated the followers of his opposite number. The members of the church depended on the proper administration of the sacraments by properly authorized clergy to pave their way to salvation. Since all clergymen had been excommunicated by one pope or the other, how could common Christians know if they were receiving an effective sacrament? How could anyone know if they were saved? Medieval society could not function without a clearly defined spiritual hierarchy. Doubts concerning papal authority opened a vacuum that begged to be filled.

The Great Schism had three important effects on ecclesiastical order. First it permitted the kings to reintroduce secular politics into the church to a degree unknown since the early eleventh century. In France, the king and his civil lawyers argued that the French church was, except for due honor and reverence, independent of the papacy. They replaced papal with royal control over the election of bishops wherever possible, and they supported conciliar theories that would have weakened the papacy in favor of the bishops, whom the king might thus the more easily control. This ecclesiastical nationalism, called Gallicanism in France, was reflected to one degree or another in the politics of England, Germany, and nearly every other country of Europe.

The second effect was that respect for the papacy greatly declined among politicians, scholars, and the people at large. The spectacle of two popes excommunicating and doing political battle with each other could scarcely elicit the same kind of awe that Innocent III or even Boniface VIII could engender. The authority of the pope had always been based on the idea that the spiritual status of the papal office transcended the man who happened to occupy the papal see; thus, the office had survived a number of under-qualified and even immoral popes, such as John XII. But for the first time in several centuries, the Great Schism caused many people to doubt the special authority of the office itself.

The third effect was the rise of conciliarism. The conciliar theory, stated in its simplest terms, is that the supreme authority in Christendom is not the pope, but a general council of bishops. The theory has its ultimate origins in the ancient idea of the collegiality of the bishops, of whom the pope is only first among equals—an idea that had always had a certain currency until the papal revolution of the eleventh century. At that time it was given impetus by certain polemicists, both anti-imperialists, who emphasized the dignity of the bishops, and imperialists, who wished to use the bishops as a curb to the power of the pope.

The kings of the fourteenth and fifteenth centuries found the idea of the collegiality of bishops attractive because it promised to limit papal interference in their countries; and it was reinforced by the ascending theories of government like those of Marsilius of Padua, who applied them in his writings directly to the church as well as to the secular power. Ultimate authority under God rested with the Christian people, who delegated it to their representatives, the bishops. The bishops then chose a pope to whom they in turn delegated certain powers. The pope was responsible to the bishops, the bishops to the people, and the people to God. Conciliar theories were worked out in great detail and sophistication and with great attention paid to the canons and traditions of the past by a number of scholars, the most influential of whom was Jean Gerson (1364–1429), professor of theology and later chancellor at the University of Paris.

The practical need to resolve the Great Schism enabled Gerson and his fellow scholars to transform theory into practice. The theory that all disputes could be referred ultimately to the pope was not convincing when there were two antagonistic popes; and the conciliarists raised other spectral possibilities: suppose, there being only one pope, he should go mad or prove a monster of depravity? Under certain circumstances at least, another authority than the pope must be able to summon and preside over a council. By 1408 it appeared that the schism was going to be interminable, and most of the cardinals, both at Rome and at Avignon, agreed to hold a council to resolve it. This council met at Pisa in 1409 and decided to end the schism by declaring both claimants deposed and choosing a new pope, Alexander V (1409–1410). But the Roman pope, backed by the southern Italians, and the Avignonese pope, backed by the kings of Scotland and Aragon, refused to abide by the decisions of the council. There were now three vicars of Christ.

The situation, already intolerable, showed signs of growing worse: it seemed that the number of popes possible at one time was unlimited. With a sense of great urgency, the conciliarists pressed their doctrines and, with the aid of the Emperor Sigismund (1410–1437), induced the Pisan pope, John XXIII, to call another general council. This, the sixteenth ecumenical council, assembled at Constance in 1414 and, in an effort to escape the intolerable pressures of the schism, passed the decree *Sacrosancta* (1415), which fulfilled the dearest wishes of the conciliarists. "The holy Council of Constance," said the decree, "declares...that it is a General Council...and that therefore it has its authority immediately from Christ; and that all men, of every rank and condition, including the Pope himself, are bound to obey it in matters concerning the Faith, the abolition of the schism, and the reformation of the church of God in its head and its members." The council went on in 1417 to depose all three claimants to the papacy and to appoint a pope, Martin V (1417–1431), who after further difficulties was at last generally recognized throughout Europe.

The triumph of the conciliarists was short-lived. At the Council of Ferrara-Florence, which met from 1438, the pope reasserted his power and domination; the decree *Frequens* of Constance calling for frequent general councils was ignored. In 1439, conciliarists elected an anti-pope, who took the name Felix V, but few people in Christendom were willing to acknowledge a second pope so soon after the Great Schism. When Felix abdicated in 1449, the conciliar movement effectively ended. In 1460 Pius II in his bull *Execrabilis* declared that the notion that a council was superior to the pope was rebellious, poisonous, erroneous, and detestable.

The monarchy of the papacy over the church continued to grow in the fifteenth and sixteenth centuries, but at the same time the general influence of the papacy in society was greatly diminished. Royalism and nationalism enjoyed successes more permanent than those of conciliarism; the papacy became again immersed in petty Italian politics; popular disaffection was widespread. The papacy's failure to regain either political or moral leadership in society resulted ultimately in the Protestant Reformation of the sixteenth century.

Movements that had begun in reaction to the rise of ecclesiastical order now grew stronger with its decline. On the one hand secularism and indifference to religion spread. It is an absurdity to suppose that everyone in the earlier Middle Ages was pious and spiritual, but few cared overtly to deny or to scoff at the principles of religion. But from the eleventh and twelfth century, poets, many of them students or even ordained priests, produced quantities of light literature that was overtly worldly, ironically skeptical, or sometimes simply blasphemous—like the piece called "The Council of Remiremont," in which a group of nuns debate whether a layman or a priest makes a better lover. The ethic of courtly love, invented by the poets of the mid-eleventh century and for centuries taken up by the nobility with varying degrees of seriousness, was, when taken at face value, idolatrous in making the noble married lady an object of worship and adoration to her lover—who obeyed her, trembled in her presence, and in every way treated her as if she were God.

Some took these games less seriously than others, and neither the student songs nor the courtly love ethic represents a formal break with Christian orthodoxy. But they are representative of the growing secular spirit, which took quite serious and important forms in the later Middle Ages, in the wholly worldly politics of the princes and in the wholly worldly commercial interests of the merchants.

Diametrically opposed to secularism, yet like secularism encouraged by the decline of ecclesiastical order, was the advance of the prophetic spirit among both the clergy and the laity. As in the Protestant Reformation, the spirit of prophecy in the fourteenth and fifteenth centuries moved with particular vigor among the laity. Lay piety was already robust in the twelfth and thirteenth centuries, as we have seen, and its later strength is in part the result of a natural growth. But the increased popularity of lay piety in the later Middle Ages is also a manifestation of the deep social dislocation brought about by the economic decline and by the terrible famines and plagues of the time.

Some popular piety, indeed, became grotesque. The obsessive preoccupation with death is visible in its personification in art, and even more in the ghastly mementos of decay that appeared everywhere. It became common, for example, to decorate tombs with representations of the dead being eaten by worms or toads. A favorite device was to sculpt a tomb on two levels: on top, an effigy of the dead person clothed and recumbent in peace; underneath, often behind a grille, a representation of the same person rotting, or as a skeleton. What monstrosities were perpetuated at the less permanent graves of the simple people, we do not know; but we do know that alive they performed "dances of death" or, joined in flagellant societies, wandered about the countryside whipping one another. These perversions of the prophetic spirit have few precedents or imitations in the history of Christianity; rather than the natural outgrowth of anything in the medieval church, they represent the attunement of religious expression to the fortunately temporary needs of a society obsessed with fear of plague and famine.

There were healthier manifestations of the prophetic spirit among the laity. In the Low Countries, for example, the spiritual teachings of Jan van Ruysbroeck (1293–1381) and Gerard Groote (1340–1384) prompted the rise of a lay organization called the Brethren of the Common Life. These people lived a simple community life devoted to prayer, book-copying, and study of the Bible.

The spirit of prophecy brought forth among both clergy and laity new and powerful manifestations of Reformist dissent. It would be a mistake to suppose, as some Protestant historians have done in order to explain and justify the Protestant Reformation, that the church of the fourteenth and fifteenth centuries was any more morally corrupt than at most other times in its history. Rather, the decline of ecclesiastical order rendered the church authorities less vigorous in their efforts to combat corruption than they had been since the early eleventh century. As in the eleventh century, the result was impatience with the authorities—impatience that often drove people beyond the bounds of orthodoxy in their demands for reform. Because of increased literacy, increased popular participation in affairs, and greater social unrest, the dissent of the later Middle Ages attracted more support than had the earlier Reformist movements.

The two most important Reformists of the period were John Wyclif (c. 1320–1384) in England and John Hus (1369–1415) in Bohemia. Of the two, Hus was much more conservative; and though he was burned for heresy by the Council of Constance in 1415, the charges were unjustified even by the criteria of the time. Hus had the misfortune of challenging the leaders of the church at a time when they were still trying to deal with the issue of three reigning popes and were extremely sensitive to their own instability. These leaders reacted with impulsive severity, further enhancing their vulnerability to criticism.

Wyclif's doctrine was much more overtly revolutionary. A professor at Oxford, he attacked papal supremacy in the church, denied transubstantiation, questioned that the Mass was the center of Christian worship, and eventually expressed doubts about the need of any kind of priesthood. Wyclif encouraged a translation of the Bible into English, with the idea that every Christian ought to read and interpret the Scriptures for himself. In 1382 he was condemned by a synod in London and ordered to remain in his own parish without preaching. Wyclif had attracted a number of followers at the university and among the gentry, and for a while after his death these followers, called Lollards (Dutch *lollaerd,* "babbler"), continued to wander about preaching from the vernacular Scriptures.

Wyclif and the Lollards, like previous Reformists, wished to teach the people to regain through individual meditation and reading of the Scriptures a direct personal experience of God. The church of order, with its hierarchy, its priesthood, its sacraments, and its often unintelligible liturgy, seemed to the Lollards an impediment, rather than an aid, to grace. Though there is no direct connection between the Wycliffites, Hussites, and other late medieval Reformists and the Protestants of the Reformation, it is clear that in some areas, England and Bohemia for instance, the success of the Reformation was rendered easier by the fact that the populace was not wholly unfamiliar with these ideas.

The most profound expression of the prophetic spirit during the Middle Ages was mysticism, or more properly, contemplative spirituality. Generally speaking, the contemplative life has played a greater role in religions such as Hinduism and Buddhism, where moral law and intellectual truth do not receive as much emphasis as they have in Christianity, or, for that matter, in Judaism or in Islam. The goal of contemplative spirituality is a direct and personal encounter with God. As such, it is not encouraged by the spirit of political, moral, or intellectual order.

In Christianity, it is a fulfillment of the prophetic tradition. Christian contemplatives derive biblical justification from the withdrawal of Christ into the desert, and later into Gethsemane, to contemplate, and from the words of Christ to Mary, the sister of Martha, that she had chosen the better part by sitting quietly and hearing the word of God rather than running about doing good works. Contemplative spirituality is not the only possible kind of spirituality. The goal of traditional monastic withdrawal and spirituality in the first few centuries of the church was not direct communion with God. Rather, it was an effort to live a completely moral and worthy life by removing all worldly distractions. The aim of traditional spirituality is the living of the perfect Christian life, and this goal was achieved by saints who were not necessarily spiritual contemplatives.

And yet the spirit of traditional spirituality could not but encourage contemplative spirituality. St. Paul had urged that we empty ourselves out and bring in Christ instead, so that "I no longer live, but Christ lives in me." The systematic turning of the mind from the things of this world to contemplation of the world of God brings us nearer to the divine experience. Thus it was among those who practiced contemplation that the life of contemplative spirituality arose.

Christian contemplative spirituality was encouraged by the writings of St. Augustine, who, though not wholly a contemplative himself, was enough of one to understand it and intellectually brilliant enough to express it intelligibly. Augustine, following both Paul and Plato, believed that the phenomenal world was a less real reflection or projection of the world of ideas or the world of God. In order to attain reality, then, one must penetrate the world of appearances to the real world. But there are two ways of doing this, both requiring meditation and contemplation. One is by means of the intellect: by first examining the world around us, and then our own minds, for analogies of God, we can penetrate behind appearances to some idea, however imperfect, of reality. In this way we get at truth, and the truth makes us understand not only the nature of the cosmos but the nature of the good, truly Christian life. The intellect can thus provide us with metaphysical and moral proof. But the religious spirit is not satisfied with knowledge; it wishes not so much to *know* as to *experience* God, and to unite the soul with him. To have this experience, it is necessary to seek God not with the intellect, but with love.

The sixth-century Syrian monk Pseudo-Dionysius the Areopagite and his followers, especially John Scotus Eriugena, did much for the development of contemplative spirituality with the negative theology they had derived from that of St. Augustine. They argued that God is so wholly above the categories of the human intellect that man can never know him. The way of the intellect, though not wholly futile, cannot lead us very far in our search for God.

As long as the practical dislocations and disorders of society demanded that the church be a bulwark of social order, as long as the search for organization and structure in the church was uppermost, contemplative spirituality was not encouraged. The domination of the Christian thought of the eleventh through thirteenth centuries by rational scholasticism, with its attempt to build a complete, orderly intellectual system of the world, did not encourage contemplative spirituality. But already, from the beginning of the twelfth century, the countercurrent was running, owing to the settling of society and the consequent freeing of the monasteries from many of their utilitarian functions. The new orders, with their emphasis upon contemplation, such as the Cistercians and Carthusians, or the Dominicans and Franciscans later, gave new life to the prophetic spirit. St. Bernard the Cistercian and St. Bonaventure the Franciscan were both spiritual contemplatives, though the prevailing scholastic manner of thought encouraged them to attempt to formulate intellectual descriptions of an experience essentially ineffable. The Franciscans, whose taste ran to experience rather than to the rational metaphysics of the Dominicans, were the leaders both of scientific and of contemplative thought, and Francis himself had been one of the simplest and most direct of the spiritual contemplatives.

Earlier movements of comtemplative spirituality were for the most part centered in monasteries or among the mendicant friars. But with the general decline of ecclesiastical and intellectual order in the fourteenth century, contemplative spirituality became for the first time a common expression of Christian thought primarily among the laity, especially in the towns and cities. In England, France, Germany, Italy, and Spain, from the fourteenth through the sixteenth centuries there was a great flowering of the contemplative spirit.

Lay contemplative thought was especially evident in movements of popular devotion such as the Brethren of the Common Life. This simple spirit of contemplative spirituality was best expressed in the *Imitation of Christ* by Thomas à Kempis (1379–1471), an Augustinian canon. This treatise, because of its simplicity and personal appeal, became one of the most popular spiritual guides ever written. "Above all goods and in all things, my soul," said Thomas in his *Imitation of Christ;* "you shall rest in our Lord always"; and his advice as to how to attain this rest in God is the more convincing because of his understanding of, and sympathy with, human frailties and temptations.

Another example of the manifestation of the contemplative spirit to a simple member of the laity is the life of Margery Kempe in England (born c. 1275). The Lord said to her in her mind, she tells us, that "though I withdraw sometimes the feeling of grace from you, fear not therefore, for I am a hidden God within you, so that you should have no vainglory .... Wheresoever God is heaven is, and God is in your soul and many an angel is about your soul to keep it both night and day. For when you go to church, I go with you; when you go to your bed, I go with you; and when you go out of town I go with you. Daughter, there was never child so submissive to the father as I will be to you to help you and to keep you." This example of spirituality is significant because it allows the most common member of the Christian laity to experience a direct relationship with God without the mediation of the clergy. But Margery shared the general feeling of the Christian community that the clergy was still necessary and vital for salvation, and she never considered the alternative.

There was, beyond the simple contemplative tradition represented by Margery Kempe and Thomas à Kempis, a deeper, though no more strongly felt, contemplative spirituality flourishing in the monasteries. Meister Eckhart in Germany (1260–1327), St. Catherine of Siena (1347–1380), and in England, Walter Hilton (d. 1396) and the unknown author of the *Cloud of Unknowing* (written c. 1345–1386) are among the best-known contemplatives of the fourteenth century. The culmination of the contemplative tradition was the work of St. John of the Cross in sixteenth-century Spain.

The *Cloud of Unknowing* expresses in vivid terms the nature of the contemplative experience. God calls the Christian spirit to lose itself in him, and "how sluggish and slothful the soul that does not respond to the Lord's attraction and invitation." People are called to God in different ways, but the one who is called to the contemplative life must seek to lose oneself in God completely. In order to do this, one must begin by turning one's attention away from this world of illusion. One must put a mist of forgetfulness between oneself and the things of this world. One must forget all desires, for intellectual truth as well as for carnal things. "There is no exception whatever, whether you think of [the things of this world] as physical or spiritual beings, or of their states or actions, or of their goodness or badness." This mist of forgetfulness can only be achieved after long discipline consisting of prayer, meditation, and deliberate mortification of the desires of the flesh by means of fasting and other ascetic practices. Having achieved forgetfulness of this world, contemplatives turn their gaze to God. But they do not expect or desire to *know about* God. "'How am I to think of God Himself, and what is He?' I cannot answer you except to say 'I do not know.'" Between humanity and God there is a cloud of unknowing that cannot be penetrated by the intellect. The only way whatever that humanity has of coming to God is through love. "With a devout and kindling love…try to penetrate that darkness above you. Strike that thick cloud of unknowing with the sharp dart of longing love."

And so God, who is himself Love, is reached only by love itself. And when a person has penetrated that cloud of unknowing and come to God, and has poured out the self and filled the self with God, then the word of Paul is fulfilled that he lives no longer, but Christ in him.

The burning arrow of love is the symbol of the prophetic spirit without which the life of the church would have died. It was the burning spirit of unquenchable love that called the church again and again back to the essential Christian experience, which is the encounter of the soul with God. The spiritual contemplatives, the monks, the heretics, the missionaries, the martyrs, all kept the church warm with the warmth of their fire.

And yet, sadly, that same fire of life lit fires of death for others—for heretics, for Jews, for Muslims, and for other Christians. As the *Cloud* says: "Or, again, they experience a spurious warmth, engendered by the fiend, their spiritual enemy, through their pride, and materialism, and spiritual dabbling. And yet, maybe, they imagine it to be the fire of love, lighted and fanned by the grace and goodness of the Holy Spirit."

And so the church needed not only to pass through the refiner's fire of prophecy, but to be molded by the formative touch of the hand of order. For it was the spirit of order that restrained the excesses of enthusiasm and kept the church in touch with the needs of society, so that society might find its life expressed in the church. It was the spirit of order that, holding to the process of gradual development, kept the teachings and practices of the Christian community within the bounds of tradition.

The spirit of order and the spirit of prophecy, the conservative reformer and the progressive reformer, the orthodox and the heretic, the layman and the monk, the pious peasant and the theologian, together gave balance to the Christian religion. The differences, the tensions, even the hostility between them, produced a medieval Christianity that was neither so esoteric as to divorce itself from the needs of society nor so utilitarian as to forget the nature of the basic religious experience. Medieval Christianity had failings, like any other manifestation of the human spirit, but as a whole it was a most creative and impressive contribution to the history of religion and to the history of western civilization.

Bibliography

Baldwin, John W. *The Scholastic Culture of the Middle Ages, 1000–1300.* Lexington, MA: 1971.

Barnes, Timothy D. *Athanasius and Constantius: Theology and Politics in the Constantinian Empire.* Cambridge, MA: 1993.

Barraclough, Geoffrey. *The Medieval Papacy.* New York: 1979.

Benson, Robert L. *The Bishop Elect: A Study of Medieval Ecclesiastical Office.* Princeton: 1968.

Blumenthal, Uta-Renate. *The Investiture Controversy: Church and Monarchy from the Ninth to the Twelfth Century.* Philadelphia: 1988.

Boff, Leonardo. *Saint Francis: A Model for Human Liberation.* New York: 1982.

Bony, Jean. *French Gothic Architecture of the 12th and 13th Centuries.* Berkeley: 1983.

Brentano, Robert. *Rome Before Avignon: A Social History of Thirteenth-Century Rome.* Berkeley: 1991.

Brown, Peter. *Augustine of Hippo: A Biography.* New York: 1986.

———. *The Body and Society: Men, Women, and Sexual Renunciation in Early Christianity.* New York: 1988.

———. *The Cult of the Saints: Its Rise and Function in Early Latin Christianity.* Chicago: 1981.

———. *Power and Persuasion in Late Antiquity: Towards a Christian Empire.* Madison: 1992.

———. *Society and the Holy in Late Antiquity.* Berkeley: 1982.

Bultmann, Rudolf. *Primitive Christianity and Its Contemporary Setting.* New York: 1956.

Burr, David. *Olivi and Franciscan Poverty: The Origins of the Usus Pauper Controversy.* Philadelphia: 1989.

Bynum, Caroline. *Jesus as Mother: Studies in the Spirituality of the High Middle Ages.* Berkeley: 1982.

Cameron, Averil. *Christianity and the Rhetoric of Empire: The Development of Christian Discourse.* Berkeley: 1991.

Cavadini, John C. *The Last Christology of the West: Adoptionism in Spain and Gaul.* Philadelphia: 1993.

Chadwick, Henry. *Augustine.* Oxford: 1986.

———. *The Early Church.* Rev. ed. London: 1993.

Cohn, Norman. *The Pursuit of the Millennium: Revolutionary Millenarians and Mystical Anarchists of the Middle Ages.* London: 1970.

Copleston, F.C. *Aquinas.* London: 1991.

Dales, Richard C. *The Intellectual Life of Western Europe in the Middle Ages.* New York, 1992.

Daniélou, Jean and Marrou, Henri. *The Christian Centuries.* Vol. 1, *The First Six Hundred Years.* London: 1964.

De Vaux, Roland. *Ancient Israel.* New York: 1961.

Drake, Harold A. *Constantine and the Bishops: The Politics of Intolerance.* Johns Hopkins: 1999.

Eliade, Mircea. *The Sacred and the Profane.* New York: 1959.

Erdmann, Carl. *The Origins of the Idea of Crusade.* Princeton: 1977.

Farmer, Sharon. *Communities of Saint Martin: Legend and Ritual in Medieval Tours.* Ithaca: 1991.

Fox, Robin Lane. *Pagans and Christians.* San Francisco: 1995.

Ganshof, F.L. *Frankish Institutions under Charlemagne.* Providence: 1968.

Geary, Patrick. *Furta Sacra: Thefts of Relics in the Central Middle Ages.* Princeton: 1978.

Gilson, Etienne. *A History of Christian Philosophy in the Middle Ages.* London: 1955.

Hamilton, Bernard. *The Albigensian Crusade.* London: 1974.

———. *Monastic Reform, Catharism, and the Crusades, 900–1300.* London: 1979.

Haren, Michael. *Medieval Thought: The Western Intellectual Tradition from Antiquity to the Thirteenth Century.* Toronto: 1992.

Hatch, Edwin. *The Influence of Greek Ideas on Christianity.* New York: 1957.

Head, Thomas. *Hagiography and the Cult of the Saints: The Diocese of Orléans, 800–1200.* New York: 1990.

Head, Thomas and Landes, Richard, ed. *The Peace of God: Social Violence and Religious Response in France around the Year 1000.* Ithaca, NY: 1992.

Heer, Friedrich. *The Medieval World: Europe, 1100–1350.* New York: 1962.

Herrin, Judith. *The Formation of Christendom.* Princeton: 1987.

Hudson, Anne. *Lollards and Their Books.* London: 1985.

———. *The Premature Reformation: Wycliffite Texts and Lollard History.* New York: 1988.

Hudson, Anne, and Wilks, Michael, ed. *From Ockham to Wyclif.* Oxford: 1987.

Hughes, Andrew. *Medieval Manuscripts for Mass and Office: A Guide to Their Organization and Terminology.* Toronto: 1995.

Hussey, Joan M. *The Orthodox Church in the Byzantine Empire.* Oxford: 1986.

James, William. *The Varieties of Religious Experience.* New York: 1991.

Johnson, Penelope D. *Equal in Monastic Profession: Religious Women in Medieval France.* Chicago: 1991.

Kelly, J.N.D. *Jerome: His Life, Writings, and Controversies.* New York: 1975.

Knowles, David. *Evolution of Medieval Thought.* New York: 1988.

———. *Thomas Becket.* Stanford: 1971.

Ladurie, Emmanuel LeRoy. *Montaillou: The Promised Land of Error.* New York: 1979.

Ladner, Gerhart. *The Idea of Reform: Its Impact on Christian Thought and Action in the Age of the Fathers.* New York: 1967.

Laistner, M.L.W. *Thought and Letters in Western Europe A.D. 500–900.* Ithaca: 1966.

Lambert, Malcolm. *Medieval Heresy: Popular Movements from Bogomil to Hus.* New York: 1977.

———. *Medieval Heresy: Popular Movements from the Gregorian Reform to the Reformation.* Cambridge, MA: 1992.

Langmuir, Gavin. *History, Religion, and Antisemitism.* Berkeley: 1990.

———. *Toward a Definition of Antisemitism.* Berkeley: 1990.

Lawrence, C.H. *Medieval Monasticism: Forms of Religious Life in Western Europe in the Middle Ages.* New York: 1989..

Jean Leclercq. *Bernard of Clairvaux and the Cistercian Spirit.* Kalamazoo: 1976.

———. *The Influence of Saint Bernard.* Oxford: 1979.

———. *The Love of Learning and the Desire for God: A Study of Monastic Culture.* New York: 1982.

Leff, Gordon. *Medieval Thought: St. Augustine to Ockham.* Baltimore: 1965.

Lerner, Robert. *The Heresy of the Free Spirit in the Middle Ages.* Notre Dame, IN: 1993.

Lesnick, Daniel R. *Preaching in Medieval Florence: The Social World of Franciscan and Dominican Spirituality.* Athens, GA: 1989.

Lewis, C.S. *The Allegory of Love: A Study of Medieval Tradition.* London: 1977.

———. *The Discarded Image: An Introduction to Medieval and Renaissance Literature.* Cambridge: 1994.

Little, Lester K. *Religious Poverty and the Profit Economy in Medieval Europe.* Ithaca: 1983.

Lossky, Vladimir. *The Mystical Theology of the Eastern Church.* Crestwood, NY: 1976.

Lourdaux, W. and Verhelst, D. *The Concept of Heresy in the Middle Ages: Proceedings of the International Conference Louvain, May 13–16, 1973.* Leuven: 1976.

Louth, Andrew. *The Origins of the Christian Mystical Tradition from Plato to Denys.* New York: 1981.

Lovejoy, Arthur O. *The Great Chain of Being: A Study of the History of an Idea.* Cambridge, MA: 1970.

Luscombe, David. *The School of Peter Abelard: The Influence of Abelard's Thought in the Early Scholastic Period.* Cambridge, MA: 1969.

Macy, Gary. *The Banquet's Wisdom: A Short History of the Theologies of the Lord's Supper.* New York: 1992.

———. *Theologies of the Eucharist in the Early Scholastic Period: A Study of the Salvific Function of the Sacrament According to the Theologians, c. 1080–c. 1220.* New York: 1984.

Marenbon, John. *Early Medieval Philosophy (450–1150): An Introduction.* New York: 1988.

———. *Later Medieval Philosophy (1150–1350): An Introduction.* New York: 1987.

Markus, Robert A. *The End of Ancient Christianity.* Cambridge, U.K.: 1990.

———. *From Augustine to Gregory the Great: History and Christianity in Late Antiquity.* London: 1983.

McGinn, Bernard. *The Foundations of Mysticism.* New York: 1991.

McGinn, Bernard and Meyendorff, John, ed. *Christian Spirituality: Origins to the Twelfth Century.* New York: 1997.

McGuire, Brian. *The Difficult Saint: Bernard of Clairvaux and His Tradition.* Kalamazoo: 1991.

———. *Friendship & Community: The Monastic Experience 350–1250.* Kalamazoo: 1988.

Mellinkoff, Ruth. *Outcasts: Signs of Otherness in Northern European Art of the Late Middle Ages.* Berkeley: 1993.

Metzger, Bruce M. *The Canon of the New Testament : Its Origin, Development, and Significance.* New York: 1987.

Mollat, Michel. *The Poor in the Middle Ages: An Essay in Social History.* New Haven: 1986.

Moore, Robert I. *The Formation of a Persecuting Society: Power and Deviance in Western Europe: 950–1250.* New York: 1987.

———. *The Origins of European Dissent.* Toronto: 1994.

Moorman, J.R.H. *A History of the Franciscan Order from Its Origins to the Year 1517.* Chicago: 1988.

Morris, Colin. *The Papal Monarchy: The Western Church from 1050 to 1250.* New York: 1989.

Morrison, Karl F. *Tradition and Authority in the Western Church, 300–1140.* Princeton: 1969.

———. *History as a Visual Art in the Twelfth-Century Renaissance.* Princeton: 1990.

Murray, Albert V. *Abelard and St. Bernard: A Study in Twelfth-Century "Modernism."* New York: 1967.

Neusner, Jacob. *Judaism and Christianity in the Age of Constantine: History, Messiah, Israel, and the Initial Confrontation.* Chicago: 1987.

Nimmo, Duncan. *Reform and Division in the Medieval Franciscan Order: From St. Francis to the Foundation of the Capuchins.* Rome: 1987.

Nock, Arthur Darby. *Conversion: The Old and the New in Religion from Alexander the Great to Augustine of Hippo.* Lanham, MD: 1988.

Oakley, Francis. *The Medieval Experience: Foundations of Western Cultural Singularity.* Toronto: 1988.

———. *Omnipotence, Covenant, and Order: An Excursion in the History of Ideas from Abelard to Leibniz.* Ithaca, NY: 1984.

———. *The Western Church in the Later Middle Ages.* Ithaca, NY: 1979.

Otto, Rudolf. *The Idea of the Holy: An Inquiry into the Non-Rational Factor in the Idea of the Divine and Its Relation to the Rational.* New York: 1980.

Partner, Peter. *The Lands of Saint Peter: The Papal State in the Middle Ages and the Early Renaissance.* Berkeley: 1972.

Pelikan, Jaroslav. *The Development of Christian Doctrine: Some Historical Prolegomena.* New Haven: 1969.

———. *The Emergence of the Catholic Tradition (100–600).* Chicago: 1971.

———. *The Excellent Empire: The Fall of Rome and the Triumph of the Church.* San Francisco: 1987.

———. *The Growth of Medieval Theology (600–1300).* Chicago: 1978.

———. *The Mystery of Continuity: Time and History, Memory and Eternity in the Thought of St. Augustine.* Charlottesville, SC: 1986.

———. *Reformation of Church and Dogma (1300–1700).* Chicago: 1983.

Pennington, Kenneth. *Pope and Bishops: The Papal Monarchy in the Twelfth and Thirteenth Centuries.* Philadelphia: 1984.

Peters, Edward. *Inquisition.* New York: 1988.

Price, B.B. *Medieval Thought: An Introduction.* Cambridge, U.K.: 1992.

Reeves, Marjorie. *The Influence of Prophecy in the Later Middle Ages: A Study in Joachism.* Notre Dame: 1993.

Richards, Jeffrey. *The Popes and the Papacy in the Early Middle Ages 476–752.* Boston: 1979.

Riley-Smith, Jonathan. *The Crusades: A Short History.* New Haven: 1987.

Rosenwein, Barbara. *Rhinoceros Bound: Cluny in the Tenth Century.* Philadelphia: 1982.

———. *To Be the Neighbor of St. Peter: The Social Meaning of Cluny's Property, 909–1049.* Ithaca, NY: 1989.

Russell, Frederick H. *The Just War in the Middle Ages.* Cambridge, U.K.: 1975.

Russell, Jeffrey Burton. *Dissent and Order in the Middle Ages: The Search for Legitimate Authority.* New York: 1992.

———. *Dissent and Reform in the Early Middle Ages.* New York: 1982.

———. *Lucifer, The Devil in the Middle Ages.* Ithaca, NY: 1984.

———. *Satan: The Early Christian Tradition.* Ithaca, NY 1981.

Ryan, Christopher, ed. *The Religious Roles of the Papacy: Ideals and Realities, 1150–1300.* Toronto: 1989.

Sahas, Daniel J. *Icon and Logos: Sources in Eighth-Century Iconoclasm.* Toronto: 1986.

Schweitzer, Albert. *The Quest of the Historical Jesus.* New York: 1961.

Sikes, J.G. *Peter Abailard.* New York: 1965.

Smalley, Beryl. *Studies in Medieval Thought and Learning from Abelard to Wyclif.* London: 1981.

Southern, Richard. *Saint Anselm: A Portrait in a Landscape.* Cambridge, U.K.: 1990.

———. *Western Society and the Church in the Middle Ages.* London: 1971.

Spinka, Matthew. *John Hus: A Biography.* Princeton: 1968.

Stow, Kenneth. *Alienated Minority: The Jews of Medieval Latin Europe.* Cambridge: 1992.

Szarmach, Paul, ed. *An Introduction to the Medieval Mystics of Europe: Fourteen Original Essays.* Albany, NY: 1984.

Tanner, Norman P., ed. *Decrees of the Ecumenical Councils.* 2 vol. Washington, D.C.: 1990.

Tellenbach, Gerd. *The Church in Western Europe from the Tenth to the Early Twelfth Century.* Cambridge, U.K.: 1993.

Tierney, Brian. *Origins of Papal Infallibility 1150–1350: A Study on the Concepts of Infallibility, Sovereignty and Tradition in the Middle Ages.* New York: 1972.

Trachtenberg, Joshua. *The Devil and the Jews: the Medieval Conception of the Jew and Its Relation to Modern Antisemitism.* Philadelphia: 1983.

Ullman, Walter. *The Growth of Papal Government in the Middle Ages.* New York: 1955.

Walsh, Michael. *The Triumph of the Meek: Why Early Christianity Succeeded.* San Francisco: 1986.

Wakefield, Walter. *Heresy, Crusade, and Inquisition in Southern France, 1100–1250.* Berkeley: 1974.

Ward, Benedicta. *Harlots of the Desert: A Study of Repentance in Early Monastic Sources.* Kalamazoo: 1987.

———. *Miracles and the Medieval Mind: Theory, Record, and Event, 1000–1215.* Philadelphia: 1987.

Warner, Marina. *Alone of All Her Sex: The Myth and the Cult of the Virgin Mary.* New York: 1976.

White, Stephen D. *Custom, Kinship, and Gifts to Saints: The Laudatio Parentum in Western France, 1050–1150.* Chapel Hill, NC: 1988.

Williams, Paul. *The Moral Philosophy of Peter Abelard.* Lanham, MD: 1980

Index

A

B

C

D

E

F

G

H

I

J

K

L

M

N

O

P

Q

R

S

T